James Deitch
Disruptive Fintech

James Deitch
Disruptive Fintech

The Coming Wave of Innovation in Financial Services
with Thought Leadership Provided by CEOs

DE GRUYTER

Disclaimer: This book contains the author's opinions resulting from discussions with other executives, experiences from 30 years in the mortgage banking industry, and research. The author may have had prior, ongoing, or planned business relationships with any or all executives or companies identified in this book, and readers should assume the author is not independent with respect to any product, service, executive, or company identified within this book. The quotes from executives in this book are used by the author with their permission and the executive quotes may not be reprinted or redistributed without the express permission of the executive. None of the executive quotes in this book should be considered an endorsement of the author's opinions in this book, which are the result of discussions with executives with a variety of views. The information provided in this book is intended to be used solely as a basis for the reader's discussion with the reader's executive team and professional advisors, and not as a substitute for legal or other professional advice. The author and publisher expressly disclaim any responsibility for the results of the reader's use of the material in this book.

ISBN 978-3-11-064941-3
e-ISBN (PDF) 978-3-11-065047-1
e-ISBN (EPUB) 978-3-11-065143-0

Library of Congress Control Number: 2019952402

Bibliographic information published by the Deutsche Nationalbibliothek
The Deutsche Nationalbibliothek lists this publication in the Deutsche Nationalbibliografie; detailed bibliographic data are available on the Internet at http://dnb.dnb.de.

© 2020 James Deitch
Published by Walter de Gruyter GmbH, Berlin/Boston
Cover image: D3Damon/E+/Getty Images
Typesetting: Integra Software Services Pvt. Ltd.
Printing and binding: CPI books GmbH, Leck

www.degruyter.com

The MBA Opens Doors Foundation is a non-profit organization dedicated to aiding families with a critically ill or injured child by making their mortgage or rent payment. MBA Opens Doors currently works directly with nine children and hospitals to identify families in need.

Opens Doors holds a special place in my heart. All royalties from this book will be donated to the Opens Doors Foundation.

Acknowledgments

Thank you to Judy, my wife, for encouragement, assistance, and practical advice, and most of all, for being a role model and mother to our kids.

To my children Michael and Christina, and grandchildren Marie, Belle, Colin, Caroline, and Austin for your constant inspiration.

To Alex Henderson, my friend, business partner, and consigliere for more than 30 years, who more or less kept me out of foolish adventures, to whom I have lost many one-dollar bets on a variety of topics and who helped greatly in the concept and structure of this book.

To Don Bishop, as well, for 45 years of friendship, business, and fun, and for being a fellow entrepreneur and inspiration for so many ideas.

To Rob Peterson and Maylin Casanueva for your strategic knowledge and perspective on mortgage banking and capital markets and for helping our business partners in so many ways.

To the mavericks: A.J. George, Barrett Burns, Bill Cosgrove, Bill Emerson, Brett Chandler, Chris George, Chrissi Rhea, Dave Motley, Dave Stevens, Deb Still, Eddy Perez, Grant Moon, Jerry Schiano, Jonathan Corr, John Hedlund, Lori Brewer, Marcia Davies, Marie Gayo, Martin Kerr, Mary Anne McGarry, Matt Hansen, Maylin Casanueva, Nima Ghamsari, Patrick Sinks, Phil DeFronzo, Rick Arvielo, Rick Bechtel, Ross Diedrich Roy George, Stan Middleman, Susan Stewart, Scott Gillen, Steve Butler and Tim Nguyen. Thank you so very much for your willingness to share your thought leadership. Without your thought leadership, this book would not be possible. And when you skim through the pages, realize that your direct quotes are but a small part of your contribution. The overall discussions with you synthesized much of my thoughts throughout this book.

To Mauricio Valverde for your assistance in interviewing the Mavericks, research, and your help in finalizing the book.

To Eleni Valasis for your outstanding writing, editing, and research work. Outstanding!

To Anthony Nguyen for technical research, analytics, and helping with the production of the manuscript. Thank you to Barb Wise for all your design and graphic work over the years.

To Teraverde®'s partners, customers, and friends—you make this all possible!

https://doi.org/10.1515/9783110650471-202

About the Author

James M. Deitch founded Teraverde® eight years ago, after serving as president and CEO of five federally chartered banks for over 25 years. Teraverde® now advises over 150 clients in mortgage banking, capital markets, and financial technology, ranging from some of the largest U.S. financial institutions to independent mortgage bankers to community banks. Jim founded two national banks, including a top 50 national mortgage lender.

Jim holds a Master of Business Administration, with concentrations in Finance and Marketing, and a Bachelor of Science degree in accounting from Lehigh University. He is a Certified Mortgage Banker and practiced as a CPA until he realized mortgage banking was a lot more interesting than public accounting. Jim has been a director of both publicly traded and privately owned banks and lenders through some very interesting times.

Jim's experience in residential mortgage banking for the last three decades on a retail, wholesale, and correspondent basis led to an intense desire to learn about how technology could be applied to financial institutions. His experience includes multi-channel loan origination and sales management, mortgage product design, credit policy, hedging, securitization and loan servicing. His beginning-to-end experience and his love of high-performance aircraft has fueled his "need for speed" in applying technology to mortgage banking.

He has served on the Mortgage Bankers Association Residential Board of Governors and served as a CEO panelist and speaker for major financial institutions, financial industry associations, corporate clients, the Department of Defense, and universities. Jim is a thought leader and has published numerous articles in the industry publications, including the best-selling books *Digitally Transforming the Mortgage Banking Industry*, published in February 2018 and *Strategically Transforming the Mortgage Banking Industry*, published in October 2018. Jim lives in Naples, Florida.

https://doi.org/10.1515/9783110650471-203

Foreword

Disruptive Fintech is Jim Deitch's third book about transformative disruption in the residential lending industry. From the ancient *Oedipus Cycle* plays of Sophocles to the futuristic *Remembrance of Things Past* novels of Chinese author Liu Cixin, trilogies have made their mark in the literary world. How fitting, then, that Jim Deitch completes his analysis of mortgage banking transformation and disruption (begun by *Digitally Transforming the Mortgage Banking Industry* in 2017 and continued in *Strategically Transforming the Mortgage Banking Industry* in 2018) in this third volume, with many illustrative examples ranging from the Greek agora to China's Alibaba. We might name these books the *Residential Real Estate Lending* trilogy.

The first volume in the trilogy, *Digitally Transforming the Mortgage Banking Industry,* was an instant best seller. The book focused on technological transformation. Technology is of course a key lever of industry transformation. In 2017, the mortgage banking industry needed to take advantage of current technology to reduce costs, increase customer satisfaction, and improve profitability. Many CEOs deployed the specific approach outlined in *Digitally Transforming* and found considerable success. But technology is only one of the levers of strategy.

Jim's second volume, *Strategically Transforming the Mortgage Banking Industry*, expanded the transformation analysis to include *strategic* transformation, not just *technological* transformation. *Strategically Transforming* provided a strategic roadmap for mortgage bankers, particularly in the area of data-driven enterprises. His comparison of the strategic challenges of mortgage banking industry to those of Major League Baseball, and the use of data in both has become a classic. Once again, Jim was specific, outlining how to use the levers of strategy. And again, CEOs deploying his levers found increased success.

The current volume takes on fintech, a concept and word often used but rarely understood. Jim expands his topic to the residential real estate industry, since disruption in the real estate brokerage space is impacting mortgage lending, and vice-versa. The writing of *Disruptive Fintech* demonstrates Jim's personal use of strategy in his capacity as an author. He continues the brilliant and highly successful research strategy of the first two volumes of the *Residential Real Estate Lending* trilogy.

Once again, Jim interviewed highly successful, disruptive "maverick" mortgage industry CEOs, this time to unlock the future of fintech. As noted by reviewers of previous volumes, *Disruptive Fintech* again contains "great insights from some of the best known names in the industry" with "an amazing roster of residential real estate heavy hitters interviewed for their opinions on where the industry needs to go to stay productive and competitive." In fact, the success of the previous volumes has led the most innovative and disruptive maverick CEOs to seek out the opportunity to share their insights in this volume.

To look forward, Jim looks back. A major insight of *Disruptive Fintech* is that fintech is not actually new. It is in fact a repeat of a financial disruption process

https://doi.org/10.1515/9783110650471-204

that has occurred over and over again for hundreds of years, from the Greeks in 600 BCE, to the Medici in the 1400s to the Bank of Amsterdam in the 1600s to the East India Trading Company in the 1700s. And of course he does not stop there, but carries on to discuss the New York Stock Exchange, the Federal Reserve, Sears, Visa/Mastercard, Apple, Uber/Lyft, and other modern disruptors. Placing fintech in a historical context enables Jim to identify the patterns of disruption in the residential real estate and lending industries.

Once again, in this third volume, Jim has specific actionable advice for CEOs in the residential real estate brokerage and lending industry—this time, how to be an intentional and successful disruptor. He identifies specific steps, which are not linear, but a circular process that is continuous. One step is to identify undervalued and overvalued assets, focusing on undervalued assets that represent opportunities for disruptive effort. Another is to reduce or eliminate provincial thinking. All of us think provincially, but we can intentionally move beyond that. That leads to imagining scenarios of disruptive transformation, rather than just anticipating events. An important step is to begin with the end in mind. Visualizing future success enables the CEO to evaluate existing tasks—can they be eliminated, automated, outsourced, or optimized?

Many years ago, as a young lawyer, I represented a client who, perhaps unconsciously, operated with a version of the disruption thinking process that Jim describes. He had started, operated, bought, and sold successful businesses. In this instance, he and a tech-savvy partner had started a data-driven business in an industry that my client knew all about. A venture capital firm had invested in the business with a typical structure of financial milestones and the ability of the venture capitalists to increase their share and control of the enterprise if the milestones were not met.

As is often the case with optimistic start-ups, the milestones were missed. We were going into what I thought would be a meeting with ugly results for my client, when my client said, "Alex, you need to tell the VCs that our results have not been what I had hoped and I don't feel motivated. They need to put more money in, my base salary needs to be increased, and I need options for a bigger percentage." I explained that this was not how the VC process worked. My client patted me on the shoulder and said, "Don't worry, Alex, you can do it." He told me that he had identified the undervalued asset (himself), an overvalued asset (the VC's capital), and he had moved beyond the standard start-up capital thinking and visualized the future success of the company and immediate success in these VC negotiations. And as he visualized, "I" did it.

Jim has provided the historical context, the present examples, and the approach for residential real estate industry CEOs to continuously and successfully disrupt their industry in the world of fintech.

Alex Henderson

Contents

Introduction

I've always been an entrepreneur at heart. It may go back to my grandfather, who started a taxi business, founded a radio station, and built multifamily housing in northeast Pennsylvania in the early 1900s. He went bankrupt in the Great Depression, but then rebuilt his businesses. He retired in 1960 with little trust in banks, though he was a prolific equity investor.

I was about seven years old when I wandered into the walk-in closet on the third floor of his apartment. There were two large safes in the closet, about three feet tall and two feet wide. I found my grandfather there, getting some cash for my grandmother to go to the market. He looked up when I entered and smiled, holding up a hundred-dollar bill. PopPop (as I called him) said, "Jim, do you want one of these?" I responded with an emphatic "Yes," smiling in anticipation of a trip to the hobby store to buy new plane and car models.

Imagine the impact, then, when he replied, "Well, get off your butt and go earn it!"

That sounds like a harsh lesson, and at the time it was. Like many a harsh lesson, though, it stuck with me, and it motivated me in my teenage years to get my first job at the age of 13, working at RadioShack.

I fell in love with technology, particularly stereo high-fidelity equipment. By 16, I was buying stereo amplifiers and speakers at wholesale and reselling them to friends. My "customers" would look at equipment at Sol Kessler's Hi-Fi Shop in central Pennsylvania, and then give me the model number so I could get it for them at a discount. At the time I didn't realize it, but I was a "disrupter" while still in high school. (My mother thought I was a disrupter, too, just not in the business sense.)

Selling stereo gear and using another person's retail showroom created friction with the owners of Kessler's. We spoke, and I struck an arrangement to sell from Kessler's stock at a discount to my friends and acquaintances, earning a commission in the process. Many of my friends' parents paid me to guide them on stereo purchases and then set up the equipment for them. Selling stereo gear remained a viable business for me all the way through college.

I didn't think of myself as a disrupter, just someone who was following his grandfather's advice to find a way to earn some money. That, however, is often how disruption works.

Accidental Disruption

By 1982, businesses were beginning to invest in microcomputers. Don Bishop, my long-time friend and first business partner, and I discovered that local businesses wanted to use IBM PCs and Hewlett Packard Laser Printers, but IT departments

https://doi.org/10.1515/9783110650471-001

wouldn't authorize the purchases. Looking into the situation, we discovered that many of these businesses were government contractors that could rent PCs and printers on a short-term basis in lieu of buying them as a capital asset. (Conveniently, this also got around information technology people preventing PC purchases, as PCs competed with their need for centralized control of all computer technology at the time.)

As a result, Don and I formed Mercury Services Inc. to purchase basic IBM PCs, upgrade the memory, add a hard drive, load them up with Lotus 123 and WordPerfect, and then rent them to businesses, particularly government contractors. We also set up and delivered the equipment, and provided training, thus completing the one-stop shopping idea. Our pricing model recovered the cost of the PC in three months. We found that businesses kept the PC for about a year and then wanted to upgrade. We replaced the old equipment with new, while redeploying the older equipment at a discount to accounting and law firms.

After 18 months, we sold the business at a substantial profit. Don and I didn't realize it at the time, but we were arguably an accidental fintech, providing a technology solution to businesses on a monthly "computing as a service" business model. We didn't discern the disruptive element of our business—providing a low-cost, easily accessible workaround to businesses that couldn't wait for a solution that their IT departments couldn't or wouldn't provide.

I didn't learn about disruption as a concept until years later when I read Harvard Professor Clayton Christensen's book *The Innovator's Dilemma* in 1998. The book was recommended by two American Management Association consultants, Mike and Maryann Kipp, who then invited me to work with them on a program they were arranging for Nortel Networks. It turned out that Mike and Maryann had arranged for Dr. Christensen to present at the program, as well.

So it was that my first personal encounter with Dr. Christensen was serving on a CEO panel moderated by Dr. Christensen himself at Duke University in 1999. The panel would focus on *The Innovator's Dilemma*. Nortel Networks was sponsoring it with the goal of laying out a strategy to transform the company from a legacy telecommunications entity into a twentieth-century technology competitor.

The story of what we discovered during those panel discussions is covered in my prior book, *Strategically Transforming the Mortgage Banking Industry*, so I won't repeat it here. Suffice to say, Clayton Christensen is now one of the most well-known thinkers on disruption. In his own words:

> As companies tend to innovate faster than their customers' needs evolve, most organizations eventually end up producing products or services that are actually too sophisticated, too expensive, and too complicated for many customers in their market.

> Companies pursue these "sustaining innovations" at the higher tiers of their markets because this is what has historically helped them succeed: by charging the highest prices to their most

demanding and sophisticated customers at the top of the market, companies will achieve the greatest profitability.

However, by doing so, companies unwittingly open the door to "disruptive innovations" at the bottom of the market. An innovation that is disruptive allows a whole new population of consumers at the bottom of a market access to a product or service that was historically only accessible to consumers with a lot of money or a lot of skill.

Characteristics of disruptive businesses, at least in their initial stages, can include lower gross margins, smaller target markets, and simpler products and services that may not appear as attractive as existing solutions when compared against traditional performance metrics. Because these lower tiers of the market offer lower gross margins, they are unattractive to other firms moving upward in the market, creating space at the bottom of the market for new disruptive competitors to emerge.[1]

Christensen followed up *The Innovator's Dilemma* with many additional works, focusing on solving the innovator's dilemma, but also branching out to examining specific segments such as manufacturing, the primary educational system, and even health care in the United States. In my opinion, his first work was his best work and resonates to this day in the conversation around disruption, which I hope can evolve further through this book.

Why I Wrote This Book

My son bought a new home in San Diego for his family in December 2018. During his home search, we spoke several times about how the residential real estate buying process works for buying, building, or renting a home. He considered all three. As he concluded his purchase, rates fell dramatically. He ended up refinancing away from his original lender. He concluded, "Your industry is really screwed up. It costs too much and is too slow." He had other observations that amplified his conclusions.

His reaction was almost identical to my daughter's reaction several years earlier. She had the same view of the home financing process. These similar reactions spurred some thinking, so I reached out to many participants in the financial services industry. I also reached out to participants that were connected to the real estate transaction, but were outside of the lending industry. I also began historical research spurred on by Stan Middleman, CEO of Freedom Mortgage.[2]

---

1 http://claytonchristensen.com/key-concepts/
2 I owe a large debt of gratitude to Stan Middleman. Stan repeatedly emphasized to me the need to carefully consider the role of history when attempting to anticipate the future. Stan's most memorable quote is, "The industry is full of bad historians... for now."

My son paid closing costs (both direct and indirect) that exceeded the cost of a new automobile. This was in a perfectly visible market. This struck both of us as an economic situation that was just crazy.

My research led me to how, why, and when disruption occurs. It fascinated me that the residential real estate market has been largely immune to disruptive forces that have roiled and remade other industries such as music distribution, film entertainment, retailing, mobile phones, and personal computing.

In my career, I've lent money to borrowers from all walks of life, and I enjoy hearing and learning from their perspectives. One professional football player spoke about why he wanted a short amortization on his home purchase. He said something to the effect of "I'm a professional football player in the NFL. And NFL means 'not for long.'" He wanted to pay off his home quickly because he knew most players had relatively short careers, and their playing days were "not for long."

I think that the current residential real estate model—the process used for buying, selling, building, financing, conveying, and insuring a home—has the same implication as those NFL initials: "not for long." It will change, especially in the pricing model that results in a very high transaction cost structure for consumers.

Consumers eventually will not pay 10% or more in transaction costs to buy a home. This book is the story of the "why," and how the coming wave of fintech innovation will drive the disruption of the residential real estate model to the tune of about $100 billion in cost reductions for consumers per year. It will affect just about everyone in the real estate value chain, as the cost to the consumer is revenue to the industry.

Chapter One
The Drivers of Disruption

Many consider technology the driver of disruption. It's a common mistake. After all, technology feels as if it's the driver of so much in our culture today. When it comes to disruption, however, it is not.

What is the true driver of disruption? Thought leadership. Yes, thought leadership may *manifest itself* by using technology, but technology is usually just the tool of disruption, not the core driver.

I've interviewed over two hundred chief executive officers and "C-Level" executives as research for my books. The thought leadership apparent in many of these executives indicates that the intersection of culture, strategy, process, and people is the "secret sauce" leading to disruption. The use of technology as a catalyst to thought leadership and as a tool for disruption is clear to me. The thought leadership of these executives in the form of transformative thinking distinguishes them as "mavericks."[3] It's a misconception that technology itself is a disruptor.

It's no surprise that many consider Amazon a technological disruptor. It was and is nothing of the kind. Jeff Bezos, the CEO and founder of Amazon, advanced thought leadership when Amazon boldly billed itself as the "Earth's biggest bookstore" even though sales initially were drummed up solely by word of mouth, with Bezos himself assembling orders and driving the packages to the post office.[4] Of course, Amazon used technology to create the marketplace by converging a large selection of books with the logistics to deliver those books anywhere, anytime. Bezos's disruptive act, however, was the thought leadership of conceiving of a marketplace so pervasive as to be the "Earth's largest bookstore."

Amazon's Challenge to Retailing

The first major online challenge to powerful department and chain stores (including bookstores) was Amazon. At the time, most regarded Amazon as a curiosity in the emerging technology known as the internet. Internet was dial-up, and internet speed

[3] The definition of "Maverick CEO" is set out in my book *Digitally Transforming the Mortgage Banking Industry*. A maverick can best be described as a groundbreaker, a pioneer. A maverick takes calculated risks to grow, to invoke change. In many ways, a maverick is an initiator, someone willing to explore unfamiliar territory, and try on innovative ideas when and where others are not. While some in the mortgage industry maintain an "If it ain't broke, don't fix it" mentality, an increasing number of maverick thought leaders are turning to transformation, be it via process, technology, or product innovation.

[4] https://www.history.com/this-day-in-history/amazon-opens-for-business

https://doi.org/10.1515/9783110650471-002

at 56,000 bytes per second was regarded as fast. (Today, 15 megabits per second is considered average, but it is in fact fast enough to stream a high-definition movie.) All in all, the internet of the time was clunky, and dominated by AOL.

As Christensen noted, Amazon was an entrant at the bottom of the market, with lower margins, a small target market of internet shoppers, and a simple model that focused on books. Amazon was initially a very inferior method of shopping for most Americans. "I love to page through a book before buying it. This Amazon thing won't work," an acquaintance of mine insisted back in 1999. Based on this belief, he even shorted the stock—a bad idea, it turns out.

Amazon's trajectory moved rapidly. According to History.com, Amazon.com launched in July 1995. By the end of 1996, Amazon had racked up $15.7 million in revenues, and in 1997, Bezos took the company public with an initial public offering that raised $54 million. In 1998, Amazon extended beyond books and started selling music CDs; by the following year it had added more product categories, such as toys, electronics, and tools.[5] Despite all of this, however, book-selling superstores Borders and Barnes & Noble were not worried.

In a 1998 *New York Times* article, Elizabeth Babin, Barnes & Noble Vice President and Treasurer at the time, contended that the advantages of internet selling were overemphasized. "The money saved by direct sellers on stores and inventory is only part of the picture. Amazon does not have to carry the $1.5 billion of hard assets that Barnes & Noble does. But it does have to pay to generate 'virtual foot traffic' in its virtual marketplace." According to the *New York Times*, Amazon spent $39 million in 1997, more than a quarter of its total revenue, on marketing and selling, $21 million of it for advertising, including banners on popular Web sites like Yahoo and Excite, to attract customers.[6]

"This is the same as paying for location to increase foot traffic," Elizabeth Babin said. Going forward, those traffic-creation costs would be much harder to forecast for Amazon than for Barnes & Noble. Joy Covey, Amazon's chief financial officer, said in the same article that she had little idea how much the company would have to spend on its relationships with Yahoo and others. The players' bargaining power is evolving from day to day, she asserted: Next year it could be Amazon calling the shots, or it could be Yahoo, or America Online, dictating prices and terms.[7]

An Amazon screenshot from October 13, 1999 doesn't seem to auger what Amazon had in store for Borders and Barnes & Noble, nor for the retail industry as a whole. The page is a time capsule back about 20 years. See at the bottom of Figure 1.1 the "Library of Literature" and "Scads of Sports Stuff" description under the "Many Merchants, Fabulous Finds" heading.

---

5 https://www.history.com/this-day-in-history/amazon-opens-for-business
6 https://www.nytimes.com/1998/07/19/business/investing-it-does-amazon-2-barnes-nobles.html
7 Ibid.

Figure 1.1: Screenshot of Amazon's home page as of October 13, 1999.[8]

Elizabeth Babin did not recognize the $1.5 billion in inventory that Barnes & Noble carried to cater to its higher end and demanding customers would turn out to be a liability. Christensen's theory that catering to high-end customers that preferred physically shopping in the store would "unwittingly open the door to 'disruptive innovations' at the bottom of the market. An innovation that is disruptive allows a whole new population of consumers at the bottom of a market access to a product or service that was historically only accessible to consumers with a lot of money."

A screenshot of February 18, 2004 turns up an Amazon branded Visa card, as well as Amazon's "1-Click" transaction innovation. Notice that books are now not the focus of the Amazon home page in Figure 1.2.

---

8 This Amazon screenshot and those following were provided though the "Wayback Machine," an internet archive of webpages captured from various points in time. See https://archive.org/web/

Figure 1.2: Screenshot of Amazon's home page as of February 18, 2004.

The Amazon home page shows a push to online versions of books via the Kindle in Figure 1.3. Kindle was even available for a Blackberry. (Innocently, a young millennial researcher for this book asked, "What's a Blackberry?" during the drafting of this text. Time flies!)

Skipping ahead ten years, the February 1, 2014 Amazon home page in Figure 1.4 brings us Kindle again and promotes gift watches and NFL tee shirts. No physical books in sight.

Finally, Figure 1.5 is Amazon's home page on May 31, 2019. It's a simple, clean look that features ease of search, and free shipping as fast as today. Search and free shipping are the beginning of the purchase process, culminating in fast and free delivery to your home or office door.

Amazon's stock was initially offered at a split-adjusted $1.97 and is currently just under $2,000 per share. Amazon's market capitalization is about $900 billion, up from just over $50 million at its initial public offering.

In 20 years, Amazon grew from a small online bookseller to one of the world's largest e-commerce sites. Amazon's Gross Merchandise Value sold in 2018 was

Figure 1.3: Screenshot of Amazon's home page as of February 18, 2010.

about $240 billion.[9] This compares to Walmart's $514 billion in sales.[10] During that same 20-year period, the list of major book, music and video retailers that failed[11] included:

- B. Dalton
- Blockbuster Video
- Borders Books
- Camelot Music
- Crown Books
- Disk Jockey
- Hollywood Video

9 https://www.fool.com/investing/2018/12/26/the-7-largest-e-commerce-companies-in-the-world.aspx

10 https://www.statista.com/statistics/183399/walmarts-net-sales-worldwide-since-2006/

11 http://self.gutenberg.org/articles/list_of_defunct_store_chains_of_the_united_states

Figure 1.4: Screenshot of Amazon's home page as of February 1, 2014.

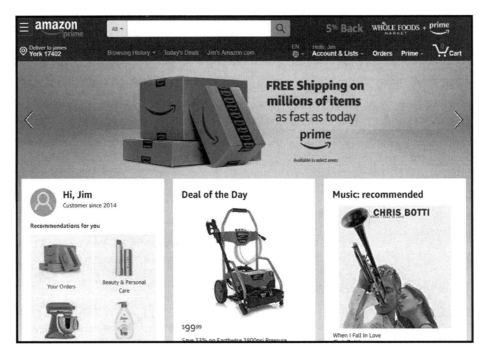

Figure 1.5: Screenshot of Amazon's home page as of May 31, 2019.

- Media Play
- Sam Goody
- Tower Records
- Virgin Megastores
- Waldenbooks
- Wall to Wall Sound and Video

On June 7, 2019, Barnes & Noble was acquired by hedge fund Elliott Advisors for $638 million, closing another chapter in the bookseller's history and a far cry from Amazon's $900 billion market capitalization.[12]

The Amazon Effect: Beyond Books

According to a *Wall Street Journal* article published on May 30, 2019, Blockbuster failed to see the transition from companies spending big mainly to get bigger to companies spending big to get smarter.[13] Getting bigger—or scale for scale's sake—does not necessarily result in economies of scale. While Walmart scaled, it did so by continuously optimizing its supply chain efficiency and pricing power. Like Amazon, logistics (not size) is a differentiator for Walmart. The Walmart logistical engine drove the demise of many retailers, from small-town mom-and-pop stores to chains like K-Mart and Sears.

Walmart learned from and adopted the lessons available in the wake of the Amazon Effect. It deployed scale as a competitive weapon.

A disruptor in China has done the same thing. Alibaba Group Holding Limited, a Chinese multinational conglomerate holding company, specializes in e-commerce, retail, internet, and technology.[14] What's more, Alibaba has a global focus, and attempts to eliminate friction in business-to-business commerce on an international scale. The company was founded in April 1999. Like Amazon, Alibaba offers electronic payment services, a variety of security and delivery services, shopping search engines, and cloud computing services.

As of 2018, Alibaba's gross merchandise value was estimated in excess of $768 billion,[15] more than Amazon and Walmart combined. Amazon and Alibaba created a combined $1 trillion in gross merchandise value sales in 2018. Neither company existed at the beginning of 1995.

That's the power of disruption.

---

12 https://www.nytimes.com/2019/06/07/books/barnes-noble-sale.html
13 John D. Stall, *Wall Street Journal*, "Behind Big Deals: No One Wants to Be Blockbuster Video," May 30, 2019.
14 https://www.alibabagroup.com/
15 https://www.fool.com/investing/2018/12/26/the-7-largest-e-commerce-companies-in-the-world.aspx

Creative Destruction

Joseph Schumpeter's 1942 book *Capitalism, Socialism, and Democracy*[16] was prescient in describing an entrepreneurial effect that he called "creative destruction." He described the concept as an inherently organic process carried out by entrepreneurs in a "perennial gale":

> The opening up of new markets, foreign or domestic, and the organizational development from the craft shop to such concerns as U.S. Steel illustrate the same process of industrial mutation—if I may use that biological term—that incessantly revolutionizes the economic structure from within, incessantly destroying the old one, incessantly creating a new one. This process of Creative Destruction is the essential fact about capitalism.

Schumpeter did not foresee Amazon, per se. What he did do was describe a free market's perennial tendency to eliminate companies and jobs as an inherent process of economic pruning. More agile and adaptive companies replace the vanishing companies, with an accompanying increase in employment in the new companies offsetting the loss of employment in the old companies. This is the brutal reality of disruption.

Richard Alm and W. Michael Cox, in an article entitled "Creative Destruction," argue that:

> Herein lies the paradox of progress. A society cannot reap the rewards of creative destruction without accepting that some individuals might be worse off, not just in the short term, but perhaps forever. At the same time, attempts to soften the harsher aspects of creative destruction by trying to preserve jobs or protect industries will lead to stagnation and decline, short-circuiting the march of progress. Schumpeter's enduring term reminds us that capitalism's pain and gain are inextricably linked. The process of creating new industries does not go forward without sweeping away the preexisting order.[17]

The impact of creative destruction isn't limited to technology improvements in recent times:

> Transportation provides a dramatic, ongoing example of creative destruction at work. With the arrival of steam power in the nineteenth century, railroads swept across the United States, enlarging markets, reducing shipping costs, building new industries, and providing millions of new productive jobs. The internal combustion engine paved the way for the automobile early in the next century. The rush to put America on wheels spawned new enterprises; at one point in the 1920s, the industry had swelled to more than 260 car makers. The automobile's ripples spilled into oil, tourism, entertainment, retailing, and other industries. On the heels of the automobile, the airplane flew into our world, setting off its own burst of new businesses and jobs.

> Americans benefited as horses and mules gave way to cars and airplanes, but all this creation did not come without destruction. Each new mode of transportation took a toll on existing jobs

---

16 Joseph Alois Schumpeter, *Capitalism, Socialism, and Democracy*, Wilder Publications, 2018.
17 https://www.econlib.org/library/Enc/CreativeDestruction.html

and industries. In 1900, the peak year for the occupation, the country employed 109,000 carriage and harness makers. In 1910, 238,000 Americans worked as blacksmiths. Today, those jobs are largely obsolete. After eclipsing canals and other forms of transport, railroads lost out in competition with cars, long-haul trucks, and airplanes. In 1920, 2.1 million Americans earned their paychecks working for railroads, compared with fewer than 200,000 today.[18]

With the creative destruction of disruption comes pain and gain. While reducing employment in the ranks of Teamsters driving horse carriages and blacksmiths forming horseshoes, this disruption in the world of transportation eliminated one very frustrating and even dangerous byproduct of so many horses: manure.

Repeating one of my favorite stories from my prior book, *Strategically Disrupting the Mortgage Banking Industry*, let me share with you a tale that focuses on that very byproduct of horses. The story was written in the *New Yorker* magazine[19] by author Elizabeth Kolbert. Kolbert writes:

> In the eighteen-sixties, the quickest, or at least the most popular way to get around New York was in a horse-drawn streetcar. The horsecars, which operated on iron rails, offered a smoother ride than the horse-drawn omnibuses they replaced. New Yorkers made some thirty-five million horsecar trips a year at the start of the decade. By 1870, that figure had tripled.

> The standard horsecar, which seated twenty, was drawn by a pair of roans and ran sixteen hours a day. Each horse could work only a four-hour shift, so operating a single car required at least eight animals. Additional horses were needed if the route ran up a grade, or if the weather was hot. Horses were also employed to transport goods; as the amount of freight arriving at the city's railroad terminals increased, so, too, did the number of horses needed to distribute it along local streets.

> By 1880, there were at least a hundred and fifty thousand horses living in New York, and probably a great many more. Each one relieved itself of, on average, twenty-two pounds of manure a day, meaning that the city's production of horse droppings ran to at least forty-five thousand tons a month. George Waring, Jr., who served as the city's Street Cleaning Commissioner, described Manhattan as stinking "with the emanations of putrefying organic matter." Another observer wrote that the streets were "literally carpeted with a warm, brown matting . . . smelling to heaven." In the early part of the century, farmers in the surrounding counties had been happy to pay for the city's manure, which could be converted into rich fertilizer, but by the later part the market was so glutted that stable owners had to pay to have the stuff removed, with the result that it often accumulated in vacant lots, providing breeding grounds for flies.

> The problem just kept piling up until, in the eighteen-nineties, it seemed virtually insurmountable. One commentator predicted that by 1930 horse manure would reach the level of Manhattan's third-story windows. New York's troubles were not New York's alone; in 1894, the Times of London forecast that by the middle of the following century every street in the city would be buried under nine feet of manure. It was understood that flies were a transmission vector for disease, and a public-health crisis seemed imminent. When the world's first international urban-planning

---

18 Ibid.
19 Elizabeth Kolbert, "Hosed," *New Yorker* Magazine, November 9, 2009.

conference was held, in 1898, it was dominated by discussion of the manure situation. Unable to agree upon any solutions—*or to imagine cities without horses* [my emphasis]—the delegates broke up the meeting, which had been scheduled to last a week and a half, after just three days.

Then, almost overnight, the crisis passed. This was not brought about by regulation or by government policy. Instead, it was technological innovation that made the difference. With electrification and the development of the internal-combustion engine, there were new ways to move people and goods around. By 1912, autos in New York outnumbered horses, and in 1917 the city's last horse-drawn streetcar made its final run. All the anxieties about a metropolis inundated by ordure had been misplaced.

It can be difficult to envision a way through disruption and its paradigm shifts. Few people saw the transformation of transportation in the major cities from horse-drawn carriages. Henry Ford didn't try to disrupt urban transportation. It just happened as a result of the automobile. Quicken Loans didn't start out as an online direct-to-consumer lender.

Bill Emerson, vice-chair of Rock Holding Inc, and former CEO of Quicken described his early strategy at the company. Initially, Quicken was a traditional lender focusing on growing the retail branch business, the economies of scale, while exploring online lending.

I started with Rock Financial in 1993. We were a branch originator. And by the time 1998 rolled around, we had about 30 branches around the country. And there was an e-mail that Dan [Gilbert, Chairman of Rock Holdings Inc.] sent internally to a group of people in 1998 that basically said "We are behind the eight ball. The internet is the way to go."

He had read an article about a company that was trying to do some stuff on the internet and that we needed to get on it and start figuring out this business model or we'd get left behind. Now, this is 1998. So, when we started out, we took about six, seven smart people, put them in a room, and started building a website. And that website was called Rockloan.com. And actually, that was a website, that back in 1999, you could literally have credit pulled, you could lock in interest rate if you wanted to.

Dan [Gilbert] was wandering by the room where the group had built the website and asked what was going on. He asked, "How many people were visiting the site?" Somebody said, "We had about 50 visits." Dan said, "50 visits! We're shutting down all the branches and we're going to the internet only." Then somebody goes, "Wait, wait, Dan. Forty-seven of the fifty were just testing the website." Dan said, "I don't care. We are getting out of the branch model and going to the internet only."

The reality of it is something along those lines, but we really did say we've got to start focusing on a centralized model and we did decide to go out and shut down every branch outside of the state of Michigan.

That strategy evolved to allow Quicken to be a direct online lender and focus on developing technology and processes in order to excel at customer service. Quicken gave up on their prior loan-officer-focused retail strategy and focused solely on direct-to-consumer lending. This focus propelled Quicken to impressive growth, allowing the company to achieve economies of scale, as well as outstanding customer service. While Quicken is privately held, it is well understood that Quicken also attains superior profitability.

Many in the mortgage industry today can't envision a future where the production cost of a mortgage loan is $1,000 or less and the loan commitment (not a preapproval) happens in seconds, but it is likely the future for the industry, as we will discuss in a future chapter. For now, let's look at how disruption occurred again in the transportation industry, and how another disruption in the urban transportation industry quickly and seriously affected a segment of the financial services industry.

Financial Services Disruption

More recent disruption in the transportation industry led to the failure of several financial institutions in New York state. If anything, these examples show just how quickly disruption can transform an industry. As the pattern of 'creative destruction' perpetuates itself, this transformation can even extend to related industries, as was the case with the recent ascendance of Uber.

As a bit of history, New York City began licensing taxicabs to limit the number of taxis on the streets of New York, and as a source of license revenue to the city coffers. By 2015, over 13,000 taxi medallion licenses were in use in New York City.[20] You needed a medallion to pick up a rider off the street in Manhattan.

Uber arrived on the scene in 2015 and arrived with gale-force winds in the urban transportation scene, especially in New York City. Ridership of New York City-licensed yellow cabs fell precipitously. In fact, Uber's ridership had surpassed New York yellow taxi ridership by May 2017. This feat was accomplished in under three years. Other ride-hailing services such as Lyft, Juno, and Via entered the New York market to capitalize on Uber's market expansion success.

Figure 1.6 shows the changes in ridership for taxi and ride share services. The increase in competition has benefited the New York consumer; the total number of individuals using a form of ride services, in the form of a yellow taxi or other for-hire vehicles, has increased, as shown in Figure 1.7.

This increase in ridership, however, ended up having a significant, deleterious effect on the financial services industry. In order to understand how this happened, we need to look at the structure of the yellow cab system.

---

20 https://www.taxiintelligence.com/the-history-of-new-yorks-taxi-medallions/

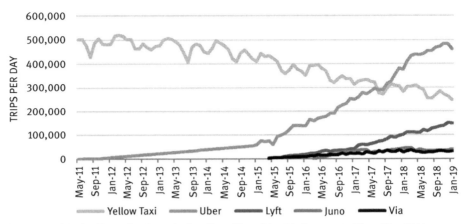

Source: NYC Taxi & Limousine Commission; Note: Uber ridership is protected from May 2011 (Uber's entrance in New York market) to December 2014 as the TLC does not track this data prior to January 2015.

Figure 1.6: New York City Yellow Taxi versus ride hailing services.

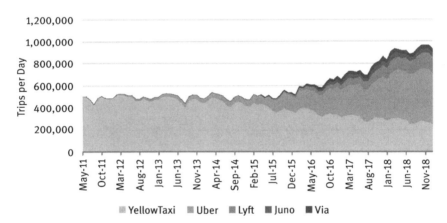

Source: NYC Taxi & Limousine Commission; For Hire Vehicles include: Uber, Lyft, Juno, and Via.

Figure 1.7: Total New York City ridership for licensed Yellow Taxis and "for-hire vehicles".

New York City—as well as Chicago, Boston, Philadelphia, and other cities—regulate cab hailing [21] via "taxi medallions." The increase in competition and its impact on New York yellow taxi ridership is evident in the following chart.

---

21 Cab hailing means flagging down a cab on the street as opposed to going to a cab stand or calling a taxi company to send a car. Cities regulate cab hailing ostensibly to protect citizens from unscrupulous limo drivers and potential criminals. Cities also regulate cab hailing as a source of licensing revenue.

Source: 2013–2019 Medallion Transfer from NYC Taxi & Limousine Commission

Figure 1.8: Median monthly New York Taxi medallion sales price.

There is a direct and opposite correlation between yellow taxi ridership and taxi medallion price, the value of which depends on the cash flow streams generated for the driver from rider fares. Fewer riders taking yellow taxis equates to less income from fares and tips collected by the taxi drivers. This ultimately depresses the demand and prices for taxi medallions. Its negative impact on New York taxi medallion prices is shown in Figure 1.8. New York has two classes of taxi medallions: individual and corporate. Note: Trend lines were added for certain months which had no sales activity.

Figure 1.8 illustrates the decline in taxi medallion prices over the five-year time span, coinciding with the arrival of ride share services like Uber.

In the past, credit unions and other financial institutions originated loans secured by these taxi medallion assets. They viewed them as lower-risk loans largely due to the stability and continued upward appreciation of the taxi medallion prices to back these loans. For years, prices of taxi medallions escalated, just like home prices through 2006.

Then. . . Uber.

The sudden change in the ride services landscape changed the status quo. Financial institutions holding loans backed by taxi medallions faced a dilemma— the $1,000,000 loan that they originated and hold on their balance sheet is now backed by an asset worth $200,000. What if the borrower decides to stop paying, such as in strategic default, or is unable to make payments on the loan due to the decrease in monies collected from fares?

The impact has been and continues to be significant and widespread. Table 1.1 shows those financial institutions no longer in existence as a result of carrying these assets.[22]

22 These financial institutions failed. Many others suffered large loan losses due to the depreciation of medallions but did not fail.

Table 1.1: Financial institutions that failed primarily because of defaults on taxi medallion loans.

INSTITUTION NAME	HEADQUARTERS	DATE CLOSED, LIQUIDATED, OR PLACED INTO CONSERVATORSHIP	ASSET SIZE IN DOLLARS (AT TIME OF CLOSING
Montauk Credit Union	New York, NY	September 2015	162,000,000
Melrose Credit Union	Briarwood, NY	February 2017	1,700,000,000
LOMTO Federal Credit Union	Woodside, NY	June2017	236,000,000
First Jersey Credit Union	Wayne, NJ	February 2018	86,000,000

The reach of "creative destruction" is wide. Fortunately, the counterbalance of the innovation that comes with it—and its benefits to the consumer—makes up the difference in the gestalt.

When an Industry Demands Disruption

A discussion I had with Dr. Christensen on disruption in 1999 still rings true: "Figure this out: If you were a competitor, how would you kill off your business?" The last 20 years have provided many examples of disruption. Amazon stands out as a disruptor in the book distribution business. And in the publishing business. And the retail products business. And the music distribution business. And in the cloud hosting business. Seems like Amazon could keep going ad infinitum at this point. But will it?

In a discussion regarding the potential and/or imminent disruption of the residential lending business, Stan Middleman of Freedom Mortgage spoke of "bad historians" who fail to look at history to learn lessons going forward. Stan commented that executives frequently do not see disruption coming, in an actionable sense. Executives may sense something is changing, that we are on the precipice, but then, according to Stan, "Refinances have bailed us out." Stan has an important caveat to that: "That will eventually end."

Bill Emerson of Quicken Loans noted that Quicken builds close relationships with its customers. "[We use] every relationship build tool available, except one. We never meet our customers face to face. Some lenders can't imagine how we build close relationships and outstanding customer satisfaction without face-to-face meetings. It can be done and done well and done repeatedly. That is demonstrated by Quicken's number one ranking in mortgage origination customer satisfaction by J. D. Power, the independent consumer satisfaction research agency."

Brian Stoffers, Vice Chairman of the Mortgage Bankers Association and CBRE stated that:

> We have enormous strategic decisions to make, which will shape our future. The impact of technology disruptors and the financial implications they have on our decisions is incredible.... Technology helps us be more efficient and effective with our very limited time in a fast-paced business world.
>
> Homebuyers want more efficient, instant home buying information, but they still want in-person assistance as well. Technology has given homebuyers the ability to be as self-sufficient as they would like. They can even bypass traditional realtors using sites like Zillow and Redfin.
>
> Rocket Mortgage completely changed the mortgage lending landscape forever by appealing to consumers' appetite for online gratification and turbocharged the desire for every other lender to better serve their customers.

Brian has framed the glowing embers of a potential disruption—no, revolution—in the residential real estate and lending industries. Consumers will demand instant gratification and lower costs. Consumers will demand industry disruption. The current economics are ripe for a shake up in the real estate brokerage, mortgage lending, appraisal and title businesses, as well as the service businesses that support the residential housing market.

Labor costs in real estate brokerage consume roughly 80% of the brokerage revenue. Labor costs in mortgage banking consumer about 70% of mortgage banking revenue. Labor costs in the title business consumer about 75% of the title insurance premium. Labor costs in the appraisal business consume about 75% of the appraisal revenue. The cost stack of real estate transactions looks like this:

The Mortgage Bankers Association (MBA) estimates 2020 home sales and average home prices[23] as set out in Table 1.2.

Table 1.2: Home sale transaction estimates for 2020.

YEAR: 2020 (*estimated*)	
MBA Home Sales Estimates	6,381,000
Average Sales Price	$250,000
Total Real Estate Sales	$1,595,250,000,000

That's $1.595 trillion dollars of estimated annual transaction volume. How much are the total transaction fees paid by a consumer for real estate commission,

---

23 Urban Institute, Housing Finance Policy Center, "Housing Finance at a Glance: A Monthly Chartbook," February 2019.

mortgage origination fees, title insurance fees, appraisal and inspection fees, and governmental taxes and fees? Let's work through the math.

First, the MBA's total mortgage dollar amount for the purchase of homes in 2020 is estimated at $1.273 trillion dollars.[24] The difference between the total mortgage amount and total home sales is the down payment made by homeowners. The average down payment forecast by the MBA in 2020 is about 20.2%. The down payments vary from the average from as little as 3% down to much higher amounts. Mortgage lenders compute the "loan to value"[25] for a home by dividing the loan amount by the purchase price.

Transaction fees include the real estate commission of 6%. Typically, the real estate commission is internally split by the real estate brokerage into a "listing commission" and a "selling commission," known as the "listing" side and "selling" side. The typical buyer does not see the breakdown as it is internal to the brokerage.[26] For purposes of this analysis, I am considering the real estate commission as borne by the buyer, even though the seller is typically the party legally responsible to pay the fee. Nonetheless, my view is that the buyer is ultimately paying the commission indirectly.

The mortgage origination fees are computed using the MBA's average cost to originate a loan. Some mortgage fees are paid directly by the borrower, such as an application fee, processing fee and underwriting fee. The bulk of the cost is paid indirectly, through a higher interest rate, so that the lender or mortgage broker can sell the loan at a 2 to 3% premium to a mortgage investor.

Title insurance fees include the title insurance premium, notary fees, recording fees, and other fees that may vary from state to state. Appraisal and inspection fees are paid by the buyer even though the appraisal and inspections are required by the lender. Fees on real estate, mortgage, and title insurance vary by state and location, so consider the following chart as indicative of national averages which may be higher or lower than those in each locale.

Once the total sales transaction and mortgage volumes are known, the fees can be computed as set out in Table 1.3.

Consumers will likely pay an estimated $201 billion in fees related to 6.4 million home sales in 2020. Let me repeat that. Consumers will pay $201 billion in fees related to 6.4 million home sales. That equates to about 12.6% of the purchase price of a home, or $31,544 for an average home. In other words, the $31,544 of fees exceeds

24 MBA "Mortgage Finance Forecast," January 17, 2019.

25 Loan to Value is the loan amount divided by the home sales price. An $80,000 mortgage on a home purchase price of $100,000 is 80% loan to value. The higher the LTV, the greater the risk of default, as the borrower has less down payment at risk. 95% and 100% LTV loans have default rates of 6 to 8 times higher than a 60% LTV loan during the subprime mortgage crisis of 2006 to 2010.

26 The commission is visible as a divided commission if the borrower uses a "buyer's agent" solely representing the buyer, though this arrangement is not common in the United States.

Table 1.3: Total fees by provider for both private provider and governmental taxes and fees.

REVENUE TO PROVIDER OF THE FOLLOWING SERVICES	FEE AS A PERCENT	HOME SALES OR MORTGAGE VOLUME	DOLLARS	CUMULATIVE DOLLARS
Total Real Estate Commissions	6.000%	$1,595,250,000,000	$95,715,000,000	$95,715,000,000
Total Loan Origination Fees	3.750%	$1,273,000,000,000	$47,737,500,000	$143,452,500,000
Total Title and Related Fees	1.250%	$1,595,250,000,000	$19,940,625,000	$163,393,125,000
Appraisal and Inspection Fees	0.375%	$1,595,250,000,000	$5,982,187,500	$169,375,312,500
Subtotal Private Provider Fees			$169,375,312,500	
Total Taxes and Government Fees	2.000%	$1,595,250,000,000	$31,905,000,000	$201,280,312,500
Total Transaction Fees			$201,280,312,500	
Percent of Home Purchase Price			12.6%	
Average Cost per Home			$31,544	

the 5% or 10% down payment of many first-time borrowers. The fees in a typical real estate transaction put the typical first-time borrower "underwater" (meaning the mortgage amount exceeds the value of the home after fees are deducted from the selling price).

The fees are paid to private providers (about $169 billion) and governmental agencies (about $32 billion). Of the $169 billion dollars of fees paid to private providers, about $135 billion went into commissions and compensation for loan officers, producing branch managers, real estate agents, title agents, and real estate appraisers. That's roughly 8.5% in compensation costs of the value of all real estate transactions projected in 2020. How long will Amazon, Zillow, Google, and other tech giants let human labor extract that kind of compensation?

Analysis of the Fee Structure in a Real Estate Transaction

With regard to the listing side of the real estate commission, the value of a listing agent used to be local market knowledge and access to MLS listing data. This information is now free on Zillow, Realtor.com, and a host of other sites. Discount real estate firms are offering listing fees as low as 1%, because there's not much work in making a listing presentation and entering the home's particulars in the multiple listing service. There is some value here, but not 3% for the listing side of the transaction.

Let's also consider the selling side of the real estate commission: In the historical paradigm, the selling agent used local knowledge to recommend homes to prospective buyers. The agent then ferried prospective buyers around, showing houses and helping the buyer to write a contract and find financing. Today, most buyers do research on neighborhoods, schools, real estate taxes, and other data. Listed homes can be researched online. Many listed homes have video tours, can be seen on Google Street view, and buyers can travel around from home to home easily via Uber. Buyers search for loans online, and most real estate contracts are "fill in the blanks." It's hard to justify a 3% commission on the selling side of the transaction. That's where discount real estate brokerages are attempting to gain ground.

The value of a loan officer used to stem from a knowledge of how to structure loans, counsel borrowers on loan options, and facilitate the transaction. But loan choices are now 30-year or 15-year fixed rate mortgages guaranteed by FreddieMac, FannieMae, or GinnieMae. What's more, structure is now tightly regulated by "Qualified Mortgage" regulations. Borrowers can obtain their credit score for free. Online resources assist borrowers in computing their eligibility for a loan. How much value does a loan officer provide in most transactions? First time homebuyers need guidance and are willing to pay for it. But for 3.5% to 4.0% fees of the mortgage amount?

That brings us to mortgage brokers, who broker loans to lenders that close the loan in the lender's name and pay the broker compensation for services. In my opinion, United Wholesale's Matt Ishiba has emerged as a mortgage lending disruptor on several fronts. Last year, Mr. Ishiba engaged in some public commentary on Quicken Loans, which was publicly rebutted by Jay Farner, President of Quicken Loans. Mr. Ishiba has been very vocal in encouraging loan originators, particularly from larger companies, to become a broker.

John Hedlund, Chief Operating Officer of AmeriHome Mortgage has some insights on these topics:

> I've heard him [Mr. Ishiba] speak a few times and he's been very open and direct about his strategy...to drive retail loan officers to become brokers, thereby growing the wholesale channel for all participants.

> The pricing incentive in early 2019 was designed to create pricing so good in wholesale that it impacted the retail LO (losing deals to their broker counterpart). Earlier in the year, when rates were up, many retail companies could not compete with the excellent pricing in the wholesale channel.

> In my opinion it was less about a short term price war and more part of the overall wholesale market share strategy (and part of the overall AIME movement). It was designed to encourage LOs to move to brokers where they can run their own business with limited overhead and better

control over compensation while signing up with several wholesalers to ensure great pricing and products. Many wholesalers assist with marketing, technology & LOS systems while giving some of the best pricing in the business. While maybe not for everyone, it is a compelling offer.

By some reports, there was growth in share for the wholesale channel in the early part of 2019. However, now only a few months later, as rates started dropping, volumes have increased for everyone and the pressure on price has abated (as operations began to get overwhelmed). Now both retail LOs and brokers are super busy. So time will tell if the wholesale channel continues taking share from retail originators in all market cycles.

Mary Ann McGarry, CEO of Guild Mortgage, describes the current state of affairs:

The industry is in a transition right now; costs are too high. The market is highly competitive, with margin compression. We need to align compensation with product complexity and business channel. Automation is taking over and there are price wars right now. That puts a lot of pressure on profitability.

I feel that brokers are growing into a bigger threat to a retail model. Technology is now being provided to the broker through the wholesale channel. This allows the broker to be a nimble, low-cost originator with access to advanced technology tools.

Dave Stevens, former CEO of the Mortgage Bankers Association, discussed a LinkedIn post that questioned an overvalued asset, that being of some mortgage loan officers:

It makes no sense to pay a loan officer 120 or 150 basis points when the lender ends up with 20 basis points of profit and takes all the risks. I didn't say there was no need for loan officers. What I said was the value proposition for loan officers is broken. Loan officers who make a couple hundred basis points for a one-time origination without any obligation or risk downstream for performance or duration risk. Loan officers refinance that loan repeatedly. That model makes absolutely no sense.

If you are building this from scratch, you wouldn't build the model the way it works today. Far too many bodies. Far too much cost. And particularly for sales commissions, it's absurd. It makes no sense to pay 120 to 150 basis points for what loan officers currently do, which is source transactional business.

Susan Stewart of SWBC Mortgage weighed in on compensation versus value added:

Most companies can afford to pay 100 basis points for origination, but companies are paying more than that. Without question, that is setting companies up to give away all profits. This isn't sustainable.

It would be great if some changes were made to compensation requirements. The industry needs some carve-outs for the loan officer to participate in a price concession and sharing in that. But you don't allow them to raise the price. This will correct the problem the industry has right now. And it is clearly really significant.

On the other hand, the actual lenders—those companies taking life of loan risks of default, litigation, and prepayment—earned about 18 basis points in profit in 2018. Projecting forward, shareholders and owners of mortgage lenders will earn about $2.3 billion in profits for carrying roughly $50 billion in costs of origination, assuming all the risk of repurchase, litigation, cures, reimbursements, and related costs. That doesn't seem like appropriate compensation to ownership. So, both the homebuyer and lender are pushing back on mortgage broker and loan officer commission costs.

A title agent used to provide a manual search of title records in order to ensure there were no intervening or unsatisfied liens on the subject property. Many of the transactional records are automated. The company insuring the title receives less than 10% of the total title insurance costs listed on a loan closing disclosure. The rest is labor and commissions.

Appraisers used to apply judgment and market knowledge. It's largely a lost art, and any lender that has repurchased a loan due to a so-called defective appraisal knows that most appraisals simply parrot the contract price. The data of real estate transactions owned by the GSEs and several private firms can provide a data-driven valuation of a subject property.

The Lessons of Convergence

How long will billions in fees be extracted from homebuyers? There is friction in the homebuying process imposed by regulations. Only licensed realtors can offer homes for sale. Only licensed or registered loan officers can offer mortgage loans. Only licensed title agents and attorneys can offer settlement and title services. Only licensed appraisers can offer appraisal services. Only licensed homeowner's insurance agents can offer homeowners insurance. These barriers to entry are formidable. But they will fall.

How might a residential real estate transaction occur in the future? Here are a few concepts to consider first.

Convergence: George Gilder proposed convergence in the mid-1990s. Gilder was a futurist author who penned the Gilder Technology Report,[27] covering emerging trends in technology. In 1995, Gilder believed that a mobile phone, internet browser, and email would converge onto a single device. He postulated that the device would be software adaptable, meaning new uses and upgrades could be added via software.

This was revolutionary thinking in 1995. At the time, mobile phones were analog devices of significant size. Mobile carriers were isolated companies that extracted "roaming" fees to users outside of their "home" network. Netscape was the

---

27 http://www.gildertech.com/

preferred browser, with dial-up service. America Online announced "You've got mail." A single software adaptable device was yet to come.

Gilder also postulated that personal assistants, cameras, and games would be converged into a single device. It took until 2007, but the first iPhone proved Gilder's convergence hypothesis correct. The iPhone launched the iOS platform, and Android soon followed. Both iOS and Android support convergence—the Internet of Things is the next round of convergence. Convergence, in fact, is now taken for granted.

Product logistics is getting physical goods from one location to another on schedule and efficiently. The U.S. Post Office was the first logistical fulfillment agency in the United States, offering free rural delivery to facilitate communications and commerce in the late 1890s.[28] United Parcel Service upped the ground game of logistics in the 1970s and 1980s.[29] Federal Express developed the air game for letters and small packages that needed overnight delivery.[30] In those 130 years, the logistics of physical goods became a commodity.

Data logistics on a network followed a similar path. The Defense Advanced Research Products Agency created an initial data network to exchange data related to classified research. Those protocols developed into the modern internet protocols.[31] Copper wire was replaced with fiber optics lines. Speed increased, as did capacity. The logistics of moving data, too, has become a commodity.

Payment logistics is moving payment for goods from the buyer to the seller. Payment technology started with national and international funds wired between banks, then transitioned to using Western Union[32] to move small amounts of money internationally. Credit cards provided the ability to move a payment from consumer to merchant. PayPal, Venmo, Square, and a host of other payment mechanisms have contributed to a fast and efficient way to transfer money for commerce quickly, safely, easily, and at a low cost.

Amazon's spectacular success has come about by leveraging logistics and convergence into a seamlessly integrated experience. Starting the fulfillment end of the process, Amazon mastered the convergence of physical logistics and data logistics. Physical goods can be sourced from any seller or supplier and delivered overnight to the buyer. The data logistics are married to the physical logistics such that physical presence can be accessed via data logistics. This logistics network delivered $275 billion of goods in 2018.

Amazon leveraged convergence by reducing every product offering into a searchable state and allowing for comparison of similar products as well as suggesting

---

28 https://about.usps.com/who-we-are/postal-history/significant-dates.htm
29 https://www.ups.com/cy/en/about/history.page
30 https://about.van.fedex.com/our-story/history-timeline/history/
31 https://www.internetsociety.org/internet/history-internet/brief-history-internet-related-networks
32 https://www.u-s-history.com/pages/h1801.html

other products. Product, data, and payment logistics are combined into a search engine, while browser, mobile, big data, payment technology, and observable tracking were designed in. And, miraculously, the process can be reversed for returning items. Amazon de-risked the purchase process and made it easy for the consumer to buy with confidence by ensuring that defective, unsuitable, or "I changed my mind" returns could be done quickly and easily.

As a contrast, the residential housing business has seen little convergence, largely due to friction, creating an "expectation gap" for consumers, according to David Zitting, CEO of AvenueU. At this point, consumers are expecting the same ease of use, even with more complex transactions, and feel suffocated by the complexity of a real estate transaction. What causes this? Friction from regulatory barriers is one reason. Inertial friction is another. But let's suspend friction for a few moments and imagine a future of little friction in the residential housing business, a convergence Chris George, CEO of CMG Financial, described as "the proverbial Holy Grail" for the industry.

Fintech Disruption via Convergence and Logistics: It's Already Underway

Two such shake-ups were recently announced. The following are examples of convergence of products—and convergence of customers—with logistics to create a path towards a one-stop shopping experience in residential real estate home buying and finance.

Amazon and Realogy Alliance: Amazon and Realogy announced TurnKey in a July 23, 2019 press release: "TurnKey combines Realogy's real estate expertise across its brands, including Better Homes and Gardens Real Estate, Century 21, Coldwell Banker, ERA and Sotheby's International Realty, with access to Amazon's Home Services and smart home products . . . "

Launching with select Realogy affiliated brokers and agents in 15 major markets across the United States, a buyer can now visit Amazon when they are ready to kick-off the homebuying process. The Amazon site will match an Amazon customer according to the homebuyer's profile to TurnKey agents. Upon closing on a home, Amazon connects the buyer with services and experts in their area to help make the house a home. Valued from $1,000 to $5,000 in complimentary products and Amazon Home Services courtesy of Realogy.[33]

TurnKey is a convergence of digital buyers with traditional local real estate agents.

---

33 https://www.prnewswire.com/news-releases/realogy-launches-turnkey-in-collaboration-with-amazon-300888956.html

Quicken and State Farm Alliance: Quicken continues to innovate. Quicken announced an alliance with State Farm Announces Alliance Bringing Rocket Mortgage's Award-winning Mortgage Process to its Customers in a press release dated July 17, 2019.[34]

According to the release, "America's largest property and casualty insurance provider is joining forces with the nation's largest mortgage lender. The alliance will allow State Farm agents to help more clients in more ways by originating Rocket Mortgage products for their customers. Rocket Mortgage is creating new technology that will allow the State Farm agents to offer a Rocket Mortgage loan as a licensed loan originator. State Farm agents can provide its customers conventional Fannie Mae or Freddie Mac, FHA, VA, USDA, and Jumbo mortgages. The rollout will take place over the next several months, and all new mortgage loans will be originated by State Farm Agents through Rocket Mortgage."

The alliance appears to be the convergence of the high personal touch of State Farm agents with the technology-powered relationship platform of Rocket Mortgage. Essentially, Quicken is acquiring a "ground game" of financial service product salespersons without having to hire or manage them directly.

The Convergence of Residential Real Estate Data: A Scenario

How will the convergence of data in real estate happen? Let's consider a scenario. A millennial is thinking of buying a home. Preferences and habits are gleaned from the potential buyer's internet behaviors, responding to the likelihood that the millennial is thinking about buying a home. Suitable neighborhoods and homes are proposed. The potential buyer takes the suggestions and begins an active search. The potential buyer identifies neighborhoods and properties of interest. Video tours provide a look inside, and all the statistics—school quality, crime, livability, entertainment, cultural offerings—are converged. The potential buyer sees a few properties of interest.

In the background, the potential buyer's bank has discerned that their customer may be looking for a home, and has an intelligent estimate of the needed mortgage. Checking accounts, asset accounts, and credit are updated, and the potential buyer is offered financing. The collateral values of the homes of interest are determined by the bank. The loan will be held in the bank's portfolio and serviced by the bank.

---

34 https://www.quickenloans.com/press-room/2019/07/17/state-farm-announces-alliance-bringing-rocket-mortgages-award-winning-mortgage-process-to-its-customers/#XWdOUiTXS52bePeY.99

The potential buyer accepts the financing offer, and is now a "cash buyer." The homes of interest are scheduled online, and the buyer's mobile device uses Bluetooth to open the home when the mobile device is in the immediate vicinity of the door lock.

The potential buyer selects the home and makes an offer via a mobile device app. The seller is notified, sees the buyer already has a mortgage commitment, accepts the offer, and schedules settlement. Data on home repairs, maintenance, and overall condition are accessed. Homeowners insurance is bid to ten carriers. A home warranty removes risk.

The buyer decides to close next week. The seller agrees, and the real estate is held in an LLC. No title work is required, and no transfer tax is paid. The transaction closes electronically, funds go to the seller, and the interest in the LLC is transferred by book entry. Transaction costs? Under $1,000.

Farfetched? The technology to accomplish the transaction described exists today. It requires two things: snapping together the correct elements of business process and technology so that the company makes a compelling offer to a customer, and inducing that customer to act in a way that benefits the customer and the company. Ideally, in the words of Rick Bechtel, Executive Vice President and Head of Mortgage at TD Bank:

> Unbelievably fascinating things are going on in terms of the way we will assemble data. Consumer direct particularly will change given big data. It's the predictive ability to go to consumers whether they're in your portfolio, whether they're in your bank, or whether they're just out there in the world.
>
> The predictive ability to offer a financial solution before the consumer may even realize they need the solution is at hand. Much like Netflix knows what movie I should be watching tonight, or Amazon knows what I should be buying next or that it's time to buy it.
>
> We want to solve a problem for a customer that they may not even be able to articulate. We want to achieve awareness of customer intent before they act. We want to discover that you are buying a house before you told anybody. Even a realtor.
>
> We'll know you plan to buy a house because we saw you on Zillow, we saw you on the realtor website. We saw that you rented a car in the town you looked at homes on Zillow. We saw that you have a plane ticket from your town to that town.
>
> We think you're buying a condo in Florida. And so, you're going to start seeing us pop up on ads and whatnot. The key is we don't have to advertise to millions of customers. If we can narrow down that list to the 50,000 customers that look like they're going to buy a house this year my ad budget is substantially reduced.
>
> And more importantly, we can start that relationship with a customer through a much less costly direct-to-consumer channel.

This is the essence of predictive strategy, and some lenders are applying this strategy now. Others will soon follow. This is truly a game-changing strategy.

And you can envision far more radical ways of disrupting the residential real estate market. Want to cut out the requirement to sell a home using a traditional realtor? Put the home in an LLC, and you are no longer transferring real estate. Same for transfer taxes. How should you show the LLC owning the home? Could it work via eBay or Amazon?

A bank can make a loan to a buyer, qualifying it using bank statements, residual income, or using IRS transcripts. If the real estate loan is under $250,000, no appraisal is legally required. Banks make credit decisions on a data-driven instant basis all the time via credit cards, indirect auto loans, and so on. Why not a real estate loan? (Most banks have not converged their lending business, so it's siloed into consumer, mortgage, HELOC, small business lending, etc.) If a bank is willing to extend unsecured credit to a borrower, why not secured real estate? It costs a bank under $100 to approve and issue a credit card. Why not use the same process for real estate under $250,000?

Where the Residential Real Estate Industry Is Headed

The rest of the book will explain why real estate transaction fees will materially fall (as set out in Table 1.4) and move toward a one-stop-shopping experience. Other opinions may vary, but the impact of disruption will be very favorable for the consumer. If transaction costs fall, the cost of home ownership will fall. Real estate will become more liquid and more affordable as transaction costs fall.

Table 1.4: Proforma fees for real estate transactions post-disruption.

REVENUE TO PROVIDER OF THE FOLLOWING SERVICES	FEE AS A PERCENT	HOME SALES OR MORTGAGE VOLUME	DOLLARS
Total Real Estate Commissions	2.000%	$1,595,250,000,000	$31,905,000,000
Total Loan Origination Fees	1.250%	$1,273,000,000,000	$15,912,500,000
Total Title and Related Fees	0.500%	$1,595,250,000,000	$7,976,250,000
Appraisal and Inspection Fees	0.100%	$1,595,250,000,000	$1,595,250,000
Total Private Provider Fees			$57,389,000,000
Savings versus Prior Estimates		·	$111,986,312,500

Not all fees will fall, however. Governmental taxes and fees seem to always ratchet upward. Excluded are governmental taxes and fees, because they are insulated from market forces that cause prices to move up and down. Private provider fees will fall because of the disruptive effect of fintech companies. The coming wave of innovation in financial services includes real estate transactions, mortgage lending, title insurance, and collateral evaluation such as appraisals and inspections, and related services. Table 1.4 shows the possible impact on fees in the future versus the current fees structure.

The consumer wins. Fees will likely fall by over $100 billion. Real estate brokerage operators, real estate agents, lenders, mortgage brokers, loan officers, and title agents will have to perform more transactions to make the same earnings. And of course, the weaker or less efficient participants will exit the business or fail.

This description is designed to provoke thinking and perhaps a bit of angst. You may think that the hypothesis of a streamlined residential real estate transaction is farfetched. You might conclude there are limits to Amazon and Alibaba's trading platforms. There are. But the elimination of friction from trading combined with an integrated finance and logistics platform will reduce fees to consumers.

The coming wave of fintech-driven innovation is unstoppable. And disruptive waves are not a recent phenomenon. The mantra of "disrupt or be disrupted" is the battle cry of the innovators. The first such wave of fintech innovation occurred 2,500 years ago. Surprised? Let's look at this concept in detail.

Chapter Two
A History of Disruption from 600 BCE to Today...
and Beyond

We could start our historical narrative about disruption at many points throughout history. Beginning with the Greeks provides the clearest through-line with regard to the concept of financial disruption delineated in this book. Their innovation in 600 BCE mirrors exactly many of the innovations we see today with regards to convergence and logistics.

Ancient Greece: The First Fintech

The Greeks created the largest marketplace hub in the world (at the time), as well as the financial services to facilitate the purchase and financing of goods. Think of it as Amazon without silicon chips. The Greeks converged trade, logistics, and financing into a single physical venue that served as broad areas of the Mediterranean Sea far beyond Greece. The physical trading platform offered trade of raw materials, food, wine, and pottery.[35]

Trade was a fundamental aspect of the ancient Greek world and following territorial expansion, an increase in population movements, and innovations in transport, goods could be bought, sold, and exchanged in one part of the Mediterranean which had their origin in a completely different and far distant region. Food, raw materials, and manufactured goods were not only made available to Greeks for the first time, but the export of such classics as wine, olives, and pottery also helped to spread Greek culture to the wider world.

Homer's "Iliad" and "The Odyssey," written in the 8th century BCE, evidence maritime trade (as well as war).[36] The Greeks credited Lydia, a region of western Asia Minor, with inventing coins in the early 6th century BCE. The state stamped the coins to guarantee value and identify them as genuine.[37] The Greek city states prospered, producing coinage as well as specialized merchant ships to facilitate trade.

As of the 5th century BCE, Athens' port of Piraeus became the most important trading center in the Mediterranean and gained a reputation as the place to find any type of goods on the market.[38]

35 https://ancient-greece.org/history/agora.html

36 https://www.webpages.uidaho.edu/engl257/ancient/iliad_and_odyssey.htm

37 https://www.ancient.eu/Greek_Coinage/

38 https://www.ancient.eu/article/115/trade-in-ancient-greece/

https://doi.org/10.1515/9783110650471-003

The Greek word "agorae"[39] is translated as "assemblies of people within a boundary where trading was carried on." Wheat, grain, salt, fish, wood, papyrus, textiles, glass, gold, silver, copper, and tin were all traded.

Financial services such as maritime loans enabled "traders to pay for their cargoes and the loan did not have to be repaid if the ship failed to reach safely its port of destination. To compensate the lender for this risk, interest rates (nautikos tokos) could be from 12.5 to 30% and the ship was often the security on the loan."[40]

In the article "Trade in Ancient Greece," Mark Cartwright writes:

> Regulation was in place, such that trade in wheat was controlled and purchased by a special "grain buyer" (sitones). About 470 BC [sic], the obstruction of the import of grain was prohibited, as was the re-exportation of it; for offenders the punishment was the death penalty. Market officials (agoranomoi) ensured the quality of goods on sale in the markets and grain had its own supervisors, the sitophylakes, who regulated that prices and quantities were correct.

> Besides taxes on the movement of goods (e.g.: road taxes or, at Chalkedon, a 10% transit charge on Black Sea traffic payable to Athens) and levies on imports and exports at ports, there were also measures taken to protect trade. For example, Athens taxed those citizens who contracted loans on grain cargo which did not deliver to Piraeus or those merchants who failed to unload a certain percentage of their cargo. Special maritime courts were established to tempt traders to choose Athens as their trading partner, and private banks could facilitate currency exchange and safeguard deposits. Similar trading incentives existed on Thasos, a major trading-center and large exporter of high-quality wine.[41]

Around 600 BCE, the Old Testament Book of Leviticus[42] was written. In Chapter 25, every 50th year was designated the year of Jubilee. The origins of modern real estate finance[43] are outlined:

> 13 In this Year of Jubilee everyone is to return to their own property.

> 14 If you sell land to any of your own people or buy land from them, do not take advantage of each other.

> 15 You are to buy from your own people on the basis of the number of years since the Jubilee. And they are to sell to you on the basis of the number of years left for harvesting crops.

> 16 When the years are many, you are to increase the price, and when the years are few, you are to decrease the price, because what is really being sold to you is the number of crops.

---

39 https://ancient-greece.org/archaeology/agora.html

40 https://www.ancient.eu/article/115/trade-in-ancient-greece/

41 https://www.ancient.eu/article/115/trade-in-ancient-greece/

42 https://www.biblegateway.com/passage/?search=Leviticus+25&version=NIV

43 My thanks to Lehigh Professor Eli Schwartz who guided me through the "'Theory of Interest" as my graduate school thesis. Dr. Schwartz was a caring professor who had no tolerance for lazy thinking or poor research, and I thank him for (at least partially) curing me of both. Dr. Schwartz passed a few years ago, and his passing was a loss to the financial community and to the human race.

The concepts of discounted cashflow and present value are formally introduced in the previously mentioned text. The concept of fee simple ownership, land lease-hold, and the right of rescission are also described:

23 The land must not be sold permanently, because the land is mine and you reside in my land as foreigners and strangers.

24 Throughout the land that you hold as a possession, you must provide for the redemption of the land.

25 If one of your fellow Israelites becomes poor and sells some of their property, their nearest relative is to come and redeem what they have sold.

26 If, however, there is no one to redeem it for them but later on they prosper and acquire sufficient means to redeem it themselves.

27 They are to determine the value for the years since they sold it and refund the balance to the one to whom they sold it; they can then go back to their own property.

29 Anyone who sells a house in a walled city retains the right of redemption a full year after its sale. During that time the seller may redeem it.

30 If it is not redeemed before a full year has passed, the house in the walled city shall belong permanently to the buyer and the buyer's descendants. It is not to be returned in the Jubilee.

31 But houses in villages without walls around them are to be considered as belonging to the open country. They can be redeemed, and they are to be returned in the Jubilee.

More than 2,500 years ago, the basics of modern real estate finance, as well as the convergence of trade, finance, and a legal framework for trade and ownership of real estate all existed. It may be a stretch to say that Amazon is merely the technologically powered agent of convergence of a marketplace and logistics. Nonetheless, the vertical integration of trade, markets, and finance is evidenced in ancient Greece, the Bible, and the convergence of marketplaces and financing ever since.

Discussing fintech in the historical context of the ancient or even biblical worlds may appear counterintuitive to some. Fintech, however, does not mean silicon wafers and electrons. It is not a medium defined by technology—it is a medium of exchange first and foremost. The "technology"—be it the introduction of the marketplace or the Judaic structures of real estate—serves to eliminate the friction from the human desire to trade goods and services.

A natural through-line to the future of fintech becomes more evident with the arrival of the next major fintech innovation[44] in the Western world: the establishment of the Medici Bank in 1397.

---

44 One can find many examples of fintech innovation throughout the centuries; the examples I cite are for illustrative purposes, and I do not claim that this book is a definitive chronological history of fintech.

The Medicis Dominate Italian Banking

Initially, the Medici Bank provided financial services for the wool guilds, even establishing wool factories in their own right.[45] The bank's first major innovation was pioneering the use of double-entry bookkeeping in Europe, which had been previously employed in the Middle East and Korea. The discipline of double-entry accounting helped the Bank become Europe's largest financial institution and helped the Medici family gain power and resources to control much of central Italy for generations to come.

Additionally, the Medicis were clever enough to ameliorate one particular bit of friction that existed in the European financial system at the time: the Catholic religious prohibitions against lending money. The Medicis sidestepped this sizable problem by issuing letters of credit with a time limit—typically the time it took for a ship to travel from one port to the next. The Medicis would then take advantage of different exchange rates from one bank to the next to generate a profit for the company.[46]

What is particularly fascinating about the Medici history is that the inherent bug in their system created by the Catholic Church was what drove much of their innovations, forcing them to go international and find ways around usury prohibitions. It was no small irony, too, that the Medicis' biggest customer in the end was the church, and that they eventually became powerful enough to select popes that suited their needs.

The power consolidated by the Medici family had lasting effects across Europe, many of which could never have been anticipated by the powerful family. This created what would come to be called the "Medici Effect" by Frans Johansson in the 21st century—a concept in which dynamic, unintended consequences result from the interconnectedness of different industries and disciplines. Today, many associate the Medicis with the Renaissance before fintech, but while their influence contributed greatly to the artistic resurgence that defined this era in Europe, the family never *intended* to create the Renaissance, per se.

The Bank of Amsterdam Innovates Coinage

A similar Medici effect occurred two centuries later with the establishment of the Bank of Amsterdam. This innovation presented itself as a solution to the problem of neighboring currencies[47] in Europe at the time. Many smaller nation states used the

---

45 http://www.themedicifamily.com/The-Medici-Bank.html

46 Tim Parks, *Medici Money: Banking, Metaphysics, and Art in Fifteenth-Century Florence*, W. W. Norton & Company; May 17, 2006.

47 I use "currency" and "coinage" interchangeably, though currency is generally considered paper money and coinage is generally considered as issued in a precious metal.

currencies of neighboring nation states in tandem with their own minted currency. The currency of the smaller nation states was sometimes discounted by merchants below the value of the precious metal contained in the coinage. This discount was due to the unfamiliarity of the currency, or illiquidity of the currency. Thus, the metal a currency was minted in may be more valuable that the currency's value itself.[48]

In response, the Bank of Amsterdam created bank money, or the first demand deposits. The bank would accept these various currencies, charge a fee for the transaction, and give the client a credit for the leftover amount. This bank money retained its value and, as such, was worth more than the minted currency of any one of these nation states. At the same time, Amsterdam authority backed the power of this bank money by requiring that bills over a certain sum always be paid with bank money.

East India Trading Company Innovates Convergence and Logistics

Two hundred years later, yet another major innovation again transformed the economy of Europe when the East India Trading Company became a stockholder-owned institution and further developed the concept of matching willing buyers and sellers. Once again, a close relationship with the government (or, in this case, the queen) buoyed the endeavor. A charter issued by Queen Elizabeth I allowed the founders of the company not only to establish a monopoly on all trade routes to the East Indies, but to, in essence, threaten all usurpers:

> George Earl of Cumberland, Sir John Hart, Sir John Spencer, and Sir Edward Mitchelburne, knights, with 212 others, whose names are all inserted in the patent, were erected into a body corporate and politic, for trading to and from all parts of the East Indies, with all Asia, Africa, and America, and all the islands, ports, havens, cities, creeks, towns, and places of the same, or any of them, beyond the Cape of Good Hope to the Straits of Magellan, for fifteen years, from and after Christmas 1600; prohibiting all other subjects of England, not free of this company, from trading to these parts without license from the company, under forfeiture of their goods and ships, half to the crown and half to the company, together with imprisonment during the royal pleasure, and until they respectively grant bond in the sum of 1000 at the least, not again to sail or traffic into any part of the said East Indies, &c. during the continuance of this grant.[49]

That's quite a charter. What followed was nothing short of domination of others as the British enterprise took over the sea and trade routes, as well as territories in South Asia. (They even did it with boats they had captured from the Spanish and Portuguese, adding some sting.) Britain's domination with regard to the Company consolidated its position as a European power, so much so that no less an expert

---

48 http://encyclopedia-of-money.blogspot.com/2010/01/bank-of-amsterdam.html
49 http://www.columbia.edu/itc/mealac/pritchett/00generallinks/kerr/vol08chap10sect01.html

than Edmund Burke observed that the destinies of Nation and Company were entirely intertwined, a relationship that many believe led to the Industrial Revolution.

For our intents and purposes here, however, the Queen's charter with the EIC did something else very significant—it defined the structure for the world's first corporation not only as a joint-stock corporation but also as a limited liability corporation, a fintech transformation once again.

The New York Stock Exchange Innovates Capital Markets

Yet another significant leap forward in fintech took place toward the end of the 18th century. According to what some think is an apocryphal story, 24 investors met under a buttonwood tree to sign what would become known as the Buttonwood Agreement, the forerunner to what we now know as the New York Stock Exchange.

Stock exchanges had existed in Spain previously. The Buttonwood Agreement, in contrast, was created as a control system and in response to a financial crisis that took place in 1782. Fearing that trust in the market had been depleted by panic, the 24 investors came together to develop a system whereby they could trade with one another while preserving the stability of the financial system by projecting public interest.[50]

While the first stocks traded were for banks, the Exchange eventually expanded beyond bank stocks or government bonds. As with all moments of punctuated equilibrium in fintech, the expansion of the NYSE went hand in hand with technological development, including the establishment of the telegraph network and eventually telephones.

The Federal Reserve Bank: A Payment Clearing System

Following is an annotated history of the Federal Reserve, drawn from the San Francisco Federal Reserve Bank's "What Is the Fed?"[51] The first notions of central banking in the United States came from the Secretary of the Treasury at the time, Alexander Hamilton. Despite opposition from Thomas Jefferson, who sided with rural (state) rights, Hamilton managed to draft a charter for the First Bank of the United States in 1791. The momentum was short-lived. Twenty years later, Congress failed to pass a bill to recharter the bank. What resulted was state banks stepping in, followed by various paper currencies around the country with no established value. Five years later, Congress once again tried to save the central system,

---

50 https://www.orionadvisor.com/history-buttonwood-agreement-matters-orion-eclipse/
51 https://www.frbsf.org/education/teacher-resources/what-is-the-fed/history/

establishing the Second Bank of the United States in 1816. This effort would not make it past its 20th birthday, with Andrew Jackson eventually vetoing its recharter.

Maintaining a central bank system was essential in Hamilton's time and would prove even more essential nearly 100 years later. During his time, banks did not allow the public to make deposits, nor did they give loans to the public. With only other private citizens and certain merchants available to make loans, the United States was facing a credit crisis in the aftermath of the Revolution.

In the years that followed Jackson's veto of the Second Bank of the United States, state banks with dubious rules and little consistency took over and became the only options out there for the consumer. The high cost of the Civil War demanded more reliable financing, leading to the drafting and eventual ratification of the National Banking Act of 1863. The Act created one national currency and limited the issuance of bank notes to nationally chartered banks. What it did not do was establish any kind of strong central bank structure as Hamilton had envisioned it.

By the turn of the century, this lack of centralization would once again lead to chaos and eventual panic. By the first decade of the 20th century, it was commonplace for banks to refuse to clear checks from other banks, leading eventually to the great financial panic of 1907. According to the Purposes and Functions drafted by the Board of Governors of the Federal Reserve System:[52]

> By creating the Federal Reserve System, Congress intended to eliminate the severe financial crises that had periodically swept the nation, especially the sort of financial panic that occurred in 1907. During that episode, payments were disrupted throughout the country because many banks and clearinghouses refused to clear checks drawn on certain other banks, a practice that contributed to the failure of otherwise solvent banks. To address these problems, Congress gave the Federal Reserve System the authority to establish a nationwide check-clearing system. The System, then, was to provide not only an elastic currency—that is, a currency that would expand or shrink in amount as economic conditions warranted—but also an efficient and equitable check-collection system.

You can explore this in greater depth in the Appendix 2: Financial Crises, 1775 to 2010. Suffice to say, Congress' innovation of creating the Federal Reserve System would define (for better and for worse) the U.S. financial picture in the coming century.

---

[52] https://www.federalreserve.gov/aboutthefed/pf.htm

Big Ideas, Big Impact: Contemporary Fintech Disruptive Thinkers and Practitioners

The 20th century and first part of the 21st century in the United States have been extremely productive times for what is described as fintech. This is unsurprising when you consider that the Founding Fathers themselves were the nation's first disrupters, setting the tone for the country to come and establishing the framework in which innovation could thrive.

The primary fintech innovation from the Founding Fathers was the creation of a public infrastructure, demonstrating significant thought leadership on the organizational structure of the country to come. The commercial interests of the burgeoning nation (and those of the Founding Fathers themselves) were foremost in their minds.[53] Not only did they have a vast swath of land across which they would need to establish trade routes, but they also had some sizable ocean-going trade logistics to plan out and protect. What's more, the Founding Fathers understood that any coalition between the separate states would hang on shared financial interest. In fact, their efforts in this regard were what would eventually lead to the Constitutional Convention.

In particular, George Washington knew that preserving the republic depended on the financial connectivity between the separate states. Within his own immediate region, including the Potomac, Washington saw how the river and the nearby Chesapeake could serve as crucial throughways for goods coming from ocean-borne ships to the interior of the United States. As such, he brought together leaders from the surrounding states to draw up the Mount Vernon Pact,[54] which laid out guidelines and principles for commerce and navigation in the region.

The following year saw the Annapolis Convention[55] with representatives from five different states, which highlighted the importance of trade and navigation to the future of a potential nation. Consequently, the participants planned a meeting to continue discussions the next year, in what would be the Constitutional Convention of 1787.[56]

There are more examples of public and early private fintech, but the confluence of check clearing, parcel post logistics, and product convergence that happened at the turn of the 20th century would define much of the innovation to come.

---

53 https://oll.libertyfund.org/pages/forrest-mcdonald-the-founding-fathers-and-the-economic-order
54 https://www.mountvernon.org/library/digitalhistory/digital-encyclopedia/article/mount-vernon-conference/
55 https://www.mountvernon.org/library/digitalhistory/digital-encyclopedia/article/annapolis-convention/
56 https://history.state.gov/milestones/1784-1800/convention-and-ratification

Sears

Beginning as a watch company, Sears would excel at logistics in a way no one had yet, leveraging a catalog business and United State Post Office parcel post to converge the marketplace for rural America.

As with the Founding Fathers, Sears was faced with the logistical nightmare of delivering goods across such a large country, especially considering that the rural consumer was the company's key demographic for its first few decades. Sears' innovation came in the convergence of a new postal delivery service in remote areas with a clever new way in which to market goods: the mail-order catalog.[57]

The first step was solving the conundrum of how to get consumers to their storefront. Sears' innovation, of course, was bringing the store to the consumer in the form of its now-famous catalog. The first Sears mail-order catalog in 1888 was 80 pages of jewelry and watches. By 1890 the catalogue had grown to over 300 pages and included essentials for the household, including what would become one of their most important product categories: durable goods.[58] What Sears did next was its true innovation—leveraging two U.S. postal innovations to expand their reach. In 1891, the U.S. Postal Service established a free delivery system in rural areas, followed two decades later by a parcel post rate that made delivering to these customers affordable. Eventually, Sears would become the biggest customer for the growing parcel post service, reflecting Amazon's relationship with USPS today.

As Sears' actual storefronts began taking on excess stock from the catalog, the innovators at Sears saw that the invention of the automobile would facilitate building larger stores in more suburban areas. In yet another game-changing moment of disruption, Sears began building the first parking lots adjacent to their larger, suburban locations.

By the 1910s, business was flourishing for Sears when they made another bold move and decided to offer credit to their consumers. Customers flocked to the company in droves, as most banks at the time wouldn't even give consumer lending the time of day. At this point, the Sears business was so robust that it was, in effect, an economy of its own.

Sears attempted to converge the residential real estate market in the 1980s. Coldwell Banker, Sears Mortgage, and Allstate Insurance were the converged marketplace.[59] But the logistics were missing. The retail walk-in logistical model didn't remove friction. And Sears failed, divesting their real estate financial efforts.

---

57 https://www.smithsonianmag.com/history/rise-and-fall-sears-180964181/
58 http://www.fundinguniverse.com/company-histories/sears-roebuck-and-co-history/
59 https://www.nytimes.com/1986/04/23/business/sears-mortgage.html

FICO: Defining Credit

Consumer credit would undergo yet another transformation toward the end of the 20th century. With the passage of the Fair Credit Reporting Act in 1970, consumers had access to a new transparency in their credit file. With the creation of Experian and TransUnion, in addition to Equifax (formerly RCC), however, lenders were still confronted with difficulties when it came to comparing and interpreting credit reports.

In response, the bureaus turned to Fair, Isaac, and Company, or what we now refer to as FICO.[60] The algorithm was developed by FICO to parse credit data transformed lending. It's not excessive to say that the FICO score is the underpinning of virtually all credit decisions in credit card, installment, auto finance, and mortgages. FICO is nothing less than the underlying core credit-scoring algorithm for the credit evaluation of Loan Prospector and Desktop Underwriter alike.

Credit scoring both democratized credit availability and provided a consistent and fair method of evaluating an applicant's likelihood to repay their debt. As an example, a credit score of 800 suggests that 99 out of 100 applicants with this credit score will not become seriously delinquent in the foreseeable future. What about a credit score of 500? Less than 60 out of 100 applicants with this credit score will not become seriously delinquent in the foreseeable future. This innovation sped up and unified the credit underwriting process.

FICO does not consider income of an applicant, so that part of underwriting is still largely manual in the mortgage lending process. The changing demographic of potential borrowers has also impacted credit scoring—for that reason, FICO is not without its challengers. VantageScore is making inroads with a different approach to credit valuation, serving as a broader scoring engine.

Barrett Burns, CEO of VantageScore, had the following observations on millennial and non-traditional borrowers:

> Historically speaking, those with higher income and assets were correlated with "thicker" credit files and more credit usage.[61] Lenders also often viewed thin-file consumers as riskier than those with thick files and they were often placed into the highest risk products (i.e., higher interest rates and modest loan limits).

> Now we see that millennials with thin files—unlike any other generations before them—on average have income and asset levels consistent with their thick-file counterparts.

> VantageScore data and the recent NY Federal Reserve data also shows that, despite the fact that the millennial cohort of the population is expected to be the largest generation by size,

---

60 https://blog.myfico.com/history-of-the-fico-score/

61 According to Mr. Burns, "'thick-file" consumers have three or more credit accounts reported and "'thin-file" consumers have two or fewer credit accounts. Typically, thick files have many more than three credit accounts. Traditional credit scoring models rate thick-file borrowers making payments as agreed much more favorably than thin-file borrowers making payments as agreed.

many appear averse to debt. Specifically, millennials have low numbers of active accounts (based on VantageScore data) and according to the New York Federal Reserve data, millennial total debt is low relative to other generations. In fact, paying down student loans and not applying for new credit is prudent credit behavior.

Notwithstanding this prudent behavior, conventional models and lending strategies might actually be penalizing millennials simply because thin-file consumers have been traditionally scored.

The take-away is this: Users of credit scores for lending decisions should carefully assess whether they should reconsider models based on legacy beliefs. In particular, trended credit data could help because it better analyzes recent credit activity on what limited accounts these consumers do have versus reliance on "length of active accounts" and "credit mix" to determine their scores. By definition, millennials and those new to credit (immigrants) will be penalized if the scoring models used rely heavily on these attributes.

Visa/Mastercard: Expanding Payment

It's hard to believe now, but when Bank of America issued its first bank card in 1958, it planned on limiting its scope to California. What in fact followed was the convergence of card issues and payment logistics, helping to develop the descendants of that first card into worldwide credit card and payment providers.

We'll cover the evolution of Visa and Mastercard a little later in the book.

Apple iPhone: Bringing Everything Together

Steve Jobs wasn't one to tread lightly. From what we know of the history of Apple, he was never above pitting one employee against another if it meant getting a better product in the end. While his methods may raise questions, there is no doubt that his products have been disruptive and transformative, perhaps none more so than the iPhone.

Perhaps the true genius of the iPhone came from Jobs' ability to pitch a vision. When he first suggested that the phone should operate solely via touchscreen, the naysayers were everywhere, both inside and outside of the company. No one believed that users would want to engage with anything less substantial than a physical keyboard. Jobs forced the idea through and, in his first pitch to the public, emphasized the seamlessness and elegance of the device. People were sold... and sold on a device that wasn't even ready for mass-market production yet.

Apple succeeded in getting the almost impossible iPhone to market and it changed the world—or worlds, rather: the worlds of music, video, and communication. The list continued to grow as each version arrived with enhanced features. It ended up being over six years before their closest competitor Samsung could get close to what Apple had achieved with the iPhone.

The iPhone is the ultimate in convergence: phone, camera, entertainment, music, email, and personal assistant all come together in one device. Apple even worked to execute these same principles of convergence when it came to the content on the iPhone. iTunes converged entertainment into a digital marketplace and provided the logistics to distribute music and video. The AppStore converged a software marketplace on a common converged platform, providing logistics for independent developers to expand the marketplace.

We cannot underestimate the effect of the app-based economy created by the iPhone. The mortgage banking industry saw the creation of many mobile applications for the iPhone and Android powered mobile devices. The mobile applications provided pre-qualification, document exchange and other capabilities to speed mortgage lending. The most notable application, in my opinion, was Rocket Mortgage from Quicken. This application offered the customer a fast and convenient approval from the mobile application. Rocket Mortgage helped power Quicken to the largest independent mortgage lender in the United States by 2016.

Non-Bank Payment Systems

One of the most recent disruptions in fintech could be argued as one of the most influential. Today's non-bank payment systems, including PayPal, Square, and Venmo have not only moved payments out of the banking system but have also redefined the social landscape of money.

The story of Venmo's founding (chronicled in The Hustle[62]) perhaps best illustrates how searching for a frictionless environment leads to innovation. The two founders of Venmo, Igram Magdon-Ismail and Andrew Kortina, met at the University of Pennsylvania, where they were roommates. A friend asked the two to help him launch a frozen yogurt store. Frustrated beyond belief with the clumsiness of their point of sale options, the pair began brainstorming workarounds. Finally, attending a concert one day, they realized they could design a method for purchasing digital recordings of the performance via text message. After exploring the option of sending money via text, they eventually graduated into developing the smartphone app we know and love today.

Venmo has changed our cultural landscape to the point of influencing language. Who hasn't heard a 30-something say "Venmo me the cash when you can." Venmo's business model is interesting, too—rather than place any cost burden on the customer, the company lets users transfer money for free, friend-to-friend, and instead makes their revenue from charging businesses that use Venmo payment 2.9% on each transaction.

---

[62] https://thehustle.co/how-venmo-started

Insurtech

According to Ross Diedrich, CFA and Chief Executive Officer of Covered Insurance, "The U.S. insurance industry has over $1 trillion in premiums written each year. Property and Casualty Insurance alone is a $617 billion market in the U.S., so there is plenty of opportunity for innovation and disruption. To frame the increase in innovative activity, patent filings related to insurance have increased by 116% over the last six years."

The biggest trends Diedrich sees are outlined as follows:

> Insurtech innovation will have several implications for the housing industry. The most obvious is the requirement to have homeowner's insurance in force to close on a mortgage, how borrowers shop for and purchase that insurance, and at what point in the mortgage process it is addressed. Leveraging new insurance marketplaces, like Covered, lenders can offer multiple, accurate, unbiased home insurance quotes to their borrower automatically. This provides a streamlined experience for the borrower, another value-add tool for the lender, and moves the home insurance process earlier in the closing sequence. Ultimately, this means a better digital experience with more value and shorter closings.

> Additionally, insurtechs are tackling other friction points in the mortgage process—like title, appraisals, and document verification. Consumers are expressing drastic shifts in purchase and consumption behavior. Digital adoption is accelerating, retail/brick and mortar is fading away, and relationship-based sales are far less important. J.D. Power cited consumers are now placing far more importance on choice and more products/services offered than before. Breadth, transparency, choice, and simplicity are table stakes.

So, what is happening in insurance and other areas of residential real estate?

> Fintechs are cutting costs of manual operational processing in the insurance industry through tech efficiency, while logistical mechanisms are evolving rapidly for additional efficiency and profitability. Innovation in digital and distribution means less cost-related sales support. For example, we're seeing chatbots (driven by AI and ML) handling more and more of the customer interactions, while reserving human intervention for more complex cases. Consumers will purchase financial products less on relationships with bricks and mortar salespersons and more on convenience, price, personalization, and transparency. Consumers should expect more personalized products and insurance buying experiences.

Ross offers a great summation as a look forward:

> Disruption is hitting the financial services industry. I believe change will happen in a thousand different small ways, with a few dramatic innovations. The industry is recognizing the disruptive power of fintech to drive revenues, profits, and customer satisfaction.

In fact, fintech is changing the landscape of the value proposition on many products and service providers in the residential real estate lending and financial services space. We'll expand our discussion into how fintech is changing the value of core assets in the space. Some assets are undervalued currently, and some assets are currently overvalued. Which are which?

Chapter Three
Data-Driven Identification of Undervalued and Overvalued Assets

As we have seen, convergence and logistics are important elements of disruption. But successful disruption means that the disruptor can thoughtfully develop a valuable product or service faster, better and cheaper than the competitors that are being disrupted. In essence, the disruptor can produce or identify undervalued assets to be exploited. This ability to perceive undervalued assets is a key element of in the type of thought leadership that leads to disruptive action.

Undervalued assets can take many forms. Warren Buffett has created incredible returns identifying and investing in stocks of undervalued or underappreciated companies. Real estate investors have a saying: "One makes money when the property is bought, not sold." Undervalued assets even play a role in sports—after all, major league baseball teams employ full-time scouts whose sole purpose is to search for undiscovered baseball talent.

Given the importance of this element in investing resources, we'll spend this chapter walking through the concept of undervalued assets in detail. There's the other side of the coin, too, where some assets are overvalued. Both sides of the coin work together, in many cases. In the stock investing sense, for example, you sell a stock when its value is recognized by all (arguably when it becomes overvalued), then reinvest the proceeds in undervalued assets.

I'm certain this chapter will make me no friends in some of the professions discussed herein. No one wants to be considered an "overvalued" asset. But the fact of the matter is that disruption (and creative destruction) occurs when overvalued assets are successfully replaced by undervalued assets. This replacement fosters faster and more valuable options for customers.

The concept of undervalued and overvalued assets is a key to thought leadership. What's more, it is a concept that is applicable to almost every industry. To illustrate this, we'll start with a discussion of undervalued stocks, and then walk through how undervalued major league baseball players are identified. We'll finish the discussion by taking a look at undervalued and overvalued assets in the financial services business.

Value Investing

Benjamin Graham is known as the "father of value investing." Warren Buffett described Graham as his mentor. According to Buffett, "Long ago, Ben Graham taught

https://doi.org/10.1515/9783110650471-004

me that 'Price is what you pay; value is what you get. Whether we're talking about socks or stocks, I like buying quality merchandise when it is marked down.'"[63]

In today's terms, Graham can be described as "data-driven" when looking for value in securities. In fact, Graham specifically searched for undervalued assets that he could purchase at a discount to the assets' intrinsic value. To me, "intrinsic value" is the actual value of the asset discovered after the fact. For example, Apple stock was an undervalued asset at its initial public offering, when reviewed in retrospect. The key to Graham's work was identifying undervalued assets before the fact, using data-driven analysis.

In a May 22, 2018 post on Investopedia, Emily Norris writes:

> Graham's work is legendary in investment circles. Graham was a famous author, most notably for his books Security Analysis (1934) and The Intelligent Investor (1949). Graham was one of the first to solely use financial analysis to successfully invest in stocks.
>
> Graham's losses in the 1929 crash and Great Depression led him to hone his investment techniques. These techniques sought to profit in stocks while minimizing downside risk. He did this by investing in companies whose shares traded far below the companies' liquidation value. In simple terms, his goal was to buy a dollar's worth of assets for $0.50. To do this, he utilized market psychology, using the fear and greed of the market to his advantage, and invested by the numbers.
>
> He was also instrumental in drafting many elements of the Securities Act of 1933, also known as the "Truth in Securities Act," which, among other things, required companies to provide financial statements certified by independent accountants. This made Graham's work of financial analysis much easier and more efficient, and in this new paradigm he succeeded.

Finding stocks that trade below liquidation value was the skill that worked well in 1929. Finding assets that will appreciate far beyond their current price is the modern translation of investing in undervalued assets.

In my prior book, I referred to Michael Lewis' book *Moneyball: The Art of Winning an Unfair Game* and the subsequent movie, both of which detailed the work of one Billy Beane to leverage data when building a winning team. Beane's story at the Oakland Athletics serves as an effective framework for analyzing undervalued and overvalued assets in the present business environment.

A short flashback: I happened to sit next to Billy Beane for lunch one day during a conference and took the opportunity to learn more about the data-driven strategy that he had implemented at the Athletics, or the "A's," as some call the team. He described his approach: "It's about winning games at the least cost. We're a small market team and can't afford to pay the salaries of large market teams. But we can still compete and win as long as the cost of winning a game fits our budget."

---

63 https://quotecatalog.com/quote/warren-buffett-long-ago-ben-g-npeEQKp/

I said, "So you manage differently." Billy laughed. "Our budget forced us to find a strategy that allowed us to manage differently and win." Beane found that strategy and has continued to use it successfully.

Taking the long-term view on this issue is essential. As Beane put it in our discussions, reframing his organization's view of the value of certain assets over time was the crux of implementing transformation at the A's. This is an approach that also takes its cue from another thought leader—Warren Buffett. "Warren Buffett has a long-term view and seeks undervalued companies that will outperform over time... That's our strategy. We look for undervalued assets."

Beane spoke about finding undervalued baseball players who could work in a collaborative manner so that the A's could compete with teams that had "star" players. Beane's goal, in fact, was to develop a team that could compete and win against much better financed opponents without any big-name, big-pay "stars" at all.

Data-Driven Baseball

The Oakland Athletics have a long and storied history. The A's appeared in three consecutive World Series, from 1988 through 1990, and had the highest payroll in baseball in 1991. In 1995, new owners Stephen Schott and Ken Hofmann slashed payroll. As a result, Billy Beane, by necessity, began developing a strategy to obtain relatively undervalued players. His real innovation came in valuing on-base percentage among hitters, a strategy that flew in the face of conventional Major League Baseball (MLB) scouting methods.

Beane crafted a cost-efficient but winning team. By the 2006 MLB season, the Athletics ranked 24th of 30 major league teams in player salaries but had the 5th-best regular-season record. The Oakland A's became the first team in the 100-plus years of American League baseball to win 20 consecutive games. They also won their first playoff series under Beane in 2006 when they swept the Minnesota Twins in the American League Division Series. All of this happened on a modest payroll.

Beane's strategy worked because baseball teams had accumulated a vast amount of data on every player's at-bat performance, fielding performance, tendencies, and so on. Other teams, however, did not use this data in the same way Beane used it. Beane used analytics to gain insight into what elements of performance factor into wins ("on-base percentage") so that you could obtain players that were not viewed as "stars" but had good "on base" production while being paid modestly.

As of 2018 late in the season, the strategy was still working, as the Oakland A's had the lowest aggregate payroll cost as of opening day 2018 (see Table 3.1).

Table 3.1: 2018 MLB Opening Day payroll list.

2018 MLB OPENING DAY PAYROLLS					
RANK	TEAM	PAYROLL ($ Millions)	RANK	TEAM	PAYROLL ($ Millions)
1	Boston Red Sox	235.7	16	Cleveland Indians	134.4
2	San Francisco Giants	208.5	17	Arizona Diamondbacks	132.5
3	Los Angeles Dodgers	186.1	18	Minnesota Twins	131.9
4	Chicago Cubs	183.5	19	Detroit Tigers	129.9
5	Washington Nationals	181.6	20	Kansas City Royals	129.9
6	Los Angeles Angels	175.1	21	Atlanta Braves	120.5
7	New York Yankees	168.5	22	Cincinnati Reds	101.2
8	Seattle Mariners	162.5	23	Miami Marlins	98.6
9	Toronto Blue Jays	162.3	24	Philadelphia Phillies	96.9
10	St.Louis Cardinals	161.0	25	San Diego Padres	96.1
11	Houston Astros	160.0	26	Milwaukee Brewers	90.2
12	New York Mets	154.6	27	Pittsburgh Pirates	87.9
13	Texas Rangers	144.0	28	Tampa Bay Rays	78.7
14	Baltimore Orioles	143.1	29	Chicago White Sox	72.2
15	Colorado Rockies	141.3	30	Oakland Athletics	68.5

The following (Table 3.2) are the standings in the American League West, the division where the Oakland A's play as of August 20, 2018, along with each team's cost per win:

Table 3.2: MLB American League West Standings as of August 20, 2018.

AL WEST AS OF AUGUST 20, 2018	WON	LOST	ANNUAL PAYROLL	COST PER WIN ($ Millions)
Houston	75	49	160.0	1.65
Oakland	74	50	68.5	0.71
Seattle	71	54	162.5	1.77
L.A. Angels	63	63	175.1	2.14
Texas	56	70	144.0	1.15

The Oakland A's currently have the lowest cost per win by far, at $710,000. The A's strategy is not only to use data-driven analytics to get the best players at the lowest cost but to also use data-driven analysis to coach the player into maximizing his opportunities to get on base—the precursor to runs, which are the precursor to wins.

In other words, it's all about the runs.

When A's players are about to go free-agent and become eligible for large contracts, the A's either trade them away or just refuse to offer them an expensive contract. They replace departing players with new, often minor, players who are still inexpensive.

It's a more than a workable strategy. But, more importantly, it's a strategy that is durable. It's worked for the A's over time.

The A's win games at a fraction of the high-salary teams. In baseball, at the end of the day, it's about the cost per win.

Undervalued and Overvalued Assets in the Financial Services Space

Using this framework, let's apply the concept of overvalued and undervalued assets to financial services. Looking at a variety of financial services segments, the following is my opinion of overvalued and undervalued assets. The common denominator for each of these segments is that data is undervalued and underutilized by the current participants in these segments.

You may have a gut feeling that data is important, but few current participants have really monetized the value of data. Here's my opinion of the segment list of undervalued and overvalued assets (Table 3.3):

Table 3.3: Description of overvalued and undervalued assets within the various financial services segments.

FINANCIAL SERVICES SEGMENT	OVERVALUED	UNDERVALUED
Wealth Management	Investment Fund Managers	Data, Robo-Advisors
Real Estate Brokerage	Listing Agents, Selling agents, MLS	Aggregated real estate, market and demographic data
Retail Banking	Physical Branches	Highly responsive mobile banking platform, Customer data
Appraisals	Human Appraisers	Data Driven Collateral Evaluation

Table 3.3 (continued)

FINANCIAL SERVICES SEGMENT	OVERVALUED	UNDERVALUED
Title Insurance	Title agents, notaries	Data to drive online real estate closings, indemnity versus insurance for clear title
Mortgage Lending	Mortgage brokers, loan officers, back office personnel	Data driven lending and decisioning models
Mortgage Securitization	FreddieMac, FannieMae	Mortgage loan performance data
Banking	Commercial lenders, relationship managers	Data driven lending, converged cash management and business banking platform
Homeowners Insurance	Licensed agents	Data; a neutral system to shop for the best policy
Certified Public Accountants	CPAs performing audits	Data and artificial intelligence performing audits
Law Firms	Attorneys	Structured and unstructured data, artificial intelligence doing research and drafting documents

In every segment listed above, people with high compensation levels doing work that could be eliminated, automated, outsourced, or optimized are instead overweighted. (Note that each of these occupations requires a professional license. More on that later.) Let's walk through the categories, with a few stories about current disruptive events included for your consideration.

Wealth Management

Fund Managers often underperform market averages, but earn high fees compared to index funds that duplicate the market. There is a lot of pressure on fund managers. Former highly successful fund managers such as Legg Mason are feeling the pain.

Early in my career, I worked for a young liberal arts doctoral candidate named Bill Miller. He was hired by a Pennsylvania manufacturer as an experiment sponsored by New York University to assist doctoral candidates in transitioning to business. Miller spent lunchtime at a Smith Barney office looking up stocks on the Quotron in the lobby. Much of our discussions revolved around Ben Graham and finding undervalued securities.

Miller left shortly thereafter to work for Chip Mason at Legg Mason. Miller started the Legg Mason Value Trust Fund. He beat the stock market every year from 1991 to 2005. To put that in perspective, only about one quarter of stock funds manage to beat the market in any given year—the odds of doing it 15 years in a row are astronomically low.[64]

I saw Miller at an Orioles game a few years ago. He mentioned that beating the market is much harder now, because everyone focuses on data.

It's also much harder for Legg Mason. According to an article titled, "Trian's Legg Mason Fix Is Bet on Future of Asset Managers" by Justin Baer, writing in the *Wall Street Journal* on June 17, 2019:

> Trian, which had owned a stake in the asset manager as recently as 2016, had considered launching a proxy fight before Legg Mason ceded three board seats. Trian owns about 4.5% of Legg Mason shares, the company said last month. Trian executives have said they will help Legg Mason cut costs and boost revenue, fattening profit margins that have lagged behind many of its peers. They have also argued the firm could emerge as a buyer in an industry many executives and their advisers say is rife for consolidation. Adding new investment capabilities would give Legg Mason's sales teams more to sell and reducing duplicate functions would lower expenses.

> If those ideas sound familiar, it is because numerous other money-management chief executives have promised to use a similar playbook. So far, few have succeeded.

> The popularity of low-cost mutual and exchange traded funds has dimmed the prospects of Legg Mason and many other asset managers. Facing outflows of client money and relentless pressure to lower fees, firms have in turn looked to slash expenses. The situation became even more dire in the fourth quarter, when a market selloff accelerated the loss of assets.

Real Estate Brokerage

Listing agents schedule showings and provide listing information, market data, neighborhood characteristics, information on schools, opinions on value, and assistance in the staging and pricing of homes.

Selling agents work with potential buyers, identifying listings to consider, providing market and neighborhood data, assisting in drafting offers, and shuttling buyers around to properties. Virtually all that information is available on the web for free. And the selling agent works for the seller, not the buyer. The selling agent has an inherent conflict of interest to sell the home at the highest price, not the best value for the buyer.

One disruptor in this segment is Zillow. Zillow's initial business model was advertising-based, with realtors and mortgage lenders purchasing leads to fund

---

[64] http://money.com/money/4451841/bill-miller-fund-manager-legg-mason-fired/

Zillow's build out of massive databases of valuable information. Zillow now offers for free much of the information that realtors once had under lock and key. Little wonder that consumers question whether real estate listing services are worth 6% of the selling price of a house.

Retail Banking

Bank branches are very valuable assets if they generate considerable levels of deposits. They are not particularly valuable for most other purposes. I spoke with Jay Sidhu, CEO of Customers Bank and BankMobile. Sidhu is working diligently to create a mobile banking platform for millennials and underbanked customers in lieu of expensive branches. According to Sidhu, "When we master deposit gathering via mobile, we change the economics of banking. But we have to find a way to support low-balance checking account customers, including pricing of core banking systems that assume much higher deposit balances. Core system providers have to get more realistic on pricing."

Appraisals

Appraisers provide value by accessing the Realtor Multiple Listing System to find comparables and then visit the home, applying the comparables data to arrive at an estimate of market value... all things Zillow and other web-based services can do. Commercial systems, too, such as Clear Capital have collateral valuation models that are data-driven and free from influence or bias of human appraisers.

Title Insurance

Title insurance was created to indemnify property owners from defects in the title chain. In the last ten years, virtually all title conveyance information is maintained in electronic form, and claims are generally related to fraud and errors by title agents. About 90% of title insurance premiums are retained by the agent; about 10% or less is actually premium to the title insurance company to stand behind the title.

Mortgage Lending

Dodd-Frank commoditized mortgage lending. The credit box is tight, and 95% of mortgage loans granted in 2018 were insured or purchased by FreddieMac, FannieMae, or insured by GinnieMae. Seventy-five percent of the roughly $8,800 on average paid by a consumer to obtain a first mortgage loan is for compensation of sales and operational personnel.

Mortgage Securitization

Securitizers such as FreddieMac, FannieMae, and GinnieMae provide liquidity and interest rate risk transfer. Freddie and Fannie provide risk transfer. According to the Federal Housing Finance Agency, the regulator of Freddie and Fannie, borrowers pay an embedded base "guarantee fee" of about 50 basis points per year for the risk transfer. That's before "loan level price adjusters" that increase the fees for risk at the borrower level. In the past five years, GSE losses have been less than 3 basis points per annum. The rest of the fee goes to overhead and payment of dividends to the Treasury.

Homeowners Insurance

Homeowners insurance has traditionally been distributed by commissioned insurance agents employed by the insurer. Transformative firms like "It's Covered" are providing neutral online platforms to shop multiple insurance companies, bind the coverage, and do so in a few minutes. The transparent process is fast and easy, and is putting pressure on the traditional commissioned real estate agents.

Certified Public Accountants

CPAs have traditionally been very labor-intensive practitioners during audit work, particularly for publicly traded companies. Artificial Intelligence and bots are rapidly replacing CPA labor in many routine audit functions. This is putting pressure on audit fees as well as providing data-driven auditing that produces higher quality audits.

Mike Fenlon, Chief People Officer of PwC US, a "big four" auditing and consulting company, foresees much work done by CPA auditors rapidly being replaced with automated auditing, driven by artificial intelligence and data-driven analytics. "Our people will have to adapt and provide more value quickly," according to Fenlon.[65] Fenlon also sees the need for employees of all firms to change mindsets

---

65 From a short discussion with the author and Rick Fenlon at Chief Executive's "Disruptive Tech Summit" Massachusetts Institute of Technology, Cambridge, MA, June 10–11, 2019.

and behaviors to adapt to the power of data and data-driven decision making: "It's not an option, it's a requirement."

Lawyers

Outside of the top law firms doing mergers and acquisitions or capital markets activities, many law firms are under pressure as clients object to paying high legal fees. Much research can be done online, and artificial intelligence is deployed to do routine tasks done previously by attorneys and paralegals. Relativity, a Chicago-based software firm, makes e-discovery software to help people organize data, discover the truth, and act on it.[66] Relativity specializes in bringing order to unstructured data such as depositions, discovery documents, and testimony.

Baseball and Data-Driven Decision Making

The Oakland A's focused on the cost per win and coached their low-cost players on how to get on base which, as mentioned, can be argued as being the true driver in winning a game. In other words, the A's executed very specific coaching at a particular set of strategic baseball levers.

My prior book, *Strategically Transforming the Mortgage Banking Industry,* covered the data-driven, low cost-per-win strategy of the Oakland A's and how the A's advanced to the 2018 American League Wild Card game with the lowest cost per win in Major League Baseball. I won't repeat the analysis here, but the utilization of how data-driven strategy can be applied to every "at bat" is worth examination again.

Baseball players like to hit the ball. It's the moment that defines the game for many, and crowd-pleasing home runs and well-struck baseballs always bring the crowd to their feet. But letting each batter hit as they wish forgoes two strategic levers: opposing pitcher strategy and batter performance.

This first lever, which involves opposing pitcher strategy, is pretty straightforward: take a lot of pitches and force the starting pitcher out early.

A snippet of a coaching scene in the movie *Moneyball*[67] illustrates this concept: Mark Ellis played second base for the A's. Billy Beane tells Ellis, "You want to see

---

66 https://www.relativity.com/

67 *Moneyball* is a motion picture by 2011 Columbia Pictures Industries, Inc. Excerpts from the script are used to illustrate data-driven strategies. A short plot summary: Oakland A's general manager Billy Beane (Brad Pitt) challenges the system and defies conventional wisdom when his is forced to rebuild his small-market team on a limited budget. Despite opposition from the old guard, the media, fans, and their own field manager (Philip Seymour Hoffman), Beane—with the help of a young, number-crunching, Yale-educated economist (Jonah Hill))—develops a roster of misfits and,

more pitches and get deep into their bullpen. You want to get your at-bats off their 10th or 11th [relief] pitcher." Ellis says incredulously, "You want us to walk more?" Peter Brand replies, "At least once in every ten at-bats." Ellis likes to hit, so he says, "Or ... " Beane replies, "Triple-A Sacramento is only 80 miles away," meaning, if Ellis doesn't follow directions, he'll be demoted to the minor leagues. In order to implement a high-level strategic approach, Beane has to ask baseball players to work against what they've always thought about the game.

The second strategic lever involves getting on base more by analyzing each batter's performance, or when the batter attempts to hit the ball.

Ray Durham also played second base for the A's. Peter Brand shows Durham a chart of data-driven analytics regarding Durham's batting averages depending on when he swings at a pitch. "Basically, these are all your at-bats. This is you versus righties, you versus lefties ... and then, of course, all your count knowledge, okay? In an 0-0 count [meaning the first pitch is coming now], you're batting .290. In an 0-1 [first pitch was a strike], you average .238. In an 0-2, .159. When you're 1-0 [the first pitch was a ball], you're batting .324. Understand what I'm saying?"

Durham's response is telling. "But I'm a first-pitch hitter. I like to swing at fastballs." Brand tells him, "And that's the way you've been trained. But it's a habit we'd like to break you from. We're trying to design the game to your strengths. This has nothing to do with you being a great hitter—you're a great hitter. We just want to get you on base."

Beane tells the players, "I'm interested in you getting on base. If you do that, we win. If you don't, we lose."

Beane told me that the movie is pretty accurate with regards to his strategy, though he said that he is more personable and better-looking than Brad Pitt, who played him in *Moneyball*. "Find out the key metric in any business, and design strategy around that key metric. In baseball, the key metric is getting on base."

Statcast Democratizes Baseball Data

Major League Baseball (MLB) has adopted and democratized big data better than just about any industry I can think of. According to MLB's Statcast primer, "Baseball will never be the same. MLB Network features revolutionary real-time tracking."[68]

According to Paul Casella, writing at MLB.com:

---

along the way, forever changes the way the game is played. https://www.sonypictures.com/movies/moneyball

68 www.statcast.com

Statcast, a state-of-the-art tracking technology, is capable of gathering and displaying previously immeasurable aspects of the game.

Statcast collects the data using a series of high-resolution optical cameras along with radar equipment that has been installed in all 30 Major League ballparks. The technology precisely tracks the location and movements of the ball and every player on the field at any given time.

The result is an unparalleled number of figures and information, covering everything from the pitcher to the batter to any defensive players—and everything in between. Statcast has been deemed by MLB Network analyst Brian Kenny to be "a revolutionary technology that will change the way fans around the world view our national pastime."[69]

Imagine coaching your team with this degree of data-driven insight. Imagine artificial intelligence finding additional insights. According to MLB, each baseball game played generates 2.5 terabytes of structured and unstructured data. MLB houses this data for ten years, and Statcast provides free access to this data for MLB fans.[70]

You can research virtually any situation in baseball and search through ten years of data. For example, I searched the 2019 season for pitchers throwing 4-seam fast balls, with batters ahead in the count,[71] with the pitch hit to right field resulting in the batter getting on base, all for games played by the Oakland A's. A portion of the results are listed in Table 3.4.[72]

Table 3.4 shows the pitch as FF, a four seam fastball, with a pitch speed in miles per hours; with an exit velocity after being hit in miles per hour; the pitcher's name; batter's name; how fast the ball was spinning in revolutions per second; the launch angle of the hit off the bat; the pitching zone (a rectangular representation of whether the pitch was "inside," meaning near the batter's body, "low," meaning well below the hitter's beltline; the game date; the count; and the "plate appearance" result. Best of all, if the video is a Y for yes, you can watch high-resolution video of the play on-demand.

That's an incredible search engine of both structured (numerical data) and unstructured (video) data. And it's free to baseball fans. Just think of what Billy Beane has at his fingertips.

---

69 Paul Casella, "Getting to Know Statcast," MLB.com, June 15, 2015.
70 You can get a sense of where data-driven decisioning is heading by exploring Statcast, which at this writing is available at https://baseballsavant.mlb.com/statcast_search and is free.
71 The "count" is the number of balls and strikes at a given time during a batter's turn in the batter's box. "Ahead in the count" mean the batter has a favorable ratio of balls to strikes. For instance, a count of 3 balls and 1 strike is "'ahead." No balls and two strikes are "behind" in the count.
72 https://baseballsavant.mlb.com/statcast_search

Table 3.4: Statcast pitch summary, including results of the pitch.

PITCH	MPH	EV MPH	PITCHER	BATTER	DIST	SPIN RATE	LAUNCH ANGLE	ZONE	GAME DATE	COUNT	PA RESULT
FF	96.4	80.7	Frankie Montas	Tim Beckham	231	2406	27	4	6/15/19	2-1	Tim Beckham doubles (15) on a line drive to right fielder Chad Pinder. Omar Narvaez to 3rd.
FF	95.6	95.8	Frankie Montas	Rafael Devers	189	2267	14	14	4/29/19	2-1	Rafael Devers singles on a line drive to right fielder Stephen Piscotty

Residential Lending Cost Data

Data-driven decision making is undervalued in residential lending, to the peril of many lenders. Tom Finnegan, a principal at consulting firm Stratmor, noted the disparity in the cost to originate mortgages at large banks compared to independent mortgage bankers. The cost disparity produced amazingly high losses per loan at large banks.

Large banks lost $4,803 per retail mortgage loan originated in 2018 compared to large independent lenders, which earned on average of $376 per loan.[73] According to an MBA NewsLink staff article reported on June 21, 2019, Finnegan stated that:

> Large banks experience a significant disadvantage in the expenses we categorize as "corporate administration," he said, noting corporate administration costs amounted to $3,654 per loan in 2018 at the largest banks versus only $1,213 per loan for the large independents, resulting in a $2,441 per loan disadvantage for the large banks.

> Portfolio loans, and jumbo loans specifically, are being priced aggressively by the banks, leading to imputed revenue that is lower than might be expected otherwise. Large banks as a group do not focus on FHA and VA lending to the same extent that independents do, and a few have virtually abandoned FHA lending due to the perceived risk of regulatory enforcement actions. Because FHA and VA loans typically offer the ability to price with wider margins, not participating in this loan segment can also contribute to lower per loan revenue.[74]

Customer retention is another issue in which large banks lose advantage, according to Stratmor's June Insights Report.[75] Stratmor estimated large banks captured only 4% of the available mortgage volume from their customer base, compared to 8.1% at regional banks. Similarly, large banks recaptured only 12% of their own customers who paid off an existing mortgage, compared to a retention rate of 30% at the large independents.

The Insights Report stated that large banks are often slow to react to changes in the marketplace in an industry that is notoriously cyclical. Many are simply not geared toward origination of purchase mortgages, a much more reliable production source than refinances. "When our industry becomes dominated by purchase money mortgages, the large banks' natural advantage in terms of new loan opportunities dissipates," Finnegan said.

Additionally, the report says that many bank loan officers are not incented to pursue leads from referral sources outside the bank, such as realtors. "The type of

---

73 https://www.mba.org/mba-newslinks/2019/june/mba-newslink-friday-6-21-19/stratmor-large-banks-lag-far-behind-competitors-in-mortgage-profitability?_zs=VCbwB1&_zl=m9HA5
74 https://www.mba.org/mba-newslinks/2019/june/mba-newslink-friday-6-21-19/stratmor-large-banks-lag-far-behind-competitors-in-mortgage-profitability?_zs=VCbwB1&_zl=m9HA5
75 https://www.stratmorgroup.com/Insights/

loan officer who is attracted to the somewhat less entrepreneurial environment inside a large bank is often not well-suited to compete for external leads," the report said.

By sharp contrast, "the lifeblood of independent lenders is their aggressive marketing to referral sources," Finnegan said, noting that large bank policies tend to work against this type of personal marketing. "The legitimate quest for branding consistency and regulatory compliance can get in the way of personalized marketing and rapid response to the needs of the real estate community," he said. "Moreover, mortgage origination must compete for marketing dollars with other areas of the bank, and often does not come out on top."

Despite spending more than four times what their nonbank rivals spend on technology, $1,724 per closed mortgage for the large banks versus only $437 for the large independents, "large banks appear to have great difficulty translating technological expertise and resources into efficient technology support for the mortgage origination business," the report said. "Large banks' IT projects appear to get mired in process considerations and take years to roll out, if they are rolled out at all. Clearly, this is an area that many of the largest banks should review."

So what assets are overvalued at large banks? What assets are undervalued? Large banks should have a natural strategic advantage in residential lending. Large banks have low cost of funds to hold mortgages during securitization or in portfolio. They are generally not required to deal with state licensing and having every originator licensed by each state where the originator does business. They have a large deposit base and information on customers from their checking account activities. They can cross market effectively and can afford advanced data analytics and electronic marketing, among others. But many banks can't make it work.

Rich Bennion, Executive Vice President of HomeStreet Bank, is a long-time friend and worked hard to make mortgage banking work within HomeStreet. According to Rich, the business didn't make strategic sense in the current and foreseeable markets, and the sale of substantially all of the non-core mortgage banking business was completed in June 2019 to HomeBridge, a large independent mortgage banker.

Peter Norden, Homebridge Chief Executive Officer, said, "With Homebridge's focus on customer satisfaction and a culture of growth and collaboration, we see the HomeStreet Mortgage team as a seamless fit. We look forward to the opportunity to incorporate the HomeStreet Mortgage team into our leading retail mortgage platform."[76] The sale involved 241 branches, 2,400 employees, and about $6 million of purchase price paid to HomeStreet.

According to a *HousingWire* piece by Ben Lane published on February 15, 2019, HomeStreet Bank's initial decision to sell the mortgage banking business occurred about four months prior to my discussion with Rich Bennion. *HousingWire* reported:

---

76 https://www.housingwire.com/articles/49280-homebridge-expands-mortgage-business-by-acquiring-retail-loan-centers-from-homestreet-bank

Mark Mason, chairman, president, and CEO of HomeStreet, said the decision to sell off its retail mortgage business was "difficult," but said the bank feels it is necessary:

"The Board of Directors made the difficult decision to explore the potential sale of our mortgage banking business after extensive deliberations, ultimately concluding that this potential change would be in the best long-term interests of the company and its shareholders," Mason said in a statement.

"We are considering a sale at this time after having taken substantial steps in the last two years to improve the profitability of our mortgage banking business while expecting a near term recovery in industry volume and profitability," Mason continued.

"Unfortunately, it is still unclear when, and to what extent, industry conditions will improve. Single-family mortgage loans remain an important part of our asset diversification strategy and part of a broad array of products that we offer to our customers," Mason concluded. "Assuming the sale of our mortgage banking business, we will continue to offer mortgages, but the scale of this business line will be substantially smaller, focused on our retail deposit network and regional markets, and positioned for ongoing profitability."

According to the bank, it is making this move due to the "persistent challenges facing the mortgage banking industry." The bank cites "the increasing interest rate environment," which has reduced the demand for refinances, and higher home prices that have decreased the affordability of homes.

"Both factors continue to put downward pressure on mortgage origination volumes," the company said. "In addition, historically low new and resale home inventories in many of HomeStreet's primary markets continue to adversely impact the volume of available purchase mortgages."

Figure 3.1 illustrates the decline in market share of depository banks versus independent mortgage bankers, or conversely the increase in market share by nonbank originators.

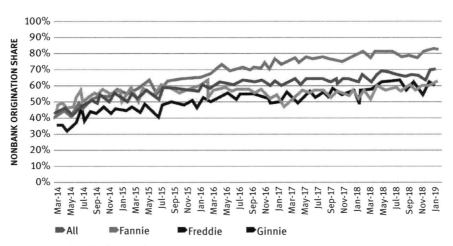

Source: eMBS and Urban Institute.

Figure 3.1: Nonbank origination market share for purchase loans.

Over the last ten years, independent mortgage bankers have substantially increased market share at the expense of large banks. Public stock analysts generally dislike the mortgage business due to profit cyclicality and perceived risk of enforcement and litigation. And many times, these risks are real.

But let's look a little deeper. First off, not all large bank mortgage platforms perform as poorly as described in the Stratmor Report. That means some banks perform better—much better, in fact—and some perform much worse. You have to ask why some banks even bother to compete in the space.

For Jay Plum of Huntington National Bank, banks will "fill in the blank" when it comes to looking out for the community and delivering to underserved sectors moving forward:

> Folks used to view that they had a community responsibility. And when it's all on the internet and it's based off of who comes in as the lead, it can be very different… [Some of the fintechs] that emerged in the early 2000 since lead aggregators feel a different sense of reaching out to communities by providing education as well as an opportunity to get a loan… and the financial education they provide is valuable to the consumers that go there… and then there are other sites that focus on loan generation and pay lip service to affordable housing. And some of those are not helpful for the industry at all. I think it's going to be up to mortgage bankers, mortgage brokers as well as banks, to make sure that the entire community is served.

In addition to Peter Norden at Homebridge, other large independents are seeking bargains in the residential lending space.

Stan Middleman, CEO of Freedom Mortgage Company, is investing and growing in the residential lending business. I spoke with him in June 2019:

> You have to understand the fundamental economics of the industry. You have to understand the fundamental drivers of risk. You also have to understand the fundamental factors that move events in an industry.

> For example, every American president puts pressure on the Federal Reserve to move rates lower as an election nears. That's the reason that I expected rates to move lower by next summer. In preparation for the lowering of rates, Freedom was ready to act. It was a surprise that President Trump pushed for lower rates at the earliest point in an election cycle, ever. But we were ready, and pleasantly surprised with the resulting drop in rates in 2019.

Freedom purchased RoundPoint in a deal announced on May 19, 2019. According to *HousingWire*, RoundPoint—which services and subservices about $91 billion in mostly agency loans—is a wholly-owned subsidiary of Freedom, a full-service, non-bank mortgage lender and servicer.[77]

---

77 https://www.housingwire.com/articles/49128-freedom-mortgage-to-acquire-roundpoint-mortgage-servicing

Middleman said that this acquisition, along with that of JG Wentworth's mortgage business earlier this year, will vastly enhance originations due to Freedom's advanced technology and customer accessibility:

> The great benefit is that each loan officer will be that much more effective. Our technology will allow a loan officer to produce in multiples of what they're able to do today from an origination standpoint.

> The RoundPoint deal adds $91 billion of servicing to Freedom. And servicing is a scale business. With the combination of servicing portfolios, the merger makes the company the seventh largest U.S. mortgage servicer nationwide. You need considerable servicing rights to generate the cash flow to make servicing a viable business long term.

> More importantly, our data-driven technology will allow us to drive costs way down, to the benefit of the customer and to Freedom. I see a day where a loan officer can handle 1,000 units a month, and an underwriter can underwrite 50 loans a day.

Middleman is a visionary, but I asked him to confirm his numbers, which he did.

> It won't happen right away, but it will happen. And here's how. Rocket Mortgage and others define a generic and tight credit box to easily approve and close loans. That's the sweet spot. There is a place for lenders to work on more difficult deals that need much more attention. There's a place for technology and a place to work on more difficult loans for borrowers, and we will continue to do both at Freedom. But you can see the value of starting with a tight box and iterating it out. That's how technology works. Harder loans will be done by specialists, with more straightforward loans done by technology-assisted generalists.

I have tremendous respect for Stan as one of the industry's best and most outspoken visionaries. He thinks broadly about technology and business:

> Figuratively speaking, technology does not solve any issue in any industry trying to take ten pounds of crap and trying to fit it into a two-pound box. That's too hard to do. Anybody that tries to do that is taking a long walk down a short pier. Technology works best on generic problems, and then one iterates out to more difficult problems.

Stan sees further consolidation, volatility, and innovation in the industry, as well as some challenges:

> Interest rate volatility will continue, as well as volatility in asset values. The drop in rates (as of June 2019) was a surprise. Freedom will take advantage of the rate drop to recapture clients that want to refinance, and build the long-term value of our servicing portfolio. Long term, lenders have to retain their customers. Once one gets a critical mass of servicing, one becomes a long-term player in the lending space. You can't sell your customers off and only originate long term.

> I expect we'll see falling home prices at some point in some locations. Diversification and liquidity to handle market volatility is key. History provides the lessons, as long as you pay attention.

> And make no mistake about it. It's all about the data. Data is rapidly becoming the fuel that drives this business.

Data as the Fuel that Drives the Real Estate Business

Maylin Casanueva, Chief Operating Officer of Teraverde, has a view on data:

> Our industry mostly relies on static historical data. The residential loan application is a picture in time, not a video of a consumer's journey up to the moment of truth: financing a new home. The same type of data is involved in the loan servicing space. It's a snapshot of prepayments and non-performing loans, not necessarily identifying the patterns and the financial journey of a borrower making mortgage payments each month. I think the key data elements—such as trending data, demographics, and predictive analytics—will provide information that is disruptive to the mortgage industry.

> But what of trended data? The information collectively gathered to identify and classify frequent characteristics into cohorts. For example, it's not just whether the borrower is current on a mortgage. When do they pay? Do they pay on the fifteenth of the month, the last day before a late fee? Before the first of the month? What if they were paying on the first, but now they're paying just before the fifteenth? Is something happening with this borrower that a lender could help with? Think of utilizing the information gathered about the borrower and the relationship value of a check-in with a borrower and helping mitigate a possible delinquency. Maybe somebody is distressed, but if they're paying, that person will likely still have a good credit score, but trouble is brewing.

> This is the power of data. We need to be thinking about really acting in the borrower's interest in a proactive way to mitigate losses as opposed to just say, "hey, you're late, you're now paying a late fee." That's punitive, versus a touchpoint to deepen a relationship and truly assist borrower when unforeseen life events occur.

Data in the residential real estate industry is everywhere. Who can monetize it?

Zillow has become a real data-driven force in the residential real estate market. Zillow is publicly traded with a market capitalization of about $9 billion as of June 24, 2019.[78] The size and scope of Zillow's data and reach is simply amazing. More importantly, Zillow has found a way to be paid by advertisers, realtors, lead aggregators, and others while building its massive data sets. Zillow collected $1.3 billion in revenue in 2018 while assembling a very disruptive set of data on dwelling units in the United States.

Zillow's mission is "to build the largest, most trusted, and vibrant home-related marketplace in the world."[79] That sounds suspiciously like Jeff Bezos's initial thought for Amazon: to build Earth's largest bookstore.

According to *GeekWire*, Zillow Group CEO Rich Barton said, "Zillow is taking a cue from companies like Amazon, Uber, and others that have created a 'one click, magic happens' expectation. That's what the new Zillow is trying to offer for buying

---

78 https://www.nasdaq.com/symbol/z

79 https://www.geekwire.com/2019/zillow-mortgage-lender-real-estate-giant-going-funnel-buying-house/

a house, with simplified mortgages tied in, just like payments are integrated into Uber." Zillow is accelerating its shift from media and advertising to moving further down funnel and closer to the real estate transaction to create better consumer experiences, paraphrasing Zillow's 2018 Form 10-K.

According to Zillow Group's SEC filings:

> Zillow's living database of approximately 110 million U.S. homes, including homes for sale, homes for rent and homes not currently on the market, attracts an active and vibrant community of users.[80]

> Individuals and businesses that use Zillow's mobile applications and websites have updated information on more than 80 million homes, creating exclusive home profiles not available anywhere else. These profiles include detailed information about homes, including property facts, listing information and purchase and sale data.

> Zillow provides current home value estimates, or Zestimates, and current rental price estimates, or Rent Zestimates, on approximately 100 million U.S. homes. Zillow generated revenue of $1.3 billion in revenue in 2018.

According to its Form 10-K:

> Zillow Group, Inc. operates the largest portfolio of real estate and home-related brands on mobile and the web which focus on all stages of the home lifecycle: renting, buying, selling and financing. Zillow Group is committed to empowering consumers with unparalleled data, inspiration and knowledge around homes and connecting them with great real estate professionals. The Zillow Group portfolio of consumer brands includes Zillow, Trulia, Mortgage Lenders of America, StreetEasy, HotPads, Naked Apartments, RealEstate.com and Out East. In addition, Zillow Group provides a comprehensive suite of marketing software and technology solutions to help real estate, rental, and mortgage professionals maximize business opportunities and connect with millions of consumers.

> Beginning in April 2018, Zillow Offers provides homeowners in certain metropolitan areas with the opportunity to receive offers to purchase their home from Zillow. When Zillow buys a home, it makes certain repairs and lists the home for resale on the open market. In October 2018, we completed the acquisition of Mortgage Lenders of America, L.L.C. ("MLOA"), a licensed mortgage lender, through which we originate residential mortgages to consumers.

A careful read of Zillow's public SEC disclosures shows a company moving to control search and data access to every residential dwelling in the United States, as well as providing access to rental, home ownership, construction, real estate valuation, mortgage banking, real estate listings, and related information.

If Zillow CEO Rich Barton is thinking about Amazon and Uber, he's thinking about taking friction, cost, and humans out of the residential shelter business. It's

---

80 http://secfilings.nasdaq.com/filingFrameset.asp?FilingID=13243830&RcvdDate=2/21/2019&CoName=ZILLOW%20GROUP%2C%20INC.&FormType=10-K&View=orig, page 3.

worth reading Zillow's 2018 10-K in detail if you're interested in seeing the vision of how the residential shelter business may be transformed.

Thinking back to the cost stack in residential real estate, disruption comes as market players find ways to tap undervalued assets. In residential real estate transactions, many overvalued assets are represented by the human assets performing transactional (as opposed to relationship) services, and the undervalued asset is transactional activity driven and powered by data.

As Stan Middleman of Freedom Mortgage says, "It's all about the data." It really is.

Chapter Four
A Conceptual Treatment of Fintech

For the purposes of our conversation in this book, I want us to take a moment now to consider a conceptual treatment of fintech.

The term "fintech" has no specific definition. Some consider an online mortgage application or mobile-enabled loan application to be fintech. Some consider eDisclosure (a consumer consenting to receiving loan disclosures electronically as opposed to paper) fintech. Mobile banking, mobile bill pay, Venmo, and even bitcoin may be considered fintech, as well. Fintech can even be a generic term that describes a technology company that is assigned a high earnings or revenue multiple simply because investors perceive the company as being a play in an investment space that may offer outsized capital gains. It's a term that is still finding its meaning, in many ways.

So, in this chapter and moving forward, I want us to consider a concept of fintech as a holistic technology (electronic or otherwise) that enables an end-to-end business process. Using this definition, the field narrows with respect to technology, but broadens with respect to business process.

In speaking with financial services providers throughout the U.S. and Canada, I am often surprised that many think that an integrated sales and financing platform is a recent phenomenon. Or that trade finance with risk premiums is a recent phenomenon and that the infrastructure of the secondary mortgage market is a recent phenomenon. They are not.

As we have already discussed, there is much historical precedent for this concept of fintech. The ancient Greek end-to-end marketplace, for one, included the convergence of product choices, trade finance, and logistical infrastructure. In the context of its time, this marketplace could be considered fintech. Why? The physical process of trading goods was augmented with a vertically integrated logistics model (transportation, a regulatory infrastructure) and a financial infrastructure to facilitate trading of goods, including the creation of coinage (the bitcoin of the day), financing of transportation and trade, and a workable banking system to gather resources to lend to merchant ships.

Silicon wafers and fiberoptic cable may have been missing, but the thought leadership of creating a marketplace with vertical integration, a method of financial exchange, lending, and a store of value qualify as fintech as of 600 BCE. The refinement of gold and silver, along with the creation of coinage containing precious metal as a store of value and a medium of exchange, was fintech at the time. The pricing of risk and the financing of merchant shipping was an advanced use of existing fintech, given that risk-based pricing of financing was aggressive thought leadership at the time.

https://doi.org/10.1515/9783110650471-005

The combined concepts of convergence and logistics created great wealth for the Greeks and a resulting increase in the standard of living for Greek citizens, as well as a structured city-state political environment. Whether in 600 BCE or 2020 CE, the elements of fintech revolve around convergence of product and the logistics to price, deliver, diligence, and risk manage the overall buying experience. So now that we have detailed the historical precedents, let's dive into this conceptualization of fintech in more detail.

I think of fintech in a broader sense than it is more commonly used today. A conceptual model for fintech could be described as follows.

Fintech is the convergence of a marketplace of product discovery, including identification of features and benefits, with a price discovery mechanism, facilitated by a means of exchange, logistics for delivery, risk management, and a regulatory or governance framework for the process. The ancient Greek marketplace qualified as fintech, as did the Medicis' and similar marketplaces, up to contemporary silicon and internet-powered fintech marketplaces.

Table 4.1 identifies my opinion of the fintech ecosystem, as well as an analysis of both ancient and contemporary fintech markets. You will note that many contemporary fintech companies provide some or all the functions of my definition of a fintech ecosystem. As the fintech ecosystem matures, the elements converge.

Table 4.1: Summary of fintech ecosystems from Greece 600 BC to Amazon 2019.

MARKET FEATURE	GREECE 600BC	MEDICI 1300 AD	*AMAZON* 2019
Product Convergence	Athens	Florence, Italy	Internet
Price Discovery	Physical market	Physical market	Website Market
Medium of Exchange	Coinage	Coinage	Fiat Currency
Financing	Trade finance	Trade Finance	Credit Card, Affirm
Risk Management	Shipping Indemnity	Guilds, Transaction Control	Free returns, product warranty
Legal Transaction Framework	Greek City States	Italian City State	Sovereign Government

Stan Middleman of Freedom Mortgage has a keen mind for looking back through history for cues as to what the future may hold. I appreciate Stan's thought leadership in the residential lending marketplace, especially. As I shared earlier, his advice to look at the historical narrative was the genesis of my foray into the early history of convergence and logistics.

Stan also understands the cyclical nature of financial systems such as the residential lending space. Fintech marketplaces and fintech participants ultimately fail through creative destruction or else through disruption arising from overzealous regulation, crushing taxation, the emergence of systemic fraud and cheating, and/ or the violence of war. The Greek and Roman Empires fell, as did the Medicis, Bank of Amsterdam, precious metal backed currency, and the Dot.com bust. One way or the other, fintech ecosystems morph over time. That's Schumpeter's creative destruction at work.

In research for this book, I was surprised to find that the mortgage banking industry was remarkably well developed in the late 1800s. As you review this short history, note that strategies such as standardization, diversification of funding sources via securitization and whole loan trading, and mortgage product niches were firmly in place 125 years ago. Though advanced technologies had not yet emerged, the strategic thought of how to serve customer segments for the good of the customer and the industry were clearly present, a fact that bodes well for the industry if and when it can leverage this conceptual modal of fintech and self-transform.

Mortgage Banking in History

The industry was divided into two segments: "farm mortgage banking" to fund agricultural expansion in the Midwest and Great Plains and "urban mortgage banking," which funded a nationwide trend toward ownership of single-family homes beginning about 1900.[81]

> Farm mortgage bankers used informal recourse arrangements to ameliorate the risks and informational asymmetries investors faced when purchasing whole loans; these intermediaries did so by developing and maintaining reputations to buy back troubled loans they had originated and serviced, so that their investors suffered no losses.[82]

It is interesting that the desire on the part of the Farm Mortgage Bankers to protect their reputations by repurchasing non-performing loans protected investors, with the Farm Mortgage Banker foreclosing on the property and recovering its funds through the subsequent sale of collateral.

> Urban mortgage bankers, in contrast, developed explicit mortgage insurance products to deal with the same issues. Second, over time, mortgage bankers in both the farm and urban markets found it advantageous to move beyond the "retail" business of selling whole loans by forming long-term, exclusive relationships with life insurance companies.[83]

---

81 Dr. Kenneth A. Snowden, The Research Institute for Housing America; Special Report, 2014, "Mortgage Banking in the United States, 1870–1940."
82 Ibid., page 3.
83 Ibid., page 4.

Finally, mortgage bankers in both sectors experimented with private mortgage securitization, but in different forms. In the 1880s, large western farm mortgage bankers established their own covered mortgage bond programs, and the same innovation was later introduced in the urban market. But after 1910, urban mortgage bankers also began to use participation certificates to combine or divide, and even to create tranches, from the payment streams of specific mortgage loans.[84]

Many of the leaders I spoke with were surprised to learn that participation certificates to parse individual loans, as well as a form of a derivative collateralized mortgage security, existed before the Great Depression. Many of these innovations were lost during the Great Depression and did not resurface until more recent times.

What is the relevance of this discussion to today's financial services industry? Let's examine convergence and logistics in financial services in more depth.

Convergence and Logistics in Greater Depth

It seems human nature to want choices and variety. That's where product discovery comes in. My friend Don Bishop introduced me to wine, particularly red French wine. At a wine dinner, the features of red wine suddenly became clear: the tannins, the terroir (French for the characteristics of the soil and exposure of the vineyard), the various aromas and fruit attributes, and alcohol level.

My discovery of wine progressed to French-style Napa red wine blends. One particularly notable discovery was tasting Joseph Phelps's wine with Joe Spellman, a master sommelier. Joe brought the individual components Phelps's Insignia, the 2002 Wine Spectator Wine of the Year. It was fascinating to have Spellman walk through the nuances of each grape component from a barrel sample of just that grape. The magic was blending the five components together. I owe Don Bishop a debt of gratitude for the initiation into wine. In this case, the wines and their components physically converged at a wine tasting at Josephine's on June evening in 2005.

Note that once you get comfortable with producers of French wine, you can experience the financial services market underlying French Bordeaux wine. The French wine market is an example of convergence of quality wines from about one hundred producers, as well as the logistical framework to distribute those wines, including the financial aspects of cash flow management for the wineries, and the physical distribution of the wine.

Thomas Jefferson was thought to be an early aficionado of French wine.[85] Napoleon created the 1855 Classification of French Bordeaux wine by segmenting

---

84 Ibid.
85 https://www.npr.org/templates/story/story.php?storyId=95087999

the wine into five categories, from "first growth" to "fifth growth," with first growth being the finest wine in Napoleon's classification.[86] The 1855 classification endures today as a method of classifying the quality of French wine. The better French wineries (Chateau for oenophiles) produce wine and distribute via négociants.[87] French wineries offer négociants tastings of wine shortly after the vilification process takes place. The négociants estimate the quality of a vintage, as well as estimating retail demand and offer to purchase the wine "en premier," or while still in the barrel at a specific price.

This is a form of the futures market. The négociants then offer the wine to wholesalers around the world, as "wine futures." That is, you buy wine two years ahead of its bottling and release. You hope that the futures price is favorable compared to the retail price when offered to consumers in retail wine shops. Sometimes it is, sometimes it is not. This is a form of convergence and logistics. Convergence in the sense that the wine futures are offered for over 100 chateaus in a unified market, competing against other chateaus. Logistics provide the ability for the chateau to sell to négociants to obtain current cashflow, deliver the wine two years later to wholesalers, then pass the wine to retailers who sell to the public. The wholesalers also fulfill sales to retail buyers who purchased the wine en premier.[88]

My wife Judy often asks why I buy wine futures. My explanation is that I am participating in a historically significant market demonstrating both convergence and logistics going back almost two centuries. Sometimes the futures market provides great value: I explained to Judy that the 2009 and 2010 Leoville Barton wines purchased en premier are worth three times the original futures price. The 2013 futures purchases, not so much value as the wines turned out to be so-so. I tell her, "At least I can drink my mistakes." And I do!

eBay provides an example of convergence electronically, not physically, together with a logistics system to facilitate payment and delivery of purchases. An anecdote to illustrate this: I rekindled my early passion for stereo gear about 15 years ago. I found myself on the hunt for a Scott 299a stereo vacuum tube powered amplifier—my first stereo amplifier, purchased used from a stereo dealer with a little help from my grandfather in 1964.

The Scott 299a used vacuum tubes to produce a very warm and inviting sound. But how do you find a 50-year-old amplifier? There aren't many antique stereo dealers in Lancaster, Pennsylvania. A search on eBay quickly yielded many examples offered by sellers across the United States, Asia, and Japan. I purchased three Scott 299a models over the course of two years and enjoyed restoring them to original condition. eBay handed the payment to the three sellers.

86 https://www.winespectator.com/articles/the-1855-bordeaux-classification-3491

87 https://blog.vinfolio.com/2016/06/22/what-is-a-wine-negociant/

88 https://vinepair.com/articles/bordeaux-en-primeur-explained/

eBay provided ratings for the sellers, too, delivering on diligence when buying a product at a distance from a seller you have never met. Pictures and descriptions, as well as purchase insurance provided by eBay, provided the convergence and the logistics to bring buyers and sellers together. PayPal allowed for easy purchase.

Move from eBay to residential real estate lending for a moment. Most mortgage lending websites provide convergence of product feature and benefits on a single site. Logistic capability is provided in some respect, as many sites permit the loading of borrower documents, receipt of disclosures, and so on. But the lender sites are not a marketplace, per se. The borrower has to move from site to site to compare features and benefits. So, let's transition back to fintech attributes in general.

Terms of Transfer

eBay provides convergence as well as structured "terms of transfer." The marketplace sets requirements, disclosure of terms and conditions, feedback regarding reliability of both seller and buyer, dispute resolution, as well as a variety of payment methods (such as credit card or PayPal). Transportation, tracking numbers and terms of shipment are also presented. eBay is a converged and vertically integrated platform offering a converged marketplace with simultaneous logistics to pay for and deliver a purchase. A framework for satisfaction and returns are available.

I recently was shopping for a watch, and discovered that I could pay for a watch by credit card, PayPal, or I could finance the purchase using Affirm, which had me extremely interested. eBay also serves as a de facto marketplace for watches, as many discrete sellers also listed their products in eBay in addition to their own websites. Several of the watch sellers have physical locations. Govberg in Philadelphia has the option to shop physically or via the web for the same price and on the same terms. As a salesperson from Govberg told me, "We're omni-channel," summing up the miracle of convergence at a retail location as well as on a website, with integrated logistics.

Risk Management

Risk management includes due diligence into the transaction and seller. It can include insurance where the buyer obtains insurance against seller failure to deliver the product, loss of product, or product function. The ability to perform diligence and achieve recourse on an electronic marketplace likely accounts for their growth.

As Bill Emerson of Quicken said, "We use every tool to create a close relationship with a customer except that we never meet that customer face to face." This is true, too, for marketplaces like Amazon and eBay. The ability to post specifications, owner's manuals, pictures, and videos for physical products builds on Emerson's thoughts—a potential buyer can examine all aspects of a product, including specs, function, price, and terms. The only thing the customer can't do is physically handle the product prior to purchase.

Return policies, insurance, buyer protection, and warranties are risk management tools. These tools help the buyer overcome reluctance to purchase the product because the buyer can't touch or inspect the product prior to delivery.

The disruptive element of eBay, Amazon, and Quicken is that they provide a customer a way to transcend the physical meeting, inspection, or building of a relationship without any face-to-face or physical access to a product.

The transformative aspects of price, terms, and risk management without physical presence are the factors that drive online everything. The Founding Fathers never contemplated the internet, but did establish a method of exchange, a framework for national commerce, and a legal framework that helped disruptive technology and practices to exist.

Government Regulation

There is a place for a transparent and well-thought-out role for government in providing a framework for legal ownership, transfer of ownership, and a method to perfect titles of major assets. Such regulations make commerce more efficient and predictable. This framework also comes with costs such as taxes on the sale, use, or transfer of an asset; fees on the sale, use, or transfer of an asset; and imposition of policy objectives achieved by regulation of transactions. These policy objectives can include fairness, non-discrimination, anti-fraud and anti-abuse, and other goals which serve a public purpose. These policy objectives provide public benefit. Sometimes regulatory overreach has adverse impacts. I'll speak to some of the adverse impacts of regulations that can have material unintended consequences, especially when such regulations are applied in novel or unanticipated manners.

One such misapplication of the False Claims Act has a very disruptive impact on the FHA lending marketplace. The U.S. Department of Justice brought False Claims actions against many FHA lenders in the wake of the mortgage meltdown. The False Claims Act was aimed at government defense contractors. The Obama-era Justice Department used it as a cudgel against lenders, most of which were large lenders who winced and settled since "resistance is futile."

One lender, Quicken, went on the offense. The CEO at the time, Bill Emerson, stated, "I will never admit to actions that never occurred to settle a dispute. It's a question of reputation and honesty." Quicken sued the Justice Department, and at each turn, Bill described the government's case as becoming smaller and smaller. Finally, on June 14, 2019, after four years of fighting the Justice Department, the case was dismissed without Quicken admitting to anything.[89] A token payment (if you can consider $32 million a token) was made by Quicken to permit the Justice Department to save some face, but it was clear Emerson administered an embarrassing blow to inappropriate use of False Claims.

The Justice Department, however, bagged many large bank lenders for similar allegations. Chase settled the matter for $614 million and was the subject of Justice Department reputational drubbing for "violating the False Claims Act by knowingly originating and underwriting non-compliant mortgage loans submitted for insurance coverage and guarantees by the Department of Housing and Urban Development's (HUD), Federal Housing Administration (FHA), and the Department of Veterans Affairs (VA)."[90] Chase substantially reduced originations in the FHA and VA programs. It's no wonder that large bank participation in mortgage lending has been curbed over justifiable fear of overly aggressive enforcement. The impact of cavalier and overly aggressive enforcement can stifle innovation and curb competition. There are many other examples of this impact, as will be covered later.

Payment Technology

Some parts of the logistical elements of fintech have emerged and grown rapidly. Payment technology, beginning with Visa and Mastercard, have flourished internationally and domestically in the United States. In 2018, Visa and Mastercard collectively issued 6 billion cards, and handled about $17 trillion in payment volume. By contrast, PayPal has about 277 million users worldwide.[91]

In 2013, Silicon Valley was awash in speculation about so-called "mobile wallets." In an article in *Barron's*, Tae Kim wrote:

> "I think it's just getting started," Tim Cook, the Apple CEO, told analysts at the time, leaving Wall Street thinking of a major disruption. But when Apple Pay arrived 18 months later, there was no sign of a revolution. Rather than start from scratch, Apple decided to partner with Visa (ticker: V), Mastercard (MA), and American Express (AXP). The new payment feature built into iPhones was just one more way to make payments at cash registers and websites via the existing payment networks. Disruption gave way to incremental change.[92]

89 https://www.housingwire.com/articles/49337-quicken-loans-agrees-to-pay-325-million-to-resolve-fha-loan-allegations-with-doj

90 https://www.justice.gov/opa/pr/jpmorgan-chase-pay-614-million-submitting-false-claims-fha-insured-and-va-guaranteed-mortgage

91 Tae Kim, "Big Tech Wanted to Dethrone Credit Cards. Why It Failed, and Who Wins Now," *Barron's*, May 24, 2019.

92 Ibid.

Apple executives still showered Apple Pay with characteristic praise; iPhone users could now "start making payments with the touch of a finger." Yet the rollout confirmed the real powers behind digital payments: Visa and Mastercard.

Rather than being cut out of the equation—as investors had feared—the existing payment networks were being endorsed by the country's most powerful tech company. "Early adopters in the space have learned the hard way," Visa's head of innovation told Barron's at the time. "Payments are just hard."[93]

The consolidation of the infrastructure supporting payment technology is undergoing rapid consolidation. According to S&P Global Intelligence, two massive mergers occurred in the payment processing space: the marriage of Fiserv Inc. and First Data Corp., and Fidelity National Information Services Inc. and Worldpay Inc. These mergers will likely reshape the payment processing landscape.

In late May 2018, a merger between Total System Services Inc. and Global Payments further reshaped the payments infrastructure landscape. This acquisition also cemented Global Payments in Total's payment-centric issuer processing business, their merchant acquiring practices, and prepaid cards, creating another two-sided network platform of merchants and financial institutions.[94]

While earning a good deal of word of mouth in recent years, cryptocurrency is not performing at the same level. According to *Barron's*, "Cryptocurrencies have also not gained traction in consumer payments because of relatively slow transaction times and the lack of recourse for fraud or stolen funds. Moffett Nathanson (a U.S.-based boutique independent research company) estimates that a payments system based on Bitcoin can handle only about seven transactions per second versus Visa's more than 65,000 transactions. And then there's the extreme price volatility of digital currencies."[95]

The breadth and scope of the global payments fintech system described above dwarfs the U.S. residential lending space, with about 6 million home sales and about $1.3 trillion in mortgage volume.

Payment technology facilitates international trade on platforms offering convergence of products. Amazon and Alibaba are examples. En premier wine futures are also served via payment technology. Place your order with a wholesaler, and you can pay for wine futures with a credit card, debit card or PayPal. Payment technology is truly fascinating as a lubricant for international trade. My wife and I traveled to Easter Island, Chile; American Samoa; Australia; Papau New Guinea; Cambodia, Dubai, India, Tanzania, and Morocco. One credit card worked in all locations; no

---

93 Ibid.

94 Rachel Stone, "Next fintech megamerger could be $20B tie-up announced within days," S&P Global Intelligence, May 24, 2019.

95 Tae Kim, "Big Tech Wanted to Dethrone Credit Cards. Why It Failed, and Who Wins Now," *Barron's*, May 24, 2019.

worries with exchange rates or acceptance. It's truly a miracle of convergence and logistics to think that the first credit card issue happened less than 60 years ago.

Payment technologies are important for in the residential real estate marketplace not as a method of paying for real estate, but as an analog of how quickly the convergence and logistics of transferring value can change. The story started in 6th century BCE Greece and has evolved quickly in the past ten years.

A Tale of Two Financial Products

Let's examine the path of two financial products: auto finance and home finance. Auto finance is largely one-stop shop point of sale. Real estate finance is not.

General Motors pioneered the convergence of automobile marketing. From entry-level Chevrolet to top of the line Cadillac, a common denominator was choice and ease of financing a purchase. General Motors Acceptance Corporation ("GMAC," now Ally Bank) was formed in 1919. According to GMAC's self-described role, "In the early 1920s, people looking to buy a car or truck had to pay cash or secure their own financing from banks that didn't typically issue loans for automobiles. We made it convenient for customers to get financing right at the dealership."[96] By 1924, GMAC financed over 4 million cars![97] In 1920, the U.S. population was just over 100 million persons.[98] With an average family size of four,[99] about 25 million families purchase 4 million GM cars financed by GMAC. Talk about fast market share growth.

Thus, GMAC disrupted banks out of the profitable auto lending and leasing business. It's easy to see why. I decided to purchase my first new car in 1976, and walked into see a loan officer at First Pennsylvania Bank in downtown Philadelphia. The loan officer sneered at me, and wondered aloud why a young person would expect that First Pennsylvania would deem him an appropriate borrower. I walked out, and got a lift from my uncle to a Ford dealer.

Media Ford in Media, Pennsylvania was happy to sell me a car, and to finance it on the spot. Virtually all cars are now financed at the dealer, with either a captive finance company like GMAC offering loans or leases. Banks have been reduced to buying auto loans as indirect lenders, paying the dealer a premium to provide a loan be sold to the bank. Auto financing is now point of sale.

Mortgage financing is not. Many have tried, but few have succeeded with one-stop shopping for home financing. Sears tried it in the 1990s. Cendant tried it in the 2000s. Zillow is trying it now. A common barrier is that customers want a 30-year fixed rate loan. Enter Fannie, Freddie, and Ginnie, and their secondary market

96 https://www.ally.com/about/history/

97 https://www.ally.com/about/history/

98 https://www.census.gov/history/www/through_the_decades/fast_facts/1920_fast_facts.html

99 https://qz.com/1099800/average-size-of-a-us-family-from-1850-to-the-present/

requirements outlined in thousands of pages of selling guides, with processes that date back to the 1930s. Buy a car and financing is approved in 60 seconds. Buy a house and financing is approved in 60 days.

National Mortgage News Editor-in-Chief Austin Kilgore pointed out that lenders and technology developers have made considerable progress improving the customer experience when applying for a mortgage. This observation is made in the context of housing finance, not buying a car or getting a credit card.

The user experience with an online or mobile mortgage application process, however, is just a first step. "Few, if any, of the fintech startups entering the mortgage arena have focused on the work that happens after a loan file reaches the hands of an underwriter, largely because it's the hardest part of the process to address. But it's where the biggest efficiency gains can be made," Kilgore wrote in his story. "While there hasn't been much digital mortgage love for the mortgage back office, the lenders and vendors that crack this code will have a competitive advantage over their peers as the first wave of digital mortgage technology becomes table stakes."[100]

The Complexity of Mortgage Finance

Nima Ghamsari, CEO of Blend (provider of a mortgage point of sale system), has views about why the mortgage lending industry has not yet transformed the entire mortgage lending process:

> I think the biggest, the hardest part... there's always this Nirvana view of the future, of "here's how good this could be if we solved all these problems at once." That has two sorts of pitfalls to it that I think are worth thinking about for companies that are undergoing this journey. The first is not every problem has been solved by companies that are out there. There's a long way to go. There's a lot more to solve. And the industry is enormous. There are so many participants. There are so many parts of the process.

> Meaning, that having a clear roadmap of the customer experience, process, and workflow lets one deploy solutions to the most pressing issues now and then undergo continuous improvement to reach the ultimate destination. So many projects fail by attempting to implement segments that are just too large.

> If we waited for everybody to solve all these things before we released our product, we'd be having this conversation in 2030. It would be a long time before we solved it. But also, what that means for the organization is that even within the organization they don't even need to use everything that we or others have to get started. So, by that I mean [some lenders] need everything integrated and everything perfect before I get started. But actually, the incremental

---

100 Austin Kilgore, "How to solve the digital mortgage divide," National Mortgage News, September 20, 2017.

value and the incremental benefit to your customers, if you're a financial institution, of getting something up and running that allows [customers] to get that simplicity and transparency is big enough on its own.

Said another way, it's important to have the overall experience, process, and workflow documented, but to undertake implementation in steps. Constant improvement towards the right vision, towards that perfect Nirvana world that everyone wants... but don't wait for the Nirvana world before you make a move. It's critically important that the overall experience, process, and workflow be understood and documented so that the highest value technology components can be implemented first.

Ghamsari is correct in that the process of obtained a mortgage loan is very complex due to secondary market requirements.

From Consumer Interest in a Mortgage to Application

The process used by a lender involves moving from the very beginning of the customer's interest in your company all the way through taking the application to closing the loan, establishing the loan servicing experience, and serving that customer's financing needs for life.

Workflow is how the lender's process is translated into the order of the individual tasks necessary to complete the loan. Workflow extends to the lowest common denominator of each task within the process. Most lenders' workflows appear to have a large amount of variability when it comes to the what and how of accomplishing each task. Most loan origination systems support milestones as a form of workflow management, but the tasks within each milestone are generally not planned and executed as they would be in a typical manufacturing operation.

Many CEOs conceive of mortgage lending as dividing into two segments. The first segment is consumer interest in a mortgage loan, through the completion of the application process. As shorthand, we'll call this "Interest to App." The second segment is the Application to Investor Funding, or "App to Fund" (Figure 4.1).

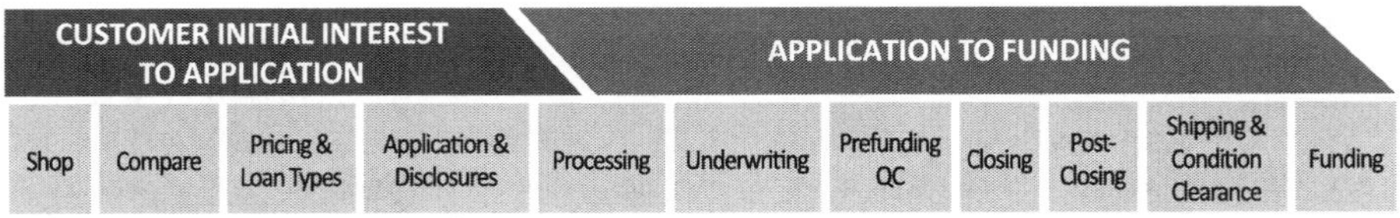

CUSTOMER INITIAL INTEREST TO APPLICATION				APPLICATION TO FUNDING						
Shop	Compare	Pricing & Loan Types	Application & Disclosures	Processing	Underwriting	Prefunding QC	Closing	Post-Closing	Shipping & Condition Clearance	Funding

Figure 4.1: Segmented view of the mortgage lending workflow.

"Interest to App" is an exciting segment. It's where the prospective borrower shops, compares, and prices a loan. It's where most of the technology innovation has taken place to date. Whether it's Rocket Mortgage, Blend, BeSmartee, Roostify,

Maxwell, SimpleNexus, or others—it's largely about transparency and ease of use for the customer.

In looking at the overall process, Jonathan Corr of EllieMae noted, "There's a lot of folks that are attacking the 'Interest to App' segment, that front-end of the process. It's exciting to see all the innovation and focus on that initial customer experience and leveraging technologies that are out there: instant asset and deposit data, and income verification. That's going to create a better experience for the consumer. But when we look at the overall mortgage origination process, that's but a fraction of the time and the cost and complexity that runs through a lender's operations."

But as Austin Kilgore noted, not much has been invested in the "App to Fund" process, delivering predictable and expensive results. Just as the end-to-end payment systems are hard, residential lending is complex and very difficult. Many lenders resort to applying "human spackle" as described by Jonathan Corr. Point of sale front-end systems such as Blend, Roostify, BeeSmarty, Maxwell, and SimpleNexus have removed some degree of friction to the mortgage application process, but little progress has been made as the loan begins the underwriting process as well as with all of the processes from underwriting through securitization of the loan. That's why the cost of originating a mortgage has been on a relentless climb since 2009. Figure 4.2 illustrates the rising cost per loan.

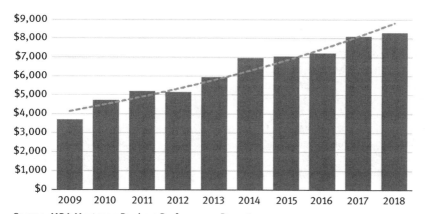

Source: MBA Mortgage Bankers Performance Report

Figure 4.2: Lender's cost per loan from 2009 to 2018.

Thought Leadership in Digital Transformation

You could start a discussion on digital transformation by reviewing the failures of effective digital transformation.

In the March 2018 Massachusetts Institute of Technology publication, Thomas H. Davenport and George Westerman write:

> Several key lessons emerge when heavy commitments to digital capability development meet basic financial performance problems. A clear one is that there are many factors, such as the economy or the desirability of your products, that can affect a company's success as much or more than its digital capabilities. Therefore, no managers should view digital—or any other major technological innovation—as their sure salvation.
>
> Second, digital is not just a thing that you can you can buy and plug into the organization. It is multi-faceted and diffuse, and doesn't just involve technology. Digital transformation is an ongoing process of changing the way you do business. It requires foundational investments in skills, projects, infrastructure, and, often, in cleaning up IT systems. It requires mixing people, machines, and business processes, with all of the messiness that entails. It also requires continuous monitoring and intervention, from the top, to ensure that both digital leaders and non-digital leaders are making good decisions about their transformation efforts.
>
> Amid the excitement and uncertainty of a new technological era, it can be very difficult to distinguish between investments you need to make ahead of the market and investments that must be in sync with market readiness. As a CEO it can be tempting to think about the early phases of radical technological change as a chance to dominate a new market rather than learning about the market. Investing ahead of the curve makes sense when we know what the curve is. But with digital transformation there's a lot of exploration and understanding to accomplish before the curve starts to take shape.
>
> When digital investments don't quickly pay off, CEOs can feel that the issue they've encountered is about not spending enough, rather than the company (or the market) not knowing what the end state actually looks like. They can fear that reducing a highly public commitment to the new business could be seen as failure rather than smart decision-making. They may double down on their chosen strategy rather than pivoting toward the profitable approach, hoping to bully the market rather than learn about it.
>
> In time, markets learn more about what they want, producers learn how to deliver it, and the way forward is clearer than it was before. At this point, it is much easier to make clear-headed decisions about digital. But funding a "big digital" strategy during the figuring out process can take more patience than investors have.

A Walk Through Digital Transformation of Residential Lending

My first book covered digital transformation in detail. I'll be brief here, and use an example of the mortgage lending segment for discussion purposes. Figure 4.3 illustrates the steps from consumer "interest" (that is, shopping, comparing loan terms, obtaining rates and fee quotes to application) and then the steps from application to close.

Chrissi Rhea, CEO of Mortgage Investors Group in Tennessee, envisions conquering the application to closing processes as a "make or break" scenario for

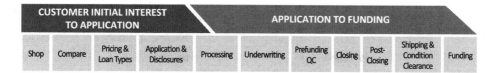

Figure 4.3: Loan process from first consumer contact through funding.

businesses: "I think that any lender in the next few years that asks for W2s and pay stubs and bank statements, while taking weeks to close a loan will be out of business." Chrissi has distinguished herself by building a profitable lending business over 30 years by focusing on the needs of the customer.

According to Chrissi:

> We are all seeing where technology is taking us in other industries. Customers want instant gratification. Retail shopping is rapidly heading online.
>
> We are on the innovation wave in mortgage lending to really gain efficiencies through re-engineering business process and improving the usefulness of technology. When I first started the company thirty years ago, we didn't have much technology. We used a few computers. We had a fax machine. That was about it.
>
> As Mortgage Investors Group has grown, we've adopted a variety of technologies. We were an early adopter of FannieMae's Day 1 Certainty. We're using a Customer Relationship Management system and a Customer Point of Sale system.
>
> We've concentrated on relationship-based lending, and have a significant market share in Tennessee. We've recently opened a direct-to-consumer division to help serve our customers in Tennessee and beyond—however, the customer wishes to interact with us. But we have to up our game.
>
> Technology is hard, because the mortgage lending process is hard. Origination for the secondary market is very complex. It's especially difficult to integrate the various technologies because the requirements to originate a loan cover so many specifics and require specific data.
>
> We've had great success at Mortgage Investors Group by focusing on the customer, and making it easy for the customer. We're embarking on a transformational initiative that is the most exciting project of my career. It's an end-to-end review of our business processes and technology systems. The goal is to create a process whereby a customer can close as loan as fast as permitted by disclosure regulations—about ten days. Everything is on the table.
>
> And that transformation is required. Customers won't accept the cumbersome and extended process of getting a mortgage. They expect a lender to be able to make it easy, to use direct sourced data for asset, income, and employment verification and to make decisions very quickly with a minimum of conditions. This transformation will be the most exciting project I've undertaken in my career.

Tim Nguyen, CEO of BeSmartee noticed the inefficiency of the mortgage banking business in the "Interest to App" space. According to Tim:

> I got into the mortgage business by accident during college. I was hanging out with a buddy one day who was a real estate appraiser who said he needed to run off and do a job. He asked if I wanted to hang out and wait for him, or if I wanted to come with him. So, I said yeah, I'll come with you. He comes back, and he picks up a three-hundred-dollar check. And he introduced me to the real estate business. That's how I got started in the business, but the reason why I stayed in this business is that I noticed tons of inefficiencies and very little innovation.

> I believed it was going to be exciting to use technology to really change the game. And that's the reason why BeSmartee exists—to make mortgages better, faster, and cheaper for the consumer, and for lenders as well. Our goal is to shift the paradigm and change the way people look at originating loans whether as a consumer or whether as a lender. Look at E-Trade who changed the game for self-service brokerage. Look at someone like Wealthfront who is changing the way people invest their money. Amazon. Expedia. The models are out there. All these models disintermediate as many third parties as possible, bringing in as direct to consumer experience as possible and using automation and big data to make it as quick, clean, and high-quality as possible.

> It's been there for years in many different industries. It just so happened that [the mortgage industry] is one of the last to really grab hold of it. And if you really look at history, technology has always been the game changer. Whether it was how we collected cotton, making the process more efficient with the cotton gin, it's always been technology making things easier faster and cheaper. And you know that is just the natural next step for our industry.

So, the Interest to App segment seems pretty well served. But then that digital, efficient, and transparent world hits its analog equivalent: application to funding. One CEO suggested App to Funding is where we throw mortgage banking back to the last century—largely manual processes that meander toward closing, followed by a crisis of having to close a loan and all hands jump on deck to make it so. And then repeat for the next loan.

Jonathon Corr, CEO of Ellie Mae, noted:

> As we go through the [App to Funding] process, invariably things change. The number of underwriting submissions and resubmissions, clear to close submissions, and pre-funding exceptions point to poorly implemented and/or poorly automated workflow. Folks are trying to find out where those exceptions are rather than using technology to ferret out exceptions as the process goes along. You can think of that all the way through, so when we get into underwriting and coordinating the closing and the disclosures there is back and forth.

Nima Ghamsari, CEO of Blend, sees a sometimes inappropriate tradeoff between human labor and technology at many points within mortgage lending:

> There are very high-value roles in the mortgage process. The advice, the consumer, the education, the guidance, understanding different life events, and understanding the consumers. Evaluating their credit especially for people who are outside the boxes. How do you understand

somebody's credit? There's a lot of room for humans in this process but I don't think that the humans are being used effectively today. Over time, the growth in technology will make a significant impact.

In short, the relationship side of mortgage banking is one of the highest and best uses of human interaction. The other side is having humans perform low-value-added tasks, while paying the high salaries for processors, underwriters, closers, and so on. You can argue that this is inefficient, error-prone, and not customer-centric.

Eliminating entirely the human element inspires trepidation from many, including Don Salmon, CEO of TBI Mortgage, who views the human element as an essential component of customer service and when it comes to protecting the customer:

> I think the personal touch is really, really important in our industry because [buying a home] is a very large investment by our customers. . . . If we allow the technology to takeover where people really add value, it could be a tendency for consumers to reduce it to its lowest common denominator, which will be price. . . customer service will suffer. I believe customers will make bad decisions as to what loan is actually best for them.

Jay Plum of Huntington National Bank would agree:

> Professional sales still matter. I think this idea of how we all evolve and do we go fully digital, where does the person intervene is something that's worth taking a look at, because I can't see sales folks going away entirely.

Interestingly, some see the human element as a tool in developing the very technologies that will remove friction and lead us toward convergence. The human touch and technology work in tandem to streamline the process in App to Funding.

David Zitting describes a scenario his team uses for dividing consumers into quadrants based on their emotional engagement in the process:

> We go a step further with measuring and categorizing different kinds of consumers and how they will actually desire to participate within the real estate industry based on where they fall in what we call an emotional spectrum. So, if you could imagine a horizontal line. . . on the very far left, [that's] zero emotion, or *E*. On the very far right of the spectrum, we're going to put *ME*, or *maximum emotion*.

> What the industry tends to do is they tend to think this is a binary thing where consumers that have low emotion will want to go with a totally digital, totally automated experience. But what's important is that when a buying consumer lands between zero *E* and *ME* there are a thousand different variations in the spectrum.

> So the concept here is to get a sense of use data and how can we approach this scientifically to get a sense of these quadrant categories, new categories of the zero *E* to *ME* spectrum and where do [consumers] fall on that. . . [we then create] a platform built process around utilizing all of this data and we go in and we find basically entry points into the housing industry for these consumers.

Mary Ann McGarry put this rather succinctly: "We need to get in front of the data."

Matt Hansen, CEO of SimpleNexus, talks about the engagement power of an end-to-end experience:

> In order to really deliver on the borrower experience, we must view the homeownership journey in a holistic fashion. For example, how does a realtor easily make warm introductions? What about for borrowers who aren't ready to apply? Lenders need systems that blur the lines between humans and technology.
>
> Lenders, realtors, title agents, insurance agents, etc. need to join efforts to provide a single experience for borrowers. The borrower should perform their home search, run calculations, read social reviews, apply for a mortgage, sign their documents, acquire or upload insurance, and close in a single system. The borrower only needs one login. This reduces the friction of the borrower needing 4 accounts in various systems to accomplish the goal.
>
> When we think about engagement with a consumer, we think about how to make sure we are providing an experience that fosters a long-term relationship. To do that effectively, we must realize there is no end. The consumer will need help setting up services in their home. They may want help managing their home. It's likely they will need additional loan support in the future too. The relationship should be ongoing.

The Interest to App technology is well thought through and varies contextually as the customer and/or loan officer proceeds through shopping for a loan, pricing it, and making an application. Contextual means if the borrower selects "refinance," the technology takes the customer and/or the loan officer around all of the purchase questions. Think about TurboTax, and the contextual walk-through based on your personal tax situation.

Jerry Schiano, CEO of SpringEQ, has a colorful take on mortgage technology, which will serve as a transition from the customer interest to application segment to the application to loan closing segment:

> The digital app is what I call the Wizard of Oz. It sounds all-powerful, but in the mortgage world it's really not true. Few mortgage loans go from start to finish on the digital app. But in the personal loan [i.e., non-real estate secured space] the digital app is really a superhero. The personal loan application is quickly approved and funded on the app. Most loans are funded, very little gets kicked out.
>
> So that's where the home mortgage must move to, but mortgages are much more difficult products. So, at SpringEQ, we decided to use a different technology stack. We pioneered the use of BlueSage. We were an early adopter; we were probably one of BlueSage's first direct to consumer lenders. Their tech is good. The tech is probably better than the rest, but they're still new.
>
> We had to spend a lot of time attaching customer relationship management, a dialer, compliance, and a document package. The mortgage process is just hard.

That it is.

From Customer Loan Application to Closing

After the application and initial data collection, many lenders' processes have great variability when it comes to what happens and when it happens, as well as fewer service level standards. Why? Martin Kerr, CEO of Loan Vision, suggests it's because most lending CEOs have their roots in origination, and that's where the emphasis is. In simpler times, pre-Dodd-Frank, that approach had fewer downsides. The cost of regulatory, disclosure, underwriting, and secondary market exceptions and the reputation risk that comes with these exceptions prompted many CEOs to throw bodies at the issue, and hire checkers who check checkers.

Longer-term, less than optimal process can't be offset by labor—the process must be fundamentally sound. That is why it is so important to "begin with the end in mind." Start with the back-end operational processes where the poor process may impact mortgage investors' diligence and pre-funding reviews. Getting the requirements of the investor hard-coded into the operational process and workflow as the end goal then lets the process and workflow correctly assemble needed information from the borrower. That makes the process from Initial Interest to Application much more likely to gather and document required information properly the first time, and minimize or eliminate rework or new requests for information to the borrower.

Martin Kerr explains further:

> My views come from my background because I was in manufacturing and was a process engineer. It was all about doing things efficiently, and getting an understanding of every single step of what you do has to be there. The keyword is what you would call "constraints." You have a constraint somewhere, which slows everything down, and so on, which seems like common sense.

> Many mortgage banks have been started by salespeople, right? They were successful LOs who have ended up as entrepreneurs. And the whole organization is set up to keep the salespeople happy. When it comes to what mortgage bankers do, they're a manufacturer. They make the loans.

> Remember, if you have a problem at the beginning of the process then that problem flows all the way down. It causes knock-on effects all the way down the process. It absolutely must add pain to underwriting, and absolutely must add pain in processing the loan because the focus is very sales-oriented. The salespeople don't care about process downstream.

> From a technology standpoint and from an effort standpoint, CEOs will remove bottlenecks through the sales process. They will absolutely invest in CRM technology or lead generation technology, making it easier when a loan officer is working with borrower. But once that came, the application is taken, everyone else will deal with it downstream if at the first point of contact, the data wasn't managed as well as it could be.

Poorly designed and implemented process can also create other risks. Reputation risk is really worth careful consideration. Patrick Sinks of MGIC stated:

I think part of the scars of the Great Recession are that everybody's been sued. Everybody you know has had their names dragged across the newspapers and televisions. So those scars run deep, so they're paranoid. But one of the underreported stories of the Great Recession was the impact of the mortgage crisis in the boardrooms... mortgage businesses are humming along; record volumes were feeling good. You know the boards ought to feel good. All of a sudden it blows up and they're going, "Wait a minute, how does all this credit risk come back to me? Wait a minute, why are we getting sued?" And so there is a visibility on the mortgage business at board levels that I don't think I've ever seen. And so, I think when you translate that into process, it's 'dot every i, cross every t, to an extreme.

Lenders could work on the loan application to funding segment and can achieve great efficiencies. Matt Hansen, CEO of SimpleNexus, states:

People are only going to install mobile apps that provide more engagement. I don't install an app that's going to tell me the weather. I am installing my banking apps and I'm going to have my Delta app and I'm going to have my Marriott app because I'm coming back repeatedly. That means more value for people to care to use it.

In addition to a meaningful engagement, a major theme in the future is going to be process automation for the lenders. The last two, three, four years has been this digital mortgage theme, which really is meant for consumer facing technologies. The term digital mortgage is, of course, much broader as we all know. Lender margin compression means lenders are going to have to figure out how to shave costs in the back office.

Scott Gillen is Sr. Vice President of Strategic Initiatives for Stewart Lender Services. Scott has been working hard on the application to closing segment, particularly the closing elements:

The digital transformation that's kind of happening has largely been focused on the first half of the process. The point of sale and other portal-based technology solutions have allowed consumers to move to a somewhat paperless application.

I like to joke that the industry has half a digitized solution, because consumers have this expectation coming through the front end of the process until they get to the pile of paper at the closing table. But we are definitely focused on trying to change that dynamic.

It starts with leveraging digital solutions in advance of the closing. The other thing that really has driven change is E-Notes (that is, electronic loan notes instead of purely paper loan notes). You've seen the figures. I certainly expect E-Notes to be close 50,000 or 60,000 by the end of the summer (of 2019). That's been a radical change of thought that's beginning to happen within the lender community.

So, technology in the mind of title insurers, digital closings really change the risk dynamic and makes us more comfortable with using the technologies to close mortgage transactions. At the end of the day, we're the title underwriter, we're writing the insurance policy and integrating these transactions. The electronic process in our mind makes it much more secure. I think it mitigates fraud to a degree.

Rob Peterson, Chief Technology Officer of Teraverde, contemplates:

Lenders that are moving the needle in performance and decreasing the cost-per-loan metrics are those that understand the need to harness technology to determine required next steps automatically. Using methods for tracking exceptions and service levels, the ability to use data to create workflows throughout the entire process are strategic decisions to dramatically decrease human workloads to increase throughput by eliminating unnecessary review of information and manual processes (that can easily be automated).

It's Not Just Customer Facing Technology

Lori Brewer, CEO of LBA Ware, is an example of thought leadership in action. Lori earned her undergraduate and graduate degrees in architectural and structural engineering. She served in the U.S. Air Force in support of the global Lockheed C-130 fleet, a four-engine turboprop heavy-duty cargo aircraft. Captain Brewer initiated a C-130 Systems Programs Office website to assist with better communications and tracking of maintenance-related documentation and spares inventory worldwide—in 1996.

Brewer described how thought leadership in aviation support translated into LBA Ware's products for supporting CompenSafe, a leading incentive compensation and sales performance management platform:

> The issue of logistics support for the C-130 fleet is complex. The C-130 fleet has operated across the world for 60 years. The 130 can take off and land on unimproved surfaces. The aircraft serves transport, cargo, and special missions, including electronic reconnaissance. The 130 has a payload of about 45,000 pounds. The various demanding roles means maintenance and spare [parts]management is critical in ensuring aircraft are ready to perform their missions.

> I envisioned a website to enable my Air Force counterparts to access information on demand. The website was static at the time, but supplied a central messaging system for the fleet and a place to organize maintenance alerts and announcements. Nonetheless, it was an innovation that put needed information at users' fingertips, especially in more challenging environments. Maintenance data and procedures are voluminous and keeping up-to-date paper copies in locations around the world was challenging.

> Transitioning into mortgage banking, the need for automation and data transparency was acute. After the financial crisis, Dodd-Frank compensation rules, together with the nature of complex commission structures presented a great opportunity for innovation. My team developed CompenSafe to provide control and management over loan officer, operations, and management compensation—something that spreadsheets simply can't provide. Our system bridges the gap between the lender's loan origination system and payroll system. It eliminates manual data entry and computations to reduce human errors and increases accuracy and transparency. CompenSafe allows management to take back control of their corporate compensation framework to establish incentives that motivate production and drive behaviors for improved performance and profitability.

Brewer's thought leadership transformed her solution for C-130 maintenance logistical support to the lending area of compensation management. Both systems manage large amounts of rapidly changing data and provide accurate and transparent information to the field.

This type of thought leadership is needed to tame the customer application to loan closing complexities of mortgage lending.

Begin with the End in Mind: Amazon's Business Model Graphic

We'll end this chapter with a revisit of Amazon's business model graphic. The Amazon business model is one of convergence of customers, suppliers, markets, and product information, levered by a logistics system that handles supply chain, finance, customer satisfaction, product delivery, product return, and a self-service model. It is truly a shining example of convergence, logistics, and digital transformation.

In the online world, the standard of excellence may be the Amazon experience. Figure 4.4 is Amazon's business model "Canvas."[101]

AMAZON'S BUSINESS MODEL CANVAS				
KEY PARTNERS	**KEY ACTIVITIES**	**VALUE PROPOSITION**	**CUSTOMER RELATIONSHIP**	**CUSTOMER SEGMENT**
Logistics Partner	Merchandising	Convenience	Self-Service	Individual Leverage
Affiliates	Production and Design	Price	Automated Service	Group Leverage
Authors and Publishers	**KEY RESOURCES**	Instant Fulfillment with eReader	**DISTRIBUTION CHANNELS**	Global Consumer Market
Network of Sellers	Physical Warehouses	Vast Selection	Affiliates	
	Human, Web Application & Development		Application Interfaces	
			Amazon.com	
			Sale of Assets	
COST STRUCTURE		**REVENUE STREAMS**		
Low Cost Structure		E-books and Content		
IT and Fulfillment Infrastructure		Acquisitions and Investments		
Economies of Scale		Commission on Reseller Sales		

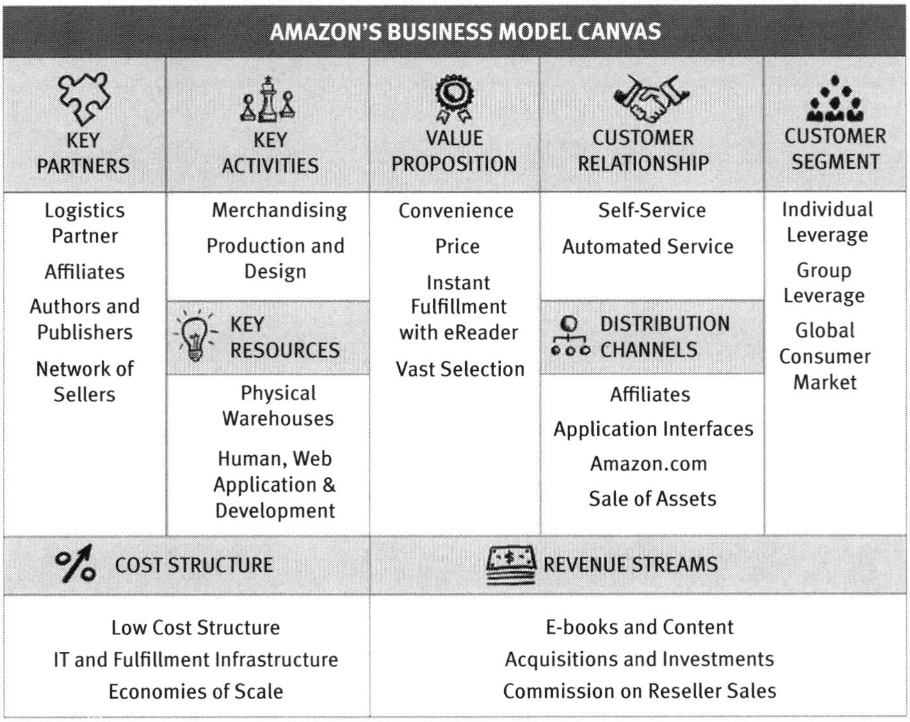

Figure 4.4: Illustration of Amazon's business model canvas.

---

101 Adapted from Alexander Osterwalden, Business Model Canvas, slideshare.net.

Convergence and logistics are tightly integrated, from the customer's first point of contact right through to ease of shipping.

Amazon offers a 'one-click' buying experience through which a customer finds what they want and—with a click—gets that item on its way to their front door. The real differentiator in this experience is that Amazon keeps the customer informed at every point along the way, keeping the customer up to speed on when the product will ship and following up with status updates to and through receipt of the product by the consumer. Whether the product is flawless or flawed, the consumer also has the ability to review the product, the seller, and the customer experience in an instant. The customer, too, has an easy way to return products that don't fit his or her needs. All of this comes in one place, and in a familiar user interface.

Wrap Up

The digital transformation is but one segment of the overall fintech ecosystem, and a brief glimpse here provides a glimpse into the overall process of intentional disruption. More on that a little later. But what of the current residential real estate market ten years after the subprime mortgage crisis? And what about millennials? Will they ever be homeowners?

Chapter Five
Demographics Driving Disruptive Forces

Americans are renting more and buying less. You see it everywhere—millennial interest in homeowning is described as "anemic," most commonly. As the legend of the millennial generation grows, can we still parse fact from fiction?

First off, a few facts. According to Statista, the average cost of owning a home versus renting a home in 2018 based on monthly payment shows that owning a home in terms of monthly payment is lower than renting in all but eight states: Hawaii, Washington DC, Colorado, Oregon, Utah, Montana, Nevada and Wyoming.[102] This comparison ignores down payment, but the statistic was surprising to me.

So, if owning a home in terms of monthly payment is less expensive than renting, why aren't more people buying homes? Is it that renters can't afford the down payment? FHA loans can be had with less than 5% down. Is it that millennials don't want to own homes? Well, it's more nuanced.

Is it true that millennials are not building wealth and not buying homes? As a whole, yes. Thanks to a significant offset (for the time being) from baby boomers, who are responsible for a whopping 244% of household growth in the U.S., the housing market remains stabilized for now. If and when interest rates begin to rise, however, will millennials be more marginalized than ever without any chance of affording a mortgage? What to do once baby boomers stop buying?

The factors influencing millennial resistance to home buying are both financial and cultural. At this point, we all know that their expectations are different when it comes to tech engagement in the sales cycle. As Rick Arvielo of New American Financial put it, "The millennial borrower is going to expect a different experience because they're used to getting answers in real time. They're used to self-serving and they're used to being able to push a button and get an answer." In tandem with this expectation of seamless ease, what we are seeing from millennials is a resistance to historical cultural norms. For one, millennials aren't settling down and getting married as quickly as prior generations, and they aren't particularly interested in having kids early, both of which traditionally correlate nicely with home buying. From a financial point of view, too, millennials are saddled with some significant burdens that didn't face previous generations. Let's start with income.

Incomes have increased steadily at a rate of 67% over the last 50 years. The rub is that the cost of living has increased much faster. Rents and housing costs have skyrocketed, while college tuition has increased by over 200% from the 1990s to today. This is particularly true in New York City, Washington DC, the Bay area, southern California, and other metro areas.

---

102 https://www.statista.com/statistics/967752/cost-of-owning-vs-renting-home-by-usa-state/

https://doi.org/10.1515/9783110650471-006

The fact that many millennials are working in the tech industry doesn't help, either. According to one assessment run by SmartAsset in 2018, the list of cities where it is most difficult to save up for a down payment is dominated by tech hubs, such as San Jose, California. There, the average household income hovers just above $100,000 and yet, the median home price is over $800,000. Running the math is simple: saving 20% of income would result in a down payment in... almost 8 years. According to research run by Clever Real Estate in the spring of 2019, 67% of millennials put less than 20% down on a home purchase, translating into significant monthly mortgage payments. While Clever also developed a "Millennial Metric" to uncover which cities were more affordable and livable for millennials, chances are it will be some time before the cultural shift that needs to happen to drive this generation to Omaha or Rochester actually happens. Or will it?

Millennials: Rent versus Buy

So, millennials rent... but at what cost? According to the U.S. Census Bureau, there is a significant cost, as shown in Table 5.1.[103]

Table 5.1: Increase of median gross rents from 1940 to 2000.

YEAR	MEDIAN GROSS RENT	COST IN TODAY'S DOLLARS
1940	$27	$471
1950	$42	$434
1960	$71	$588
1970	$108	$693
1980	$243	$758
1990	$447	$852
2000	$602	$866

In 2017? The median gross rent is $1,358. The average rent in 2018 in Washington DC was $2,600; New York state was $3,300; California state was $2,700. But New York City? The Bay area? My son rented in the Bay Area and paid over $4,000 per month for a 1950s three-bedroom home that was not updated. And buying a home, with transaction costs of 10% or more was out of the question for a mobile, young professional. (He recently moved to San Diego and bought a home.)

---

103 https://www.census.gov/hhes/www/housing/census/historic/grossrents.html

What are millennials buying when they do buy? Millennials are waiting longer and longer to buy homes and many are bypassing starter homes. When they do buy, some people of this generation are turning to larger homes that would have followed as a natural second step to a starter home in previous generations.

The tide is turning, albeit slowly. Home ownership is rising again as millennials begin to buy their first homes. Considering it is a generation raised in the depths of a financial crisis, millennials' investment in the housing market is heartening and belies the naysayers, at long last. Figure 5.1 shows home ownership is rising after falling from the all-time highpoint of 2005 to the recent low of 2016.

Figure 5.1: The homeownership rate as a percentage of the population seeking shelter in residential rental property of owned homes.

Millennials Earning College Degrees Earlier

Millennials are following a familiar enough path and moving college education to their early years. However, millennials are earning bachelor's degrees or higher much earlier in their lives than previous generations. The phenomenon may be delaying family formation, childbearing, and home ownership. As we'll see in a few graphs that follow, millennials aren't purchasing as early as prior generations, but they are still purchasing eventually.

The earlier attainment of college degrees may partially explain the student debt that has rapidly expanded in the past eight years. Another factor may be the Obama administration eliminating the federally guaranteed student loan program offered by private lenders in 2010.

In 2010, the Obama administration eliminated the federal guaranteed loan programs, which let private lenders offer student loans at low interest rates. The student loan program was effectively taken over by the Department of Education.

According to *Investor's Business Daily*, "Obama sold this government takeover as a way to save money—why bear the costs of guaranteeing private loans when the government could cut out the middleman and lend the money itself? The cost savings didn't happen. What did happen was an explosive growth in the amount of federal student loan debt. At the same time, the Obama administration made it easier to avoid paying back student loans in full. In 2015, for example, the administration expanded eligibility for the 'pay as you earn' program, which limits loan payments to 10% of income, with any debt left after 20 years forgiven."[104]

Figure 5.2 shows that millennials are attaining degrees much faster than prior generations, with the effect of delaying homeownership as we will see below.

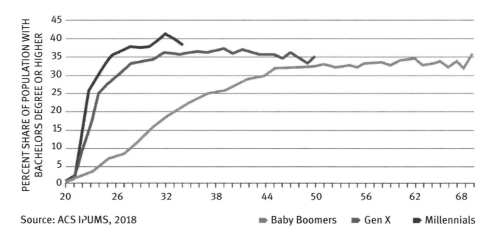

Source: ACS IPUMS, 2018 　　　　　 ⬛ Baby Boomers 　⬛ Gen X 　➡ Millennials

Figure 5.2: The speed of earning a college degree by the generation.

With Age Comes Home Ownership

Although homeownership is coming at a later age for millennials, it appears to be on a similar vector when compared to prior generations. When viewed through the lens of data, the delayed home ownership of the millennials seems much less impactful. Figure 5.3 shows that homeownership increases with age, and though millennials are presently "behind the curve," the shape of the curve appears similar to prior generations, though delayed about four years.

---

104 https://www.investors.com/politics/editorials/obama-created-student-loan-crisis-with-1-trillion-in-loans/

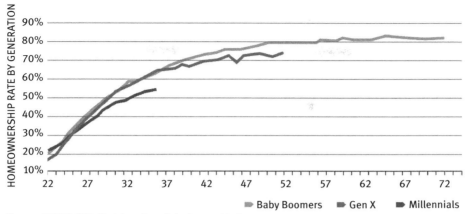

Source: IPUMS CPS, First American Calculators, 2018

Figure 5.3: As individuals age, they become homeowners due to family formation.

Downturn in Home Inventories

More worrisome is the state of affairs when it comes to housing supply. Housing inventory expressed in terms of months of supply is at pre-mortgage crisis levels, due to much reduced home building during the ten years following the onset of the crisis. The reasons are many, including a ten-year reduction in the home building rate due to the mortgage crisis, and anti-development regulations in many metro locations. Figure 5.4 shows home inventories at about four months of supply. This is a national average. Home inventories are much lower in many metro locations, especially in moderately priced homes aimed at first-time home buyers. The lack of affordable housing in high-cost metro areas such as New York City, the Bay Area, Southern California and other areas is likely depressing purchases by first-time home buyers, including millennials.

Homeowners Are Staying Put Longer

Tenure in homes is increasing—meaning that homeowners are less likely to move as frequently as in prior generations, for a variety of reasons. Reasons include the high transaction costs of buying and selling a home. All told, selling your existing home, buying a new home, and then moving your possessions can easily consume 15% of the cost of the new home.

That cost could equate to a substantial portion of your equity in an existing home. Low interest rates on existing homes may encourage homeowners to defer

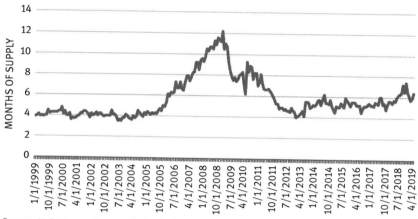

Source: U.S. Census Bureau, fred.stlouisfed.org

Figure 5.4: The national months of inventory of homes for sale.

moving. Lastly, mobility is reduced in high-cost areas. High housing costs (and high rents) dissuade homeowners from moving from their existing lower-cost areas to higher cost locales. Figure 5.5 shows that homeowners are staying in their homes ten years or more as of 2018, up from a tenure of less than five years before the sub-prime mortgage crisis.

The subprime mortgage crisis, as well as land development and zoning restrictions has reduced home inventory available for sale, especially in high-cost areas like coastal southern California, the Bay Area, New York, Washington, and others.

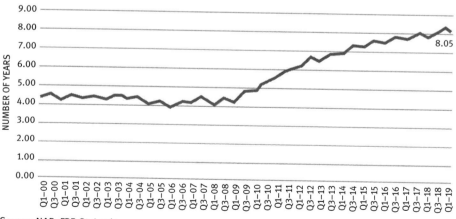

Source: NAR, FRB St. Louis

Figure 5.5: The longer tenure of homeowners in their existing homes.

Figure 5.6 expresses the lack of inventory available for sale in terms of units available for sale, with homes available for sale at a 25-year low.

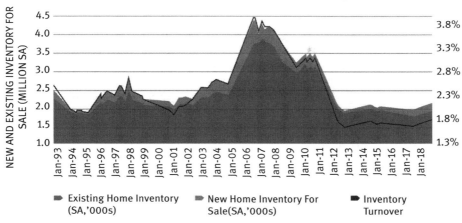

Source: NAR, Census, FRB St. Louis, First American Calculations, Feb. 2019

Figure 5.6: Home supply available for sale is at a 25-year low.

Roy George, of Taylor Morrison Home Finance, provided some great alternative insights on millennial buyers:

> Some millennials have relatively "thin" credit files. I sit fairly close to being a millennial. I grew up where I needed to make sure that I had the right credit profile because I happened to be in this industry, and I learned about it. Right? That's probably the only reason I have a leg up on some of my own age range group.
>
> But when you look at millennials, they're more inclined to worry about paying for something in full and creating an experience in their life rather than taking on a new mortgage. I know there are a lot of studies out there right now that say, oh no, the 35-year-old millennial, they want to buy a house. But I don't believe that because I'm physically speaking to these people on a regular basis, whether I'm coaching people on LinkedIn or whether I'm part of an alumni organization that has about 50,000 people in it.
>
> Their focal point is not buying a house. It's not building a credit history. It's nothing like that. It's more "Hey, I'm saving up for my next trip. I have a woman that works for me here. She's a millennial. She booked tickets to go wherever. She just looks on the internet and if something is less than a hundred dollars, she buys it. And then she asks for a day off that Friday, maybe before she's going. And she just leaves for a weekend to go to some city in the U.S. she's never been to before, but she does it all the time. She's perfectly happy living in her apartment, in her smaller space and not having to worry about all the responsibility that comes with a home and the yard, the windows and the air conditioners."

Rick Arvielo at New American Funding has a slightly different take on millennials:

> The millennial borrower is going to expect a different experience. I think our industry has to be prepared to deliver a different experience because millennials are used to getting answers in real-time. They're used to self-service.
>
> A breakdown is more likely to occur with the market practitioners because they're just not in a position to offer that real-time experience. At New American, we spent the last three years developing technology to really empower the practitioner on the street to be able to deliver the kind of service levels by pushing everything right to millennials' mobile devices.

Tax Reform Aimed at High-Tax States

A different demographic is the tax structure of a state, particularly states that have state and local income and real estate taxes that are materially higher than the average in the United States. A significant undercurrent in the conversation around supply in the housing industry is the state and local tax deduction (SALT) limitation put into place by the 2017 tax reform bill. Higher-income earners in states—such as New York and California, where local and state tax rates are high—had long relied on being able to deduct these taxes, with New Yorkers claiming average SALT deductions of $21,000, while the SALT deduction for Californians came in at just over $17,000 on average. The impact on high earners is much more significant.

With the passage of the tax bill, there were more than a few voices ready to take on the role of Cassandra in the housing industry in response. The prevailing concern was that home sales in these regions would fall and stagnate, and the result was just that. In the northeast alone, new home sales fell at a rate of 51.3% in September 2018 compared to a year earlier.[105] The results were not much better in southern California, where the sales of new homes in September 2018 were 47% below the 30-year average.

Slower growth may continue in these areas in the wake of SALT. While this may shift demand back to starter homes, the more important shift that may occur is a shift in demand from wealthier consumers, who may abandon these expensive SALT locales for greener and more lucrative pastures in the southeast and southwest United States.

The Attack of the NIMBYs and California's Housing Crisis

The effect of high-cost home price areas locks out middle- and lower-income potential buyers. Land use regulations make it cost prohibitive for builders to create low-to-moderate new home inventory in many locales.

---

105 https://www.bloomberg.com/opinion/articles/2018-10-25/housing-market-is-tanking-in-the-northeast

Affordability is constrained by the limited housing supply, resulting in home prices being bid up to record levels, especially in California. But it's not just California. It's any urban area where housing demands, especially affordable housing, exceed supply.

Of course, tax reform isn't the only villain in the California housing crisis, at least. The recent phenomena of NIMBY, or "Not in My Backyard" activism has had its fair share in slowing down the supply of housing. Serious and rather far-reaching culture wars over where and how new developments can happen have ensued.

In one of the most jarring episodes, the California state legislature found itself up against various coalitions of NIMBYs. Recognizing the seriousness of the housing shortage in the state, legislators drafted SB 827, which would limit any municipal government that wanted to restrict housing. While increasing the supply of housing near transit hubs may seem like a win-win to most, it ended up creating a firestorm in local and state politics, with NIMBYs protesting the potential existence of large (or lower income) buildings in their neighborhoods. In one of the stranger alliances, the NIMBYs even created a coalition with the Public Housing contingent, who were afraid that the passage of SB 827 would lead to less funding for public housing. In the face of this opposition, the legislation eventually died.

Would SB 827 have saved the day? According to the Mercatus Center's research, implementing SB 827 would have resulted in San Francisco housing costs that were 5.8% lower. While a nice bit of savings, it would not have been enough to make housing affordable for those in this tech hub without additional efforts. File under "too little, too late."

Credit Needs of "Non-traditional" Borrowers

A truth facing the industry is the fact that accommodations must be made for today's non-traditional borrowers.

The rapidly changing demographic landscape may mean that the majority of new potential mortgage borrowers are "non-traditional." This includes multi-generational families, recent immigrants, millennials with large amounts of student debt coupled with frequent job changes, and earners who forego traditional full-time W-2 jobs for independent contractor or "gig" economy workers. A number of factors influence this, but perhaps none more so than shifting cultural norms and the gig economy.

Eddy Perez of Equity Prime took his cultural knowledge and developed a strategy to use Equity Prime's GNMA issuer capability to better serve borrowers:

> When Equity Prime became a GNMA issuer, it's like we were promoted from the minor leagues to the majors. It gives you more ability to help borrowers. What's misunderstood about the Hispanic market is the commitment to maintain a home. I know it extremely well because I grew up 100 percent Cuban.

Lenders get caught up on ratios. Oftentimes, the calculation of DTI overstates the true family DTI. The Gig economy is real. Borrowers are making money doing extra jobs or they have family members who are contributing to the household and who are going to live there. So, you can look at a bank statement and determine if the cash flow is there to make the payment.

Why are these people's deposits so much higher than their reported income? You discover one or two family members that earn $3,000 a month. So, is the DTI really 52% or 38% with the extra liquid cash on bank statement deposits? When you're dealing with the aggregators they won't care if the people who have $100,000 in the bank get another $3,000 deposits because their 17-year-old kids are working. That's very common in the underserved market, especially in the Hispanic market. We can make those loans because we know they will perform. It's a prudent risk to take.

Credit scoring and documentation and computation of income need to be more aligned to current first-time borrowers. Some efforts are being made. VantageScore has long been a proponent of an expanded set of credit scoring criteria to score a large portion of the population. Pilot programs such as Experian Boost and UltraFICO are attempts to help borrowers who have been traditionally marginalized due to lack of credit history. Through Experian Boost, borrowers can provide access to the payment history of bills that have never been used as criteria before, including utility bills and cell phone bills. UltraFICO, on the other hand, uses bank account activity, balances, and the age of accounts as criteria by which to determine a borrower's viability.

A Decline in Foreign Buyers of U.S. Real Estate

Yet another demographic is foreign buyers of U.S. real estate. According to MarketWatch, the current tariff threats and political climate may reduce the foreign buyers. Foreign buyers purchased $77.9 billion in residential real estate between April 2018 and March 2019. This is a 36% drop from the previous year. Chinese buyers accounted for $13.4 billion in real estate purchases. In 2018, they accounted for $30.4 billion in home sales. China has the largest cohort of foreign real estate buyers.[106]

Trade wars and tariffs have a direct impact on the industries affected. Real estate purchases by foreigner buyers often represent a form of investment as well as a home. You only need to observe the Miami real estate market to see the impact of foreign buyers.

Real estate markets need a balance of supply and demand. The $13 billion or so of recent real estate purchased by Chinese buyers is about 1% of the total real estate

---

[106] https://www.marketwatch.com/story/led-by-the-chinese-foreigners-are-buying-31-fewer-american-homes-2019-07-17?mod=mw_theo_homepage

transaction volume, down from roughly 2%. The purchases tend to be in large metropolitan areas, however, at higher price points. So, the reduction could have a disproportionate impact on metro home prices in New York City, Washington DC, and California.

Final Thoughts on Demographics

My purpose in discussing demographics is to move the issue of population, state and local economies, and foreign buyers into the picture of real estate demand, as well as mortgage demand. These are by no means the only demographic factors to consider.

But you must look at demographics in general in your served markets as you seek to understand the disruptive currents of fintech. The correct demographics are literally customized to your specific market. So, this discussion is illustrative of how many factors can change residential real estate and mortgage demand.

Chapter Six
Can Disruption Be Planned and Orchestrated?

The incredible impact that intentional disruption has when planned carefully hit me on a summer day in June 1999. I sat in a seminar room at the U.S. Army War College with just over a dozen Colonels and Lieutenant Colonels from the U.S. Army. A senior Air Force and Naval Officer filled out the American armed forces contingent. Several foreign senior armed forces officers from Saudi Arabia, Germany, and the Philippines, called International Fellows, sat interspersed among the U.S. officers.

The two civilians in this seminar room, a university president and I, were invited by General Robert H. Scales, the 44th Commandant of the U.S. Army War College (USAWC) to add a civilian perspective to the discussion. As I walked the grounds of the War College during the week as a guest of the U.S. Army, I thought about graduates who walked these same grounds over the years. The hundreds of distinguished graduates of the War College include Generals John J. Pershing, Dwight D. Eisenhower, George S. Patton, Jr., Omar N. Bradley, H. Norman Schwarzkopf, and Admiral William F. Halsey.[107]

The "War College" part of the name is somewhat of a misnomer. The mission of the USAWC is to educate and develop leaders for service at the strategic level, while advancing knowledge in the global application of Landpower. The USAWC also acts as a "Think Factory" for Commanders and Civilian Leaders at the strategic level worldwide and routinely engages in discourse and debate on ground forces' role in achieving national security objectives.[108]

During our seminar, the Strategic Deterrence topic of discussion in particular generated vigorous conversation. The German officer present said something that stopped the discussion cold: "Your former President (Reagan) defeated the Soviet Union, brought down the Berlin Wall, freed millions of people in Eastern Europe, and reunited Germany without firing one shot. That is the favorable result of Strategic Deterrence."

I immediately thought of the book, *The Art of War* by Sun Tzu[109] that I had read as part of preparation for the 1999 Kipp Conference at Duke. "Hence to fight and conquer in all your battles is not supreme excellence; *supreme excellence consists in breaking the enemy's resistance without fighting.*"

Discussion ensued, and the thought of winning a conflict without firing a shot kept coming back. Looking back now, I can see that the German officer, in fact, was describing disruption without actually thinking about the term. "The fall of the

---

107 https://www.armywarcollege.edu/
108 https://www.armywarcollege.edu/
109 https://www.history.com/topics/ancient-china/the-art-of-war

https://doi.org/10.1515/9783110650471-007

[Soviet] empire," former Czech president Václav Havel wrote, "is an event on the same scale of historical importance as the fall of the Roman Empire."[110] Given that, let's look at the history of the fall of the Soviet Union.

The Fall of the Soviet Union as a Military and Political Power

In honor of Stan Middleman and his regard for history, the following is a view of how the fall of the Soviet Union—an orders of magnitude disruption with the same historical importance as the fall of the Roman Empire—was achieved.

Dr. Lee Edwards, writing for the Heritage Foundation in June 2010, stated:

> Soviet communism, the dark tyranny that controlled nearly 40 nations and was responsible for the deaths of an estimated 100 million victims during the 20th century, suddenly collapsed 20 years ago without a shot being fired... In just two years—from 1989 to 1991—the Berlin Wall fell, the Soviet Union disintegrated, and Marxism-Leninism was dumped unceremoniously on the ash heap of history. There was dancing in the street and champagne toasts on top of the Brandenburg Gate.

> It is true that Gorbachev publicly repudiated the Brezhnev Doctrine—that the Soviet Union will use force if necessary, to ensure that a socialist state remains socialist—and in so doing undercut the communist leaders and regimes of Eastern and Central Europe in the critical year of 1989.... The Soviet Union no longer possessed in 1989 the military might that it had in 1956 when it brutally suppressed the Hungarian Revolution or in 1968 when it snuffed out the Prague Spring.

> The Soviet Union desperately needed the trade and technology of the West to avoid economic collapse that it knew it would not obtain if it enforced the Brezhnev Doctrine... In January 1977, four years before he was sworn in as the 40th President of the United States, Ronald Reagan told a visitor that he had been thinking about the Cold War and he had a solution: "We win and they lose."

> He first went public with his Cold War analysis in May 1982 when he declared in a speech at his alma mater that the Soviet empire was "faltering" because rigid centralized control has destroyed incentives for innovation, efficiency, and individual achievement.... In March 1983, the President announced that development and deployment of a comprehensive anti-ballistic missile system would be his top defense priority. The Strategic Defense Initiative (SDI) was called "Star Wars" by liberal detractors, but Soviet leader Yuri Andropov took SDI very seriously, calling it a "strike weapon" and a preparation for a U.S. nuclear attack.

> Moscow's intense opposition to SDI showed that Soviet scientists regarded the initiative not as a pipe dream but as a technological feat they could not match. A decade later, the general who headed the department of strategic analysis in the Soviet Ministry of Defense revealed what he had told the Politburo in 1983: "Not only could we not defeat SDI, SDI defeated all our possible countermeasures."

---

110 https://www.heritage.org/report/ronald-reagan-and-the-fall-communism

President Reagan forced the Soviet Union to abandon its goal of world socialization by challenging the Soviet regime's legitimacy, by regaining superiority in the arms race, and by using human rights as a weapon as powerful as any in the U.S. or Soviet arsenal. . . . Lech Wałęsa, the founder of the Solidarity movement that brought down Communism in Poland and prepared the way for the end of Communism throughout Eastern and Central Europe, put his feelings about Reagan simply: "We in Poland . . . owe him our liberty."[111]

My purpose here is not to deify Reagan—rather, it is to illustrate the power of disruptive thinking on a very large scale. Reagan knew the Soviet economy could not keep up technologically with the Western economies. Reagan conceived of a space- and ground-based defense approach called the Strategic Defense Initiative (SDI) that would have a high probability of destroying many incoming nuclear missiles launched by the Soviet Union. Destroying incoming Soviet missiles by a combination of ground-based interceptor missiles, space-based interceptors, and directed beam energy weapons was technologically possible and within the reach of the United States. SDI would thus render the Soviet's threat of a first strike much less lethal, as well as ensure that the United States would retain sufficient capability to retaliate with its nuclear triad: ground-based missiles, submarine-based missiles, and aircraft carrying retaliatory strike nuclear weapons.

Given its feasibility from a technological standpoint, the Strategic Defense Initiative would change the balance of power considerably, if implemented. Reagan's brilliance was to use the carrot and stick. Reagan stood at the Brandenburg Gate separating East and West Germany and declared, "Mr. Gorbachev, tear down this wall!" It was a direct challenge to then Soviet President Gorbachev. Reagan received an ecstatic response from his audience. Two years later, the Berlin Wall fell, and Eastern Europe was free of Soviet rule, while the Soviet Union eventually crumbled worldwide.

Demonstrating what could be described as a keen instinct for brinkmanship, Reagan was quick to offer face-saving gestures to Russia in the form of diplomatic, economic, and military concessions. A side benefit of all this was that much of the defense spending from the 1980s in basic and applied technology research flowed into the economy: faster, cheaper microprocessors, memory, the commercial high-speed internet, the global positioning system, laser technology, and much more.

The review of the fall of the Soviet Union can be used as an example of disruption by examining the intended effect of Reagan: "We win, they lose." The strategy employed by Reagan was not based on creating a series of events that would be hard to stage and control. Reagan by definition did not want to engage in armed conflict that might arise from staging a series of *events* that would result in the fall of the Soviet Union. Instead, Reagan produced a strategy that achieved the *effect* of the fall of the Soviet Union.

---

111 https://www.heritage.org/report/ronald-reagan-and-the-fall-communism

Reagan recognized that the efficiency of the free market system produced more impact per dollar of spending than the Soviet Union could achieve with the same spend. An associate in the U.S. military put it quite succinctly: "For every dollar the U.S. spends, the Soviet Union had to spend two dollars to achieve the same effect. The Soviet economy was in free-fall, and the quality of their military products was inferior. It was just a matter of time until the whole system simply fell apart."

Predicting the Future

Dr. Chris Caplice, Senior Research Scientist at the Massachusetts Institute of Technology, posed a question at a recent Chief Executive Disruptive Technology Conference[112]: "If the future is uncertain, humans are bad at predicting, so what can we do?" Dr. Caplice describes sources of uncertainty (things beyond your control or influence) as falling into five groups: social, technological, economic, environmental, and political uncertainties.

The uncertainties took me back to another professor from MIT, tripped up by the very same uncertainty that Dr. Caplice referenced. MIT professor Lester Thurow wrote *The Zero-Sum Society: Distribution and the Possibilities for Economic Change*.[113] In game theory and economic theory, a zero-sum game is a mathematical representation of a situation in which each participant's gain or loss of utility is exactly balanced by the losses or gains of the utility of the other participants. In Thurow's mind at the time, scarce resources could only be redistributed (as in a zero-sum game). He envisioned macroeconomics as a zero-sum game and asserted that the American economy could not solve its problems of inflation, slow economic growth, the environment unless society forced the brunt of taxation and other government-sponsored economic actions onto individuals. Thurow's early thoughts on redistribution convinced Senator George McGovern to make income redistribution a major feature of his campaign for the Presidency in 1972.[114]

I heard Dr. Thurow present his theories in Boston in the early 1980s. He presented a laundry list of sobering predictions: The United States would run out of petroleum reserves by 2000, the northeast would be uninhabitable in the winter due to the coming Ice Age (!)[115] and energy prices would rise to oppressive levels.

---

112 Dr. Chris Caplice, "Making Sense of an Uncertain Future," lecture at Chief Executive's Disruptive Tech Summit, June 10, Cambridge MA.

113 Lester Thurow, *The Zero-Sum Society: Distribution and the Possibilities for Change*, Basic Books; New edition (April 2, 2001).

114 https://www.commentarymagazine.com/articles/the-zero-sum-society-by-lester-c-thurow/

115 The New Scientist (https://www.newscientist.com/article/dn11643-climate-myths-they-predicted-global-cooling-in-the-1970s/) According to Michael Page writing in the New Scientist on May 16, 2007, a 1971 paper by Stephen Schneider, then a climate researcher at NASA's Goddard Space Flight

Japanese manufacturing expertise would render the United States industrial base obsolete, clean water would be scarce, and the world would run out of food to support its growing population. Interest rates at the time were just coming off all-time highs, and the stock market experienced a downturn from the mid-1970s through the time of Thurow's lecture. Unfortunately, Sam Adams beer had not yet been invented, so I left the conference and had a few Budweisers to wash away the malaise from hearing a prominent economist predict such a dire future.

Fortunately, none of Thurow's predictions came to be. Figure 6.1, which shows U.S. household net worth increasing by a factor of ten since Dr. Thurow made his predictions, shreds Thurow's theories and the thought that society is a zero-sum game. This illustrates that myopia can influence the worldview of even a well-educated economist.

The story of Thurow's work illustrates how difficult predicting future events can be. Thurow's worldview missed the possibility that productivity and technology could vastly improve the standards of living for much of the world's population. In 1990, about 2 billion people in the world lived in extreme poverty. In 2018, that number is 650 million people.[116]

During that same time, the world's population increased from 5.3 billion people in 1990 to 7.7 billion people in 2019.[117] Said another way, about 40% of the world's population lived in extreme poverty in 1990 versus 8.4% in 2019. At the time of Thurow's lecture, the world's extreme poverty rate was 51%—more than half of the world's population lived on an inflation adjusted income of $40 per month. No reasonable individual would suggest that the world's economies should rest on their laurels. No one should live in poverty of any kind. And while poverty rates are much improved, much needs to be accomplished. My point on Thurow, however, is that the world economies are not zero-sum games, nor are societies, and predictions are notoriously difficult.

Center in Maryland, U.S. Schneider's paper suggested that the cooling effect of dirty air could outweigh the warming effect of carbon dioxide, potentially leading to an ice age if aerosol pollution quadrupled. This scenario was seen as plausible by many other scientists, as at the time the planet had been cooling. (global temperatures fell between 1940 and 1980). Furthermore, it had also become clear that the interglacial period we are in was lasting an unusually long time. However, Schneider soon realized he had overestimated the cooling effect of aerosol pollution and underestimated the effect of CO_2, meaning warming was more likely than cooling in the long run. In his review of a 1977 book called *The Weather Conspiracy: The Coming of the New Ice Age*, Schneider stated: "We just don't know ... at this stage whether we are in for warming or cooling—or when."

116 https://ourworldindata.org/uploads/2019/04/Extreme-Poverty-projection-by-the-World-Bank-to-2030.png

117 https://www.worldometers.info/world-population/world-population-by-year/

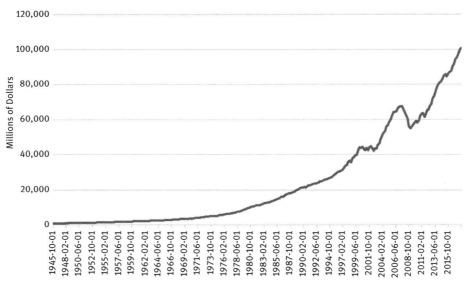

Source: Board of Governors of the Federal Reserve System (US)

Figure 6.1: The growth in collective net worth over a 70-year period.

Provincial Thinking and Recency Bias

Dr. Caplice attributes people's poor predicting ability on his view that we are all "provincials in time."[118] Caplice explains a 'provincial' as a person with a narrow point of view or outlook, countrified in the sense of being limited. The more "recency bias" (the tendency to weigh the latest information more heavily than older data) and "availability heuristic" (easier recall of an example of an event), the more people assume that the event is much more frequent or influential than it is. According to Caplice:

– We look to the future through today's lenses and we think today will go on for forever;
– We think that today will go on forever, that change happens slowly; and
– Then we forget how we got to today—it seems pre-ordained.[119]

I drowned my despair in beer after Thurow's lecture because I was, indeed, a "provincial in time." My experience was limited, and recent history had OPEC oil embargos producing a scarcity of gasoline, heating oil, and natural gas. What's more,

118 Dr. Chris Caplice, "Making Sense of an Uncertain Future," lecture at Chief Executive's Disruptive Tech Summit, June 10, 2019 Cambridge MA.
119 Ibid.

Japan was kicking Detroit's butt in automobile quality and inflation was running in double digits. It seemed like doom and gloom were preordained, and that the United States' best years were behind the nation.

Even former president of the United States, Jimmy Carter, was full of doom and gloom just 18 months earlier.

> In July 1979, lines at gas pumps stretch for blocks, and President Jimmy Carter was scheduled to address the nation on Independence Day. But when he cancels last minute and disappears from the public eye, rumors spread of a health problem or, even worse, that he's left the country. After 10 days, he reemerges with a speech—to address the energy crisis, unemployment, inflation, and something else a bit more nebulous.

> Carter said, "The threat is nearly invisible in ordinary ways. It is a crisis of confidence. It is a crisis that strikes at the very heart and soul and spirit of our national will. We can see this crisis in the growing doubt about the meaning of our own lives and in the loss of a unity of purpose for our nation."

> The speech was later dubbed the "malaise speech," even though Carter never used that word.[120]

Caplice's "provincial" thinking hypothesis can affect even the minds of presidents (and well-known economists such as Thurow). Looking back at two former presidents, Carter and Reagan, from a historical perspective provides insight on provincial thinking. Carter appeared to be bound by provincial thinking and recency bias, considering recent oil embargos, inflation, and slow economic growth. Carter was also affected, in my opinion, by the availability heuristic, in that most American were preoccupied by inflation and recession, and thus those two elements dominated thinking. Reagan appeared to break away from provincial thinking, recency bias, and the availability heuristic, resulting in the ultimate contradiction: a peaceful way to win a war against an opposing superpower.

Provincial thinking was evident in the story of horse manure in New York City cited earlier in this text. The scientific panel convened in the 1890s could not see beyond horse-and-wagon transportation and extrapolated the future without regard for technological change.

The last element of Caplice's thesis is that looking backward, the outcome will seem preordained. It will appear so obvious that few may see the end of the provincial process as having been a process. Whether it's horse manure, taxi medallion value that is destroyed by Uber, the iPhone, or other transformational occurrences, in looking backward, the process seems preordained. Provincial thinking may have extreme risk for its practitioners.

Yogurt Market Disrupted! Brand Equity Destroyed!

Rapid changes in consumer taste rattled the market for yogurt in less than ten years. Consumer product companies think in terms of brand equity over generations, and that brand equity usually equates to market share. In the period between 2007 and 2017, Greek-style[121] yogurt catapulted from less than 2% market share to over 50% market share.[122] General Mills-brand Yoplait yogurt was second only to Dannon in 2010. General Mills, Kraft Foods, and other marketing powerhouses have seen brand equity erode in the face of changing consumer tastes brought about by artisanal and organic food options, etc. Figure 6.2 shows the Greek yogurt market share in the United States over a ten-year period.

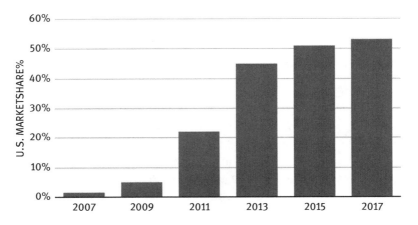

Figure 6.2: Growth in the Greek Yogurt U.S. Market Share over a ten-year period.

Brand erosion is apparent in other consumer markets. For instance, Sharon Terlep writing in *The Wall Street Journal* on July 1 reported that "Cosmetics maker Coty Inc. is taking a $3 billion write-down on CoverGirl, Max Factor and other brands it acquired a few years ago, becoming the latest consumer giant to reckon with mainstream labels that are losing their grip on American shoppers. The makeup and fragrance seller, which is controlled by European investment firm JAB Ltd., has struggled with weak sales and executive turnover. On Monday, the company said it will restructure its operations and cut jobs to ease indigestion from brands Coty bought in 2016 from Procter and Gamble."

Brand erosion is an effect of disruption and can happen quickly with very adverse financial consequences.

---

121 There are the Greeks creating disruption 2,500 year later!

122 Dr. Chris Caplice, "Making Sense of an Uncertain Future," lecture at Chief Executive's Disruptive Tech Summit, June 10, 2019, Cambridge MA.

Motorola and Mobile Communications

Mobile phones have seen a similar transformation, and provincial thinking in the boardroom of a major company contributed to its demise. Dr. Nicholas Negroponte related a story[123] that occurred when he served on the board of Motorola. (Negroponte is an architect by training and is the founder and chairman Emeritus of MIT's Media Labs.) At the time, Motorola had a rich history of innovation in radio communications and was the leader in two-way radio communications.

Motorola started when Paul and Joseph Galvin bought the bankrupt Stewart Battery Company in 1928.[124] At the time, most radios ran on batteries, but not the batteries you may be thinking of. Radios in the 1920s were powered by vacuum tubes. Vacuum tubes require three different sources of power: filament power to heat the internal filament that serves as a source of electrons for the function of the tube; high-voltage power to energize the "plate" of the vacuum tube that attracts electrons emitted by the filament; and power to set the "control grid" voltage in the vacuum tube.

A-batteries had to be about the size of a box of baking soda in order to power filaments with 6 volts of power. B-batteries were about the size of a quart of milk and provided about 90 volts of power. C-batteries were similar in size to A-batteries and were wired in reverse to provide negative voltage to the grid. In other words, batteries were cumbersome and expensive.

Stewart Battery Company had developed a "battery eliminator" consisting of a transformer that provided multiple voltages, as well as a method for converting an alternating current to the direct current required by vacuum tubes. Motorola converged the three batteries into a single power supply, solving the logistics problem of batteries essentially by eliminating them. The company then innovated by converging the radio vacuum tubes onto the same chassis as the power supply, logistically making the radio a self-contained device. Finally, Motorola converged a radio transmitter and radio receiver onto the same chassis, making a two-way radio "transceiver," or transmitter and receiver.

According to the history of Motorola,[125] the Galvin brothers rapidly grew Motorola into consumer radios for automobiles, police and fire two-way radios, and television and specialized two-way communications. The company even provided communications gear to NASA for most manned space flights. Motorola also innovated in early cell phones, making mobile analog phones for automobiles that were the size of bread boxes, before transitioning to mobile "bag" phones and handhelds that looked like a standard phone handset with a large battery attached. (This phone was deemed so trendy that Michael Douglas used the phone in the 1987 movie *Wall Street*.)

---

123 A discussion with and presentation by Nicholas Negroponte at Chief Executive's Disruptive Tech Summit, June 10, Cambridge MA.

124 https://www.motorola.com/us/about/motorola-history

125 https://www.motorola.com/us/about/motorola-history

Motorola continued to innovate, introducing the Razr mobile phone in 2005. Nokia and others made inroads into Motorola's market share, which takes us to Negroponte's story of a board meeting at Motorola in early 2007.

Negroponte had spent time with Steve Jobs from Apple vis-à-vis Negroponte's work with MIT Media Labs.[126] Jobs showed Negroponte a pre-production version of the first iPhone, and bragged about its touchscreen, computing power, and ability to run "applications" on the phone from independent developers. Negroponte received Jobs's permission to talk about this new Apple phone, in general, to Motorola.

Negroponte relates how he described the iPhone to Motorola's board. The reaction was muted, with one director stating that no one would buy a phone without push buttons, and that the director thought Apple would be lucky to sell 1 million units.

By 2019, Apple has sold more than one billion iPhones.[127] Motorola has lost billions of dollars from 2007 to 2011, and was pressured by investor Carl Icahn to split into two companies in 2011.[128] Google acquired Motorola Mobility in 2011.[129] Motorola Solutions went back to its roots of specialized communications gear. Motorola Solutions' sales of $7 billion are a fraction of its former combined company.

Motorola was a victim of provincial thinking: taking its historical success in mobile communications as "recency bias" and "availability heuristic" that colored the board's thinking. Assuming that all mobile phones required a keypad was a fatal assumption. Change happened really fast at Motorola's expense. The business model worked until it didn't.[130]

Change happening much faster than expected in the technology business doesn't always have an unfavorable ending. Andy Grove, CEO and Chairman of the Board of Intel wrote "Only the Paranoid Survive"[131] in 1999 to explain how he and Gordon Moore handled an extreme challenge to Intel's memory business. According to Grove, the book describes "a strategy of focusing on a new way of measuring the nightmare moment every leader dreads—when massive change occurs and a company must, virtually overnight, adapt or fall by the wayside."

In his book, Grove illustrates that almost anything can set off such a moment: mega-competition, a change in regulations, even a seemingly modest change in technology. That's when conventional strategic planning and ordinary rules of business go out the window. But, according to Grove, this is also an opportunity to emerge stronger than ever.

---

126 A discussion with and presentation by Nicholas Negroponte at Chief Executive's Disruptive Tech Summit, June 10, Cambridge MA.
127 https://www.statista.com/statistics/263401/global-apple-iphone-sales-since-3rd-quarter-2007/
128 https://www.cnbc.com/id/40897532
129 https://abc.xyz/investor/
130 This is a hypothesis I developed in *Strategically Transforming the Mortgage Banking Business*, published in 2018. More on this concept later in this chapter.
131 Andy Grove, "Only the Paranoid Survive," Crown Business; March 16, 1999.

Paraphrasing the book, Grove describes the extreme cost pressure on dynamic random-access memory (RAM) from offshore competition. Intel pioneered memory chips beginning in 1970 and grew the memory chip business exponentially through the early 1980s. Intel was early in the development of microprocessor chips beginning in the late 1970s. By the mid-1980s, memory chips had become extremely competitive and Intel was under extreme price pressure. Right around this time, Grove and Moore were in a conference room together when Grove asked Moore what the board would do with executives who couldn't manage the problems facing the company. "Fire them" was Moore's response. Grove suggested they ceremonially fire themselves, walk out of the room, and come back in as new management. They completed their ceremonial firing in a few minutes, and then decided to exit the memory business to concentrate on where Intel was developing a defendable competency—advanced microprocessors.

Grove and Moore divested the memory business. Grove described the emotional trauma that he, Moore, the executives, and employees felt when Intel abandoned the very business that brought Intel success. Despite that trauma, the move created tremendous shareholder value and success for Intel.

In 1985, Intel stock traded at a split-adjusted price of just $0.37 per share.[132] As of May 2019 the stock traded at $58.00 per share. Unlike Motorola, which lost billions of dollars of shareholder value through its inability to anticipate the effect of a touchscreen phone (among other things), Intel created over $200 billion in market value for its shareholders by anticipating the growth of microprocessors. An investment of $1,000 in Intel in 1985 would be worth about $157,000 today.

Let's develop disruption, convergence, logistics, and provincial thinking further as a way to evaluate business models, and perhaps to anticipate events that will spawn new opportunities.

The Business Model Works Until It Doesn't

"Your business model works until it doesn't" is a hypothesis I developed in my third book, *Strategically Transforming the Mortgage Banking Business*. This notion stemmed, in large part, from experiences I went through early on in my career.

In 1982, I worked at Air Products and Chemicals as a financial analyst. Our department used a mainframe-based financial analysis package to evaluate large-capital projects. Use of the analysis package was time consuming and inflexible. I discovered a small office that had an Apple II computer loaded with VisiCalc, or "visible calculator." VisiCalc, invented by Dan Bricklin in 1979 and published by

---

132 https://www.macrotrends.net/stocks/charts/INTC/intel/stock-price-history

Software Arts Corporation,[133] was the first electronic spreadsheet.[134] I used it for sup-
plemental analysis for capital projects. The spreadsheet size usable in VisiCalc was
limited by the 32 kilobytes (not mega or gigabytes, but 32 thousand bytes) of memory
available on Air Products' Apple II. I learned how to link spreadsheets to overcome
the 32K limit. Over a few months, it became harder for me to access the Apple II, as
other analysts found the value of the spreadsheet. Air Products then purchased IBM
PC's with Lotus 1-2-3 spreadsheet software. This combination greatly improved the
functionality of the spreadsheet and its usefulness for business. The backstory on
VisiCalc and Lotus 1-2-3 follows as an example of the speed of disruption, and where
an early disruptor becomes the disrupted. Figure 6.3 shows a screenshot of VisiCalc
as a point of reference for non-VisiCalc users or for readers born after 1965!

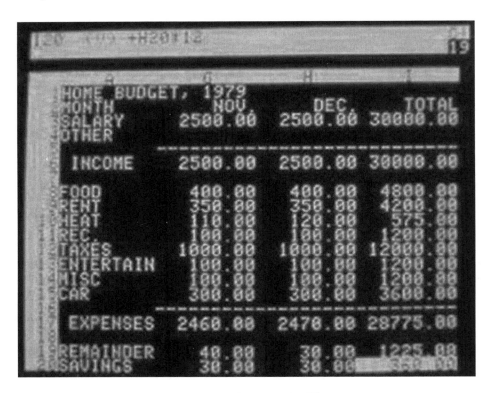

Figure 6.3: A screenshot of VisiCalc on a monochrome monitor.[135]

---

133 Software Arts Corporation was formed by Dan Bricklin and Bob Frankston in 1979. Bricklin
graduated from MIT with a degree in Electrical Engineering and Computer Science. Frankston
was an experienced programmer and MIT graduate, according to History-Computer. https://his
tory-computer.com/
134 https://history-computer.com/ModernComputer/Software/Visicalc.html
135 https://history-computer.com/ModernComputer/Software/Visicalc.html

Disruptor or Disrupted?

VisiCalc was quickly extended to a product suite, "VisiOn," and a user graphical interface. The product took off, and helped Apple sell personal computers to businesses.[136] Near the end of 1981, IBM introduced the IBM PC, initially using and Intel 8088 microprocessor, an 8-bit design.[137] VisiCalc (originally developed for the Apple II) and a product from Microsoft called Multiplan (offered initially on the Radio Shack TRS-80) were offered for the IBM PC. Air Products purchased several IBM PC, loaded with VisiCalc.

Mitch Kapor worked for VisiCorp when he recognized some of the limitations of VisiCalc. Kapor left Software Arts in late 1981 with a $1.2 million buyout, and an exception to compete with VisiCorp with a product he outlined in his separation agreement. That exception became Lotus 1-2-3.[138] Kapor introduced Lotus 1-2-3 for the IBM PC. It was an immediate success, as it took advantage the IBM PC's 16-bit microprocessor and much-expanded memory, as well as the ability to utilize the PC's hard disk to store spreadsheets. VisiCalc was slow to respond to the IBM PC and Lotus 123, and ultimately languished as Lotus 1-2-3 dominated the business market for spreadsheets by 1984.[139]

The microcomputer rental business started by Don Bishop and I took advantage of the introduction of the IBM PC and its rapid evolution. The PC was the first computing device that democratized computing technology away from the Management Information Systems department. Don and I took advantage of that shift and helped early users disrupt the access computing assets away from the MIS department.

The saga of VisiCalc is instructive in the sense that the rapid evolution of software for microcomputers occurred shortly after IBM introduced the PC for business use. The advantage VisiCalc has on Apple II computers was rapidly supplanted by Lotus 1-2-3 on the IBM PC platform. By 1985, VisiCorp was insolvent, and Lotus purchased the assets of VisiCorp and quickly threw VisiCalc into the dustbin of history.[140] The disruptor (VisiCalc) had been disrupted by Lotus 1-2-3.

Dead Men Walking

The rapid demise of VisiCalc can be explained readily by the rapid advances of technology, resulting in the death of VisiCalc. The following example of "Dead Men Walking" is a testament to provincial thinking and all its components. Who are the

136 https://history-computer.com/ModernComputer/Software/Visicalc.html

137 https://www.ibm.com/ibm/history/exhibits/pc25/pc25_birth.html

138 https://www.nytimes.com/1984/02/26/business/how-a-software-winner-went-sour.html

139 https://www.nytimes.com/1984/02/26/business/how-a-software-winner-went-sour.html

140 https://history-computer.com/ModernComputer/Software/Visicalc.html

Dead Men Walking? Fannie Mae and Freddie Mac in the summer of 2008. It's an example of "your business model works until it doesn't."

In July 2008, both Fannie Mae and Freddie Mac had issued Securities and Exchange Commission filings that essentially stated that the respective companies' loan loss reserves and capital were sufficient. Two months later both companies were essentially "dead." Both were placed in conservatorship in September 2008, despite herculean efforts of the federal government to prevent their failure.

Fannie Mae and Freddie Mac required over one hundred billion of capital assistance from the U.S. Treasury. The leadership of both companies were intelligent and respected industry leaders. How could a business model fail so quickly? It works until it doesn't. Provincial thinking. Recency bias. Availability heuristic. Huge impact. All in plain sight, such that in retrospect, the outcome of the subprime mortgage market was obvious. It even made good entertainment in the movie *The Big Short*. See Appendix 2 for a description of how quickly and unexpectedly their end came.

The Residential Real Estate Market Coming Transformation

But it doesn't have to be that way. The United States residential shelter market is under pressure, heading toward a moment that will transform the way the $26 trillion of housing units are sold and rented; how the $1.6 trillion of real estate that will be sold in 2020 may be traded; how the $2 trillion[141] of residential mortgages will be granted; how $26 trillion in insured value of homeowners insurance will be placed, how $1.6 trillion of title insurance will be purchased, how 6 million appraisals will be ordered, and how the millions of transaction services—credit reports, fraud analysis, appraisals, automated valuation reports, automated underwriting systems, loan origination system data pulls—are made. This is a run-on sentence, but it serves my point. All of these services are labor intensive and connected, and, in many cases, duplicative.

How many times are property, borrower, asset, and income assessed in a real estate shelter transaction? How many times is that information verified by a checker? How much value is really added by this process?

Brent Chandler, founder and CEO of FormFree, has views on the cost stack in mortgage lending. Like how to completely disrupt it:

> FormFree's vision is to eliminate unnecessary friction on the lending process. Account Check was the first product. It lets a lender access asset balances for a customer's bank accounts without having to provide physical bank statements.

---

141 The $2 trillion includes both home purchase and refinance transactions. Refinance transactions are not driven by home sales.

There's more to come. Game changers. What if we could provide "six pillars" of any consumer's credit in real time? Assets, identity liens and judgments, credit, income, and employment. With one authorization from the customer? The future is using data to eliminate the need to spend time and money documenting assets, income, and employment using 1930s methods.

Brent's vision is more at hand than may be immediately apparent. Maylin Casanueva, Chief Operating Officer of Teraverde, noted:

It's not just borrower data and the ability to pay that can be data-driven. The GSEs and a large number of service firms have data regarding real estate transactions, chain of title, appraisal data, multiple listing service data, real estate tax data, satellite mapping of collateral, neighborhood school, crime, and related data. In short, aside from a human walking through the home to confirm the physical condition, the entire home buying and financing process could be done electronically.

Chrissi Rhea, CEO of Mortgage Investors Group, noted:

Today's borrower may use technology a great deal more than some loan officers. The majority of borrowers, even borrowers of my mother's generation, would work online to gather documents, and not have to put together mounds of paperwork. A key point is that the borrower is ready and willing to accept technology in documenting their income and assets. In the near term, any lender that doesn't offer direct source data verification to their borrowers may be heading out of business.

Which raises the question, "How long will a consumer consent to paying 12 to 15% of a home's purchase price to complete a purchase transaction?" There are many other questions, but my point is to get your mind fertile and transitioning out of provincial thinking.

A Revisit to President Carter's "Malaise" Speech and the 1970s Oil Shocks

Before getting into the real estate shelter topic, let's examine the world automobile manufacturing industry environment when President Carter delivered his "malaise" speech. Since the beginning of the twentieth century, about the time horses were being replaced with automobiles, the price of crude oil, in nominal terms, was stable. Oil was cheap, and automobile manufacturers took advantage of that cheap gasoline.

Things changed with OPEC oil embargoes imposed in 1973 and several more times in the mid and late 1970s. Figure 6.4[142] shows the oil "shocks" that occurred in the economy. The spike in oil prices in 1979 to 1981 must have influenced Thurow's thinking. Maybe oil prices will continue their trend upward, while the world exhausts the last remaining stocks of crude oil.

142 https://www.quandl.com/data/BP/CRUDE_OIL_PRICES-Crude-Oil-Prices-from-1861

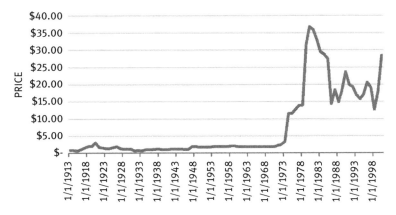

Figure 6.4: Price of crude oil over an 80-year period.

That thinking may be easily seen as faulty today, but in the period from 1975 to 1982 the trends seemed ominous and everlasting, as shown on Figure 6.4. Provincial thinking, recency bias, and information availability heuristic were at work.

During this period, the U.S. auto industry built larger and larger cars, designed to be traded in for a newer model every two years. Quality was not important and, as long as oil was cheap, efficiency was not a priority.

Conversely, most other developed nations taxed gasoline more heavily, and combined with roads that may have had their origins in the Roman empire, smaller fuel-efficient cars in Europe and Japan made sense. The oil shocks had predictable impact of U.S. car manufacturers. Mired in recession, U.S. car buyers wanted more fuel-efficient and better quality cars.

Japan had transformed its post–World War II approach to production into a fuel-efficient and quality-centric philosophy. Imported Japanese cars crushed the sales of U.S. automakers. American Motors failed; Chrysler was on the brink.

The U.S. Congress stepped into force automobile manufacturers to improve fuel efficiency, further exasperating U.S. manufacturer problems when buyers began purchasing more fuel-efficient cars of their own volition.

According to the Union of Concerned Scientists' "Brief History of U.S. Fuel Efficiency Standards":

> The U.S. Congress first established Corporate Average Fuel Economy (CAFE) standards in 1975, largely in response to the 1973 oil embargo. CAFE standards set the average new vehicle fuel economy, as weighted by sales, that a manufacturer's fleet must achieve.

> Through the Energy Policy and Conservation Act of 1975, Congress established fuel economy standards for new passenger cars starting with model year (MY) 1978. These standards were intended to roughly double the average fuel economy of the new car fleet to 27.5 mpg by model year (MY) 1985.

Additionally, the Department of Transportation set the first round of CAFE standards for light trucks (i.e., pickups, minivans, and SUVs) beginning with MY 1978.

Like most well intended government regulations, there were seeds of unintended consequences planted from the outset. One seed was the material difference between passenger car and light truck fuel standards. Few in Congress could foresee the sports utility vehicle segment spawned by the differences. Nor did many in Congress see the devastating impact that the increase in oil prices would have on U.S. manufacturers and the economy. Inflation and unemployment soared, interest rates increased, and the U.S. economy entered a deep recession.

About the same time, in 1980, Ron Harbour, now Senior Partner, Global Automotive Manufacturing of the consulting firm Oliver Wyman Group, visited Japanese automobile factories to learn the secrets of their manufacturing process. Harbour describes himself as having a first-row seat to manufacturing transformation.[143] He began authoring the Harbour Reports, gathering global factory data and building relationships with auto manufacturers and their manufacturing facilities worldwide.

Harbour Reports evaluates over 400 factories that perform vehicle assembly for car, truck, and commercial vehicles. He also evaluates facilities that perform metal stamping, engine, transmission, electric motor, and battery manufacturing.

Harbour Reports maintains a large web-based database, accessible to leadership executives at all companies for anonymized data, with private data for respective participants only. This database has been used by manufacturers worldwide to reduce auto manufacturing costs and increase quality.

In North America, manufacturing has internationalized, and the international auto manufacturers have attained approximate parity in quality. North American auto plants, save General Motors, achieve world-class standards for production efficiency. Figure 6.5 shows the relative productivity of North American auto manufacturing plants.

Quality is now built in, as opposed to being a process after manufacturing. According to Harbour, "U.S. manufacturers had quality control at the end of the production line. About 45 to 50% of cars coming off the line in the early 1980s had material defects that were corrected by 'quality control.' That was just ridiculous. Japan developed lean manufacturing, building quality into the manufacturing process. By 2018, quality standards and lean manufacturing are evident not just in U.S. auto manufacturers, but in virtually all manufacturers. You can't compete with poor quality."[144]

---

143 Ron Harbour, "Automobile Quality and Productivity," lecture at Chief Executive's Disruptive Tech Summit, June 10, Cambridge MA, and a conversation with Mr. Harbour at the same event.

144 As a side note, LoanLogics, a U.S. mortgage quality assurance firm, notes that about 50% of mortgage loans contain quality defects. Lenders employ quality assurance departments and post-

COMPANY	AVERAGE NA PLANT OUTPUT	NORMALIZED CAPACITY	AVERAGE CAPACITY LINE RATE	3C2S + 3 SHIFTS/ PLANTS
BMW	370,865	131%	75	1/1
FCA	253,133	121%	63	6/9
Ford	252,489	116%	58	7/12
GM	181,872	98%	49	7/18
Honda	200,520	99%	54	0/9
Hyundai	328,400	120%	73	1/1
Toyota	202,548	101%	54	1/8
Volkswagen	180,073	91%	54	2/4

Figure 6.5: Average Vehicle Assembly Output, which shows the relative productivity of manufacturing plants.

Unintended Consequences of CAFE, Land Use, and Federal Interventions into Real Estate

The unintended consequences of CAFE are seen in Figure 6.6. The disparity between mileage standards, relatively lower fuel prices, and consumer preference had the number of passenger vehicles sold in the United States fall below 50% of total passenger and light truck vehicles in 2014. The trend has escalated through 2018 with light trucks and SUVs comprising over two-thirds of vehicles in the United States.

The unintended consequences of government regulation almost always surprise. A few examples of unintended consequences:

Health Insurance: Most people love their doctors and medical care, but dislike the mess of the current healthcare finance system. My business partner Alex Henderson describes the current healthcare system as capitalistic on the provision of services, and socialistic on how those services are provided. So how did we get into this mess? Believe it or not, the current mess has its genesis near the end of World War II. Rick Lindquest penned "The History of U.S. Employer-Provided Health Insurance Post-World War II" on June 5, 2014:[145]

---

closing departments to correct the errors made in the origination process. This sounds eerily similar to U.S. auto manufacturers in the early 1980s.

145 https://www.peoplekeep.com/blog/part-1-the-history-of-u.s.-employer-provided-health-insurance-post-world-war-ii

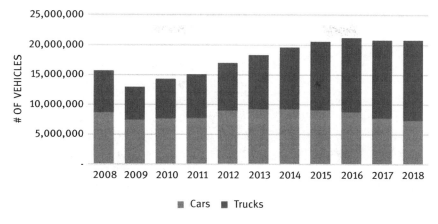

Figure 6.6: U.S. car and light truck manufacturing over a ten-year period.

The employer-provided health insurance industry that exists today is largely the unintended result of a temporary tax break from the early 1940s. This tax break became the basis for U.S. healthcare.

Prior to World War II, most Americans paid for their own medical care, either directly to the provider, or beginning in the 1930s, through the Blue Cross nonprofit health insurance entities which were created to offer guaranteed service for a fixed fee. Back then, health insurance really was insurance—providing coverage only for major items like hospitalizations that people could not afford to pay for themselves. All other expenses were paid out-of-pocket directly to the provider.

During World War II, the federal government was wary of post-war inflation. The administration saw the terrible devastation hyperinflation wreaked on post–World War I Germany and they were determined to hold it at bay through wage and price controls which they instituted during the war. In reaction to the wage controls, many labor groups planned to go on strike en masse. In order to avert the strike, in a concession to the labor groups, the War Labor Board exempted employer-paid health benefits from wage controls and income tax.

This historical accident created a tax advantage that drove enormous demand for employer-provided health insurance plans over the previously more common individual health insurance. Employers received a 100% tax deduction while the benefits employees received were exempt from federal, state, and city taxation.

As early as the 1940s, when the U.S. presidential administrations tried to end the tax break and reform healthcare, the employer-provided health industry was already dug-in. In addition, labor groups preferred the employer-provided health insurance model. By the mid-1960s, employer-provided health insurance was almost universal.

The employer model worked well while costs remained low and employees stayed with the same company for their entire career. As healthcare costs increased and employees began to change employers regularly, the system began to erode.

Thus, tax arbitrage between employer-paid and employee-paid healthcare, coupled with politicians' natural ability to shift costs of entitlements onto the private sector has resulted in the mess we have today. Numerous attempts to reform healthcare cost are mired in tax arbitrage, Medicare and Medicaid health cost-shifting, and arbitrage between for-profit and non-profit hospital systems. It's a mess that heretofore has defied resolution.

Land Use Regulations: Rational regulations for zoning, land development, and land use make sense and are in the public interest. Unfortunately, land use regulations have been weaponized by a variety of combatants. "Not in My Back Yard" (NIMBY) has long been an issue. I served 15 years on the Zoning Hearing Board (ZHB) of my township. The ZHB hears appeals of the planning commission and board of supervisors regarding land use where variances and special exceptions are required where a land use is not permitted.

Normal cases are for an addition that exceeds lot setback restrictions, signage variances in commercial zones, and permeable surface coverage. These cases are typically resolved with a listening ear and some common sense, usually satisfying opposing parties.

Even at the sleepy township level, land use issues have become weaponized. The local school district wanted to build a school where some of the land was in a flood plain, next to a sewage treatment plant. The superintendent had her own agenda, which was publicly expressed as "for the kids." We turned the plans down. Out came the lawyers, and after a battle, our school district now has a high school partially in a flood plain. There were self-interests that I won't address here, but suffice it to say this high school in my opinion was a $100 million boondoggle.

The Superintendent then had signage added that was not in the approved plan, and was aghast when the zoning officer cited the district for a zoning violation. Again, the superintendent appeared with her standard argument of it being "for the kids." Feeling a little tired of this project, which came back for serial variances and exceptions, I asked her why she had such a difficult time with following regulations. Her answer was, in so many words, "We're doing right for the kids."

After the hearing, the superintendent lectured me on why I was so unreasonable about enforcing zoning rules. I simply said, "Why not try to comply before the fact?" It didn't go well from there.

The preceding matter is a microcosm of land use issues. Here's the macro view: Industry leaders tell me that the time and cost of obtaining development permits has skyrocketed and makes affordable housing more out of reach. "Impact fees" and similar costs shift infrastructure costs onto builders, who include them in the price of housing, effective home affordability of mortgage payment, or monthly rental.

Chris George, CEO of CMG Financial and the 2019 Chairman of the Mortgage Bankers Association, noted:

Affordability's a function of inventory and local building rules. The "Not in My Backyard" discussion about housing density comes into play. And so local municipalities, cities, counties, and states impose certain rules that impact cost a developer or a builder incurs to build there. To make a profit, the price [of land use regulations] affects the price of the real estate. And once you build there, you box out home affordability. There are a number of things happening —some municipalities [are attempting] to allow a builder to build a home that is affordable to residents at the median income.

Fannie Mae has already started a pretty ambitious endeavor to educate [consumers on the cost benefits of] manufactured homes and modular homes. Those particular building techniques can reduce the cost of a home. The only way you can potentially influence the price of that home is by influencing the cost of building it. I think affordability comes by way of us being a little more creative and innovative with [affordable housing] product.

Don Salmon, CEO of Toll Brothers Mortgage, expanded on growing the housing supply:

I understand that people don't want to see any more development in their neighborhood. They want the open space. We understand that open space is important to society. But so is having a fresh stock of new housing. The population continues to grow, but housing stock continues to get older. Some houses are at the economic end of their lives, and it's time to replace them. So, it's important that we have a balance between open space and environmental issues and continuing to make sure that there's adequate housing stock to meet families' needs.

The truth is they're not making any more land. So, land is a nonrenewable resource that once it's developed, is very difficult to redevelop. There are some redevelopment opportunities, however. For example, we have taken old factories in Hoboken [New Jersey, near New York City] and turned them into magnificent condominiums.

More efforts along the lines mentioned by Chris George and Don Salmon are needed. Development moratoriums and limits on rehabilitation and higher land use intensity of existing land, especially in California, Washington state, New York, and other metro areas limit affordable housing options. Limited options produce the result that some metro areas are rapidly approaching unaffordability for most working families.

Figure 6.7 shows that in many communities, the average family would have to spend more than 40% of its total income to buy a median-priced home in that community. The Bay Area of California is a perfect example. Land use and new develop restrictions limit new inventory, and high compensation for technology workers crowd out most working-class families. I visited San Francisco about half a dozen times in the last year. Suffice it to say that the current system is not working, and the homeless problem and all of its manifestations have financial and quality of life issues that are hard to fathom.

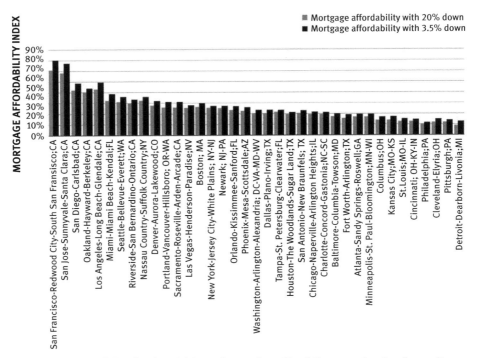

Source: National Association of Realtors, US Census Bureau, Current Population survey, American Community Survey, Moody's Analytics, Freddie Mac Primary Mortgage Market Survey, and the Urban Institute.
Note mortgage affordability is the share of media family income devoted to the monthly principal, interest, taxes, and insurance payment required to buy the median home at the Freddie Mac prevailing rate in 2018 for a 30-year-fixed-rate mortgage and property tax and insurance 1.75 percent of the housing value.
Data for the bottom chart as of Q3 2018.

Figure 6.7: Mortgage affordability by metropolitan statistical area.

Federal Intervention into Real Estate Marketplace

Fair housing and non-discrimination should be the law of the land, and prudent regulation is absolutely essential. But what are the unintended consequences? They abound. The following is a short history of some of the regulations that have unintended consequences that cost consumers dearly and restrict the availability of credit. According to Investopedia:[146]

> The Real Estate Settlement Procedures Act, or RESPA, was enacted by Congress to provide homebuyers and sellers with improved disclosures of settlement costs and to eliminate abusive practices in the real estate settlement process.

> From its inception, RESPA has regulated mortgage loans attached to one-to-four family residential properties with the objective of educating borrowers regarding their settlement costs

---

146 https://www.investopedia.com/terms/r/real-estate-settlement-procedures-act-respa.asp

and to eliminate kickback practices and referral fees that can inflate the cost of obtaining a mortgage. The types of loans included would consist of the majority of purchase loans, assumptions, refinances, property improvement loans, and equity lines of credit.

RESPA attempts to regulate settlement costs by requiring lenders, mortgage brokers or servicers of home loans to provide disclosures to borrowers that will inform them about real estate transactions, settlement services, relevant consumer protection laws and any other pertinent and timely information connected to the cost of the real estate settlement process. Any business relationships between closing service providers and other parties connected to the settlement process would also need to be disclosed to the borrower.

The Act also prohibits specific practices, such as kickbacks, referral, and unearned fees. RESPA regulates the use of escrow accounts—such as prohibiting loan servicers to demand excessively large escrow accounts. RESPA also restricts sellers from mandating title insurance companies.

Sounds like a good idea. But in practice, the impact has often been illusory. Take the huge package of disclosures that a borrower receives at application and again at closing. I'm sure regulators would be shocked to hear that consumers usually don't read them and almost never understand them.

Interestingly, automobile financing does not have any RESPA-like rules. Ford and Chrysler offer financing and leasing of vehicles in the showroom to consumers, as well as floor plan financing to dealers. Aside from disclosure of finance charges, there are no prohibitions to one-stop shopping, payment of referral fees, and so on.

Ford Motor Credit makes its mission very clear:

Our primary focus is to profitably support the sale of Ford and Lincoln vehicles. We work with Ford to maximize customer and dealer satisfaction and loyalty, offering a wide variety of financing products and outstanding service. We continually improve processes focusing on the customer and the dealer to manage costs and ensure the efficient use of capital. As a result, Ford Credit is uniquely positioned to drive incremental sales, improve customer satisfaction and owner loyalty to Ford, and direct profits and distributions back to Ford to support its overall business, including vehicle development.[147]

Chrysler Capital launched in 2013 as the full-service finance provider for FCA US LLC dealers. General Motors Acceptance Corporation failed in 2008 during the mortgage crisis and became Ally Bank.

Cost Impact of Mortgage Regulation

David Motley, 2017 Chairman of the Mortgage Bankers Association and President of Colonial Savings, noted that he was "struck by how the government plays such a huge role in our mortgage finance process. The expansive regulatory structure put

---

147 https://www.sec.gov/Archives/edgar/data/38009/000003800918000030/fmcc1231201710k.pdf

in place after the financial crisis in 2008 has really impacted consumers' ability to achieve home ownership. I see regulations and I want to do something about it."

The impact of regulation can be seen in the increasing cost of originating a mortgage set out in Figure 6.8.

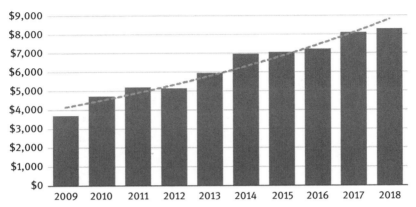

Sources: MBA Mortgage Bankers Performance Report

Figure 6.8: Cost per loan to originate a mortgage loan.

The cost increases include a roughly 50% increase in the number of non-sales personnel at a typical mortgage banker. In 2010, the personnel cost component was approximately 60% in origination personnel and 40% in operations personnel. That mix has reversed. There are now 60% in operations and 40% in origination.

Said another way, in 2010, a company of 400 employees would have about 240 origination personnel and about 160 operations personnel. In 2017, that same company would have 240 in operations and 160 in origination. Many of the additional operations personnel are compliance focused or are involved in "checking the checkers."

Lenders have had regulators chasing at their heels over the past eight years, and have simply added layers out of necessity to accommodate the added compliance burden. As Jonathan Corr of Ellie Mae has frequently said, applying "human spackle" to cover holes in the process doesn't work long-term without a significant cost impact.

I've seen various estimates of the cost of regulations imposed since 2009— regulations that stem from Dodd-Frank, the Consumer Financial Protection Bureau, and various state regulatory requirements. The estimate of $2,000 per file of increased regulatory burden cost seems about right. For a first-time homebuyer seeking a $160,000 loan, the cost is about 1.3 discount points, which equates to roughly 1/4 to 3/8% in higher interest rate. Would a first-time borrower happily agree to this higher interest rate for "regulatory benefit"? That's $400 to $600 per year in increased interest expense, supposedly for "consumer protection."

That $2,000, too, is before the cost of punitive regulation by enforcement, before the punitive cost of repurchases due to so-called technical defects that were not causal to loan performance, or the costs that the duopoly of Freddie Mac and Fannie Mae imposed via guarantee fee and loan-level price adjusters and fees set by regulators, not competition.

Another way to think about this cost is to frame it in terms of a 5% down payment loan typically sought by a first-time buyer. The $160,000 hypothetical loan down payment is $8,000. Hypothetically, how about a line item on the Loan Estimate that shows additional cash to close of $2,000 for "consumer protection expense"? I favor regulation that is flexible enough to respond to technological and demographic changes; regulation should be subject to cost/benefit analysis and transparency, regarding the cost of the regulation being borne by consumers. I am not in favor of "hard-coding" elements like debt-to-income ratio maximums that discourage innovation and assume a legislator can dictate the ratio that "protects" consumers.

This additional cost is borne by the customer in the form of higher interest rates, which increase debt to income and impair the consumer's "ability to repay." I asked consumers anecdotally how much mortgage regulations actually cost them per year; their estimates were way low.

There is also an indirect cost of regulatory uncertainty. David Motley stated, "We need clarity on rules and appropriate penalties for failing to follow them. When we have that, [lenders] will be more willing to lend outside of the four corners of the credit box."

GSE executives appear to have potential competition within the four corners of the credit box. I spoke with a senior GSE executive, at his request, about how competitors might compete aggressively with the GSEs. My reply was that the guarantee fees of GSEs appear to make no sense compared to the losses in the 2012 to 2017 vintages. Virtually no losses, but 40–45 basis points guarantee fees collected on a pristine credit book.

Here are the economics that show Fannie Mae has collected about $40 billion in aggregate guaranteed fees from 2012 to 2016 for the loans guaranteed (Table 6.1). The unpaid principal balance of defaulted loans is $781 million, not billion. 3.3 basis points of total principal balance guaranteed at issuance. This is my calculation and assumes prepayment speeds, but the economics are materially the same. There are guarantee fees of about 40 times the defaulted balances, and the defaulted balances are an unpaid principal, not actual realized losses. No wonder the jumbo and conventional spread is negative!

Several executives of bank and independent mortgage bank originators stated that the GSEs have noticed that they are selling higher balance, high credit-quality loans away from the GSEs and into the private label and whole loan markets. The

Table 6.1: Guarantee fees and loss rate on loans from 2012 to 2016.

YEAR	UNPAID PRINCIPAL BALANCE ($ MILLION)	DEFAULT UNPAID PRINCIPAL BALANCE ($ MILLION)	LOSS RATE (DEFAULT DIVIDED BY UPB)	APPROXIMATE CUMULATIVE GUARANTEE FEES COLLECTED ($ MILLION)
2012	608,103	300	0.049%	13,313
2013	483,419	246	0.051%	9,071
2014	310,374	152	0.049%	4,587
2015	421,057	72	0.017%	5,297
2016	540,409	11	0.002%	5,010
Total	**2,363,362**	**781**	**0.033%**	**37,278**

GSEs are said to have relayed that they expect a "representative mix" of the lender's loan production. They don't want "adverse selection." Yet their pricing model has no relation to the credit risk of a large segment of loans sold to the GSEs.

Guess what? We are approaching the inflection point where the GSE business model will work, until it doesn't. Despite reform attempts by the administration, the GSE model is a tough mess to overhaul. As Roy George, VP of Taylor Morrison Home Funding, observed, it may be too large a problem to shift in any way:

> I see a lot of great ideas. I see a lot of possibilities. But when you really sit down and you do the numbers, to take Fannie or Freddie public, that would be the largest IPO in the world. I don't think that that's going to happen. I don't think that they're going to be able to pull that off. I don't think they're going to be able to change gears. I think that as far as what they do, I think that's going to remain fairly the same.

Today's Real Estate Market

Borrowers expect home buying to be a single transaction. They expect all vendors to work together seamlessly and effectively. Table 6.2 lists the vendors in the process and how much each process costs for a typical home purchase with a $250,000 purchase price.

I spoke with Chris McEntee, the president of ICE Mortgage Services, about the 13% or more transaction costs related to a real estate transaction:

> The cost is just not sustainable. The cost of trading a share of stock on the New York Stock Exchange is a fraction of a cent. This was achieved by using technology and efficiency to reduce the cost of trading assets. The same can be applied to a real estate transaction.

Table 6.2: Listing of the fees in terms of percentage of purchase prices and dollar amounts to purchase a $250,000 home.

	REALTOR LISTING AGENT	REALTOR SELLING AGENT	REAL ESTATE BROKERAGE "JUNK FEES"	MORTGAGE BANKING COST TO ORIGINATE	REAL ESTATE APPRAISAL	INSPECTION FEES	TITLE INSURANCE, RELATED RECORDING COSTS	TRANSFER TAXES	TOTAL
Percentage	3.00%	3.00%	0.50%	3.75%	0.35%	0.20%	1.00%	2.00%	13.80%
Dollars	$7,500	$7,500	$1,250	$9,375	$875	$500	$2,500	$5,000	$34,500

According to a June 12, 2019 article by Ben Lane in *HousingWire*, "Intercontinental Exchange, the parent company of the New York Stock Exchange, moved into mortgages in a big way last year when the company bought MERS, which operates a national electronic registry that tracks the changes in servicing rights and beneficial ownership interests in U.S.-based mortgages. And now, ICE is increasing its presence in the mortgage business. ICE announced Wednesday that it has acquired Simplifile, which acts as an electronic liaison between lenders, settlement agents, and county recording offices, for $335 million."[148]

Simplifile digitizes the closing process for real estate transactions in over 2,000 counties that use Simplifile to electronically record deeds, mortgages, liens, releases, and other documents online.

McEntee stated the "combination of MERS and Simplifile will help the real estate industry speed the evolution from paper-based transactions toward digital ones."

Incoming Chairman of the Mortgage Bankers Association Brian Stoffers stated that many MBA members struggle with streamlining and digitizing the mortgage process.

At a recent MBA Conference, Stoffers said:

> We face strategic decisions that will shape our future. The impact of technology disruptors will be incredible. We have to adapt so that lenders will be more efficient and effective. Customers used to instant online gratification will demand it, but they still want in-person assistance as well. Technology can assist homebuyers be self-sufficient as they would like. They can even bypass traditional realtors using sites like Zillow and Redfin.

How much of the processes used in residential real estate purchase and finance be eliminated, consolidated, and automated, and how can cost be reduced from 13% to 10%? 5%? 2%?

This chapter title is "Can Disruption Be Planned and Orchestrated?" We've walked through a series of examples to consider. Chris McEntee of ICE Mortgage Services stated, "We'll see an acceleration of consolidation and efficiency through technology. The landscape will really change."

I agree. Can we influence the change and spark intentional disruption? I think so. So how can we profit from this?

---

148 https://www.housingwire.com/articles/49314-mers-nyse-owner-intercontinental-exchange-increases-mortgage-presence-by-buying-simplifile

Chapter Seven
Boot Camp for Disruption:
A Disruptor's Guide to Innovation

The hypothesis for our boot camp discussion is that history can provide guidance as to how you can identify, initiate, and profit from being a disruptor. Our dive into history provides some common themes:

1. Convergence and Logistics are the precursors to disruption—bring them together and the stage is set.
2. Disruption occurs when a particular process, method, or product becomes so compelling that it becomes ubiquitous.
3. Convergence and Logistics are the fuel for Schumpeter's "Creative Destruction." Thought leadership and creativity provide the sparks for Creative Destruction and Disruption.

Fintech has been in evidence for over two thousand years; the addition of the internet is just another facilitating tool in addition to merchant ships, coinage, indemnity agreements, and regulation. Regulation can be a facilitating tool. Yes! We have seen the disruptive disturbances of regulation in health insurance, municipal taxis, mortgages, and a few other areas.

Some definitions:

Convergence refers to the aggregating of a marketplace or method for a potential customer to perform product discovery; features identification and comparison; benefits identification and comparison; and price investigation and comparison.

Convergence can occur in a physical space. My friend Peter Manolakos explained to me that the Agora was a space in ancient Greek city-states that was open, centrally located, and available to the public. Literally translated, *agora* is "gathering place" or "assembly." In later years, shopping centers and malls functioned in a similar manner. eBay, Amazon, and Alibaba are internet-powered equivalents.

Logistics include payment terms, terms of transfer, form of payment (cash or credit), how the payment is financed (secured loan, unsecured loan, trade credit), arrangements for transportation, delivery to the customer, and whether the product will be subject to a custody or bailment arrangement. Risk management (insurance, warranty, indemnity, financial hedge) and diligence complete the logistics explication. Or do they?

Regulation adds a rules-based framework to the logistics, such as a legal ownership framework provided (direct ownership, lease, etc.), taxes on sale use or transfer, fees on sale use or transfer, and other policy objectives desired by the regulator.

Finally, thought leadership is the true catalyst of disruption. The DNA that a company accumulates can foster or inhibit thought leadership. The examples that

https://doi.org/10.1515/9783110650471-008

follow are largely historical and are not related to real estate. The reason I take this approach is to present historical examples free from recency bias, availability heuristic, and the preordained outcome distortion, as well as offer examples that most readers will not have any hands-on experience with.

Company DNA

According to Angela Zutavern, Managing Director at AlixPartners, the DNA of a company is important. Ms. Zutavern presented these ideas as part of a presentation on "How Machines Will Remake Your Business Model."[149] Companies formed before the internet could be called "born traditional." Companies formed explicitly to exploit the internet and digital technologies could be called "born digital."[150]

Traditional and digital companies have different DNA. Traditional companies may be very successful with physical convergence and physical logistics. Digital companies may be very successful at online convergence and digital logistics. *Digital logistics* describes Netflix, Spotify, and similar companies whose products are delivered in the digital domains. Some companies can be hybrids, in which there is an online convergence with an outstanding physical logistics capability. Amazon, eBay, and similar companies may be considered hybrids.

In some cases, born-digital companies struggle with domain knowledge of an industry. Several years ago, I was asked to assist a born-digital company entering the mortgage business. They had great marketing technology, great data scientists, customer experience engineers, and all the competencies you would expect in a born-digital company. There was just one key ingredient missing. Not one of the employees had executive or senior leadership experience in mortgage banking. The highest competency was a closing manager from a national lender.

Needless to say, this company struggled. The born-digital founding and executive team had difficulty envisioning a mortgage product as distinctly different from physical or streaming products. I couldn't help, since none of the leadership team had any significant domain knowledge, nor were they willing to accept the peculiar regulatory and GSE models of the mortgage lending market. The outcome was not pleasant for the executive team, as the company never really obtained traction.

Similarly, born-traditional companies can excel at domain knowledge but struggle with digital. I am familiar with a sizable and successful financial institution that decided to become digital, and literally took every physical process of deposit account opening and pushed it to their website, albeit in PDF form, with little thought

---

149 Angela Zutavern, "How Machines Will Remake Your Business Model," lecture at Chief Executive's Disruptive Tech Summit, June 10, Cambridge MA.
150 Ibid.

of why or how potential account openers would react to shuffling physical paper back and forth. Not a great success.

An Early Example of Pre-Planned Disruption: Lockheed's Skunk Works

Let's look at a company that has achieved an amazing set of technical and product achievements consistently in an intentional and planned manner. That company is Lockheed. Clarence "Kelly" Johnson was a thought leader that conceived Lockheed's Skunk Works in 1943. The Skunk Works®, by definition, was a born-traditional company as there were no born-digital companies in 1943. According to Lockheed Martin's history of the Skunk Works[151]:

> The Skunk Works division was formed by Kelly Johnson to build America's first jet fighter. German jets had appeared over Europe. Uncle Sam needed a counterpunch, and Johnson got a call. As with virtually all Skunk Works projects that followed, the mission was secretive, and the deadline was remarkably tight. Johnson promised the Pentagon they'd have their first prototype in 150 days. His engineers turned one out in 143 days, creating the P-80 Shooting Star, a sleek, lightning-fast fighter [that flew in 1945 near the end of World War II. The P-80 went on to win history's first jet-versus-jet dogfight over Korea in 1950.

> Just four years later, amidst growing fears over a potential Soviet missile attack on the United States, Skunk Works engineers—who often worked ten hours a day, six days a week—created the U-2, the world's first dedicated spy plane. It cruised at 70,000 feet, snapping aerial photographs of Soviet installations. This vital reconnaissance, unobtainable by other means, averted a war in Europe and a nuclear crisis in Cuba.

> But high altitude was not enough. By 1960, Soviet radar and surface-to-air missile technology had caught up with the U-2. President Eisenhower needed something quicker, stronger, and more elusive. Using sheets of titanium coated with heat-dissipating black paint, engineers created the SR-71 Blackbird. On July 3, 1963, the plane reached a sustained speed of Mach 3 at astounding 78,000 feet and remains the world's fastest and highest-flying manned aircraft.

The lesson from the Skunk Works is that disruption is not a technology matter. *Disruption is one hundred percent people. It's thought leadership.* When the Skunk Works was conceived, there were no computers and no internet. Johnson's engineers designed and fabricated a flying prototype in 143 days. That's just over five months. All was done in secret, with pencil, paper, and slide rules. The slide rule is an analog computer used for mathematical computations, with its first use in 1622. So, no modern technology driving disruption, though the aircraft that was produced harnessed available and advancing technology designed by thought leaders.

---

[151] https://www.lockheedmartin.com/en-us/news/features/history/skunk-works.html

Johnson thought the Skunk Works® was so distinctive, a logo was developed, shown in Figure 7.1.

Figure 7.1: Lockheed Martin Skunk Works® logo.

The power of thought leadership is evident in the success of Kelly Johnson and his team. In 15 years, Lockheed produced the first sub-sonic jet fighter, then the world's first high altitude sub-sonic jet-powered reconnaissance aircraft, then a supersonic—in fact, three times the speed of sound!—reconnaissance aircraft.

Diversity and Inclusion as Elements of Thought Leadership

A company needs a DNA that includes a diverse group of thought leaders. You can increase the likelihood of achieving disruption by intentionally including a diverse group of potential thought leaders together.

Marcia Davies, Chief Operating Officer of the Mortgage Bankers Association, is a proponent of diversity and inclusion in the workplace, especially for the purpose of developing a greater bench of thought leadership executives. Marcia Davies of the MBA explains further:

> The more diverse the group around the leadership table, the better the outcome. If you sur-
> round yourself with people who think like you and have the same background as you, you're
> probably going to come up with solutions that are in your comfort zone to tackle a problem or

seize an opportunity. But if you look at it from different angles and consider different perspectives, the opportunity opens itself up for you to consider ways you otherwise wouldn't have had the insight and advantage to consider.

We formalized the mPower program to help expand opportunities for talented women. The growth has been so explosive. I'm hoping the network continues to expand. The number of women who tell me the benefits of the network has been overwhelming. Women are doing business and seeing business results by some of the connections that they have made in the network. They are able to mentor and coach others. The energy that comes out of events where women feel like they get some real time solutions to help them navigate in the workplace. So, I would hope that our community would continue to grow and be strong and that we'll see more women rising in the ranks in this industry and more women represented on boards and more women's' voices around the table.

According to Price Waterhouse Coopers (PwC), an international consulting firm, 78% of CEOs who have invested in diversity and inclusion programs have seen a greater capacity for innovation within their organizations. Eighty-five percent of CEOs who have invested in diversity and inclusion programs saw enhanced business performance.[152]

According to Michael Fenlon, Chief People Officer at PwC, a company has to be committed to diversity and inclusion while intentionally upscaling its existing employees. Companies can close a skills gap by hiring from competitors or from outside the industry, but PwC asserts that retraining and upscaling its existing team delivers a very high ROI. More importantly, PwC is following its own advice and is investing in a variety of upscaling initiatives, including personalized training based on a skills inventory, training using social media and gamification, and enabling employees to produce "citizen-led change" to scale business activities.[153]

Another Preplanned Disruption: North American P-51 Mustang

North American Aviation produced a World War II air superiority fighter that changed the course of the European theater. The aircraft, the P-51 Mustang, was designed by Edgar Schmued and incorporated a number of thought-leading features, including a laminar airflow wing, armor plating of the pilot's seat back, self-sealing gas tanks, an oxygen system for the pilots, and a supercharged engine with a variable pitch propeller. None of these features by themselves were game changers, but when combined into the P-51, the result was a game-changing product—again, born by thought leadership.[154]

---

152 PwC: 18th Annual Global CEO Survey, 2015.

153 Michael Fenlon, "Disrupt Your Talent Strategy," presentation at Chief Executive's Disruptive Tech Summit, June 10, Cambridge MA.

154 http://aerospacelegacyfoundation.com/p51-mustang

The P-51 Mustang could fly at 40,000 feet and accompany Allied bombing aircraft to and from Germany. As a result, bomber losses were substantially reduced. Many bomber pilots affectionately referred to the P-51 as "Little Friends" that protected the bombers.[155] One squadron, the Tuskegee Airmen, became legendary flying their signature "red tail" P-51s. The Airmen were also legendary as the squadron pilots were African Americans, and the skill and ferociousness of the "red-tailed" Airmen made them feared adversaries of the Nazi opposition. The Tuskegee Airmen were an early effort at long-needed diversity within the armed forces.

I've logged about four hours in P-51s, flying with Lee Lauderback, owner of Squadron 51 in Kissimmee, Florida and John Posson, a Squadron 51 instructor pilot. The preflight inspection of Lee's "Crazy Horse" is like touring a museum of incredible technology. The landing gear machining and design are works of art, as is the Rolls Royce Merlin V-12 supercharged engine.

The takeoff roll on Runway 33 with John Posson as instructor pilot at Kissimmee Airport is spectacular. There is plenty of rudder needed to counteract the torque of the Merlin engine. The Mustang literally leaps into the air, and a left turn on climb out has the airfield slipping away below. About ten minutes later, we enter the Avon Park Air Force Range,[156] a retired bombing range and practice area for Air Force pilots from an earlier era.

With clearance to maneuver within a block altitude of 6,000 to 18,000 feet, John Posson has me demonstrate slow flight, full aerodynamic stalls, aileron rolls, barrel rolls, and full loops, following his lead. The aircraft handles like a Formula racecar. The controls are precise.

On the ground, Lee reveres Crazy Horse as well as Crazy Horse 2 and Strega, all P-51D models. "These are flying treasures. About 100 (out of 15,000 produced) are still airworthy." According to Lee Lauderback, the P-51 converged two incredible technologies: a very low-drag laminar flow wing paired with a Rolls Royce turbocharged liquid cooled engine that was fuel efficient at 40,000 feet. These two technologies produce a long-endurance, high-performance fighter. The marriage of a Rolls Royce engine from England with an American-designed airframe proved to be a formidable combination.

The P-51 went from concept to prototype in about six months, according to Lee Lauderback. North American Aviation created the logistics to build 15,000 aircraft in three years, including three substantial upgrades: the B, C, and D models.[157] Interestingly, female pilots who served in the Women's Airforce Service

---

155 https://www.collingsfoundation.org/aircrafts/north-american-tf-51d-mustang/
156 Avon Park Air Force Range is a 106,000-acre bombing and gunnery range located in Polk and Highlands Counties, Florida. The Avon Park Air Force Range (APAFR), Operating Location Alpha (OL-A), is located approximately 100 miles east-southeast of MacDill AFB, FL.
157 https://www.britannica.com/technology/P-51

Pilots (WASP) ferried some P-51s from the factory to theater mustering points.[158] The P-51 design and manufacturing would be labeled "agile" today. The impact of the P-51 was so disruptive that it changed the course of the Allied bombing campaign against the Nazis.

I haven't personally experienced a business model literally working until it doesn't. An analog is flying an aircraft into an aerodynamic stall.[159] Above a certain speed, which pilots aptly labeled the "stall speed," the wings provide sufficient lift to keep the aircraft flying. As you approach the stall speed, the initial indication of an impending stall is aerodynamic buffeting, as parts of the smooth airflow over the wing are disrupted by the high angle of attack of the wing.

That buffet is actually the disruption of smooth airflow separating from the wing, producing a turbulent "buffet" that can be felt in the aircraft. Continued application of back pressure on the control stick raises the nose further, until the speed deteriorates to the point that smooth airflow over the wing is totally disrupted and a "full stall" ensues.

In the Mustang, the full stall occurs at about 88 knots, and the stall occurs very quickly. The Mustang rolls over, the weight of the Rolls Royce engine pulls the nose toward the ground, and just one second after the aircraft was flying with a little buffet, the ground is rushing up at about 1,000 feet per minute. The first time I stalled a Mustang, I was amazed at the speed and aggressiveness of the stall. The P-51's laminar flow wing flew until it didn't. It wasn't anything like stalling a general aviation Piper Archer, which is designed to be much more docile and forgiving at stall entry.

Recovery from the stall is accomplished by relaxing back pressure on the control stick, applying rudder to stop aircraft rotation, letting airspeed build, and then applying power and a firm smooth pull on the stick to bring the nose back up through the horizon to return to smooth flight. So, the "business model" of the wing—that is, producing lift—works until it doesn't. This is unlike with company business models, where the recovery from disruption is not as simple as lowering the nose of the aircraft to regain flying speed.

Pilots practice the disruption of airflow over the wing known as a stall with plenty of altitude to provide ample time for stall recovery. Each year, many pilots and their aircraft are lost when their wings' business model—producing lift—works until it doesn't. Stall accidents usually occur when a pilot is maneuvering to land. The accident reports usually describe a common scenario. The reports cite that cause of the accident was pilot "failure to maintain airspeed and loss of control resulting in an

---

158 http://womenofwwii.com/wasps/ferry-pilot-warms-up-her-p-51/
159 An airplane stall is an aerodynamic condition in which an aircraft exceeds its given critical angle of attack and is no longer able to produce the required lift for normal flight. https://www.thebalancecareers.com/what-is-an-aircraft-stall-282603

uncontrolled impact with the ground. Contributing factors were loss of situational awareness of the aircraft's altitude and/or bank angle contributing to an aerodynamic stall." In short, a series of factors converge together, disrupting smooth airflow and resulting in an accident. The wing's business model worked until it didn't.

The time spent discussing aerodynamic stalls is to draw a strong analogy to the stalling of a business model. Borders and Barnes & Noble could feel the buffeting of Amazon nipping away at the "airspeed" of their retail business model. You can ignore the buffeting until the model simply stops "flying." Whether it was Borders, Circuit City, or Motorola, the "full stall" is a loss of control of the company, with substantial damage to employees, lenders, and stockholders.

The residential real estate industry has disruptive "buffeting" shaking the business models of competitors. The buffeting is worthy of attention.

Disruption with Intention

Some disruption occurs without intention. The failure of taxi medallion lenders is an example. Some disruption is intentional. So how can disruption be intentionally created? Intentional disruption is easier in the face of significant recognized need. The P-51 Mustang and P-80 Shooting Star are examples where significant need, convergence, and logistics created disruption in armed conflict. There are numerous other examples of disruptive advances in the military sphere, from the invention of gunpowder through the deployment of weapons of mass destruction.

Many recent disruptive technologies have been created where significant revenue is currently available, or in anticipation of significant demand to be created. Amazon, Alibaba, Netflix, and Spotify identified a large pool of revenue to be won, and won it. This is creative destruction at work. Competitors' older business models worked until they didn't. That is the lesson for initiating intentional disruption.

Sometimes disruption can occur through chance meeting. According to IBM's official history, "the Sabre (Semi-Automatic Business Research Environment) central reservation system, which was originally a part of American Airlines, pioneered online transactions. For the first time, computers were connected together through a network that allowed people around the world to enter data, process requests for information and conduct business."[160]

> Sabre got its start because of a chance meeting in 1953. A young IBM salesman, R. Blair Smith, had boarded an American flight from Los Angeles to New York on his way to a training session. He got into a conversation with the man sitting next to him, who turned out to be C.R. Smith, the president of American Airlines.

---

160 https://www.ibm.com/ibm/history/ibm100/us/en/icons/sabre/

At the time, airline reservations were written by hand on cards and sorted in boxes—an un-wieldy mess, as the industry expanded. Blair Smith knew that American Airlines had an older model computer that could only keep track of the number of seats reserved and open on a flight, but could not record anything about who was in those seats.

Blair Smith recommended a joint development project between IBM and American Airlines to create a computerized reservation system, and American Airlines president Smith agreed, and the SABRE system was born.[161]

The rest, as they say, is history.

The Sabre airline reservation system evolved and was spun off into a separate company that supports airline, hotel, and car reservations in about 140 countries.[162] Sabre is widely used by airlines, except by Southwest, which has a captive system. Travel agents can access the Sabre system to book flights, hotels, and cars for con-sumers. Sabre is also a backbone for online travel-booking sites like Expedia.

Think of Sabre as a real estate multiple-listing service, except instead of houses, Sabre listed inventories of future flights from various airlines, hotels, and rental cars as well as customer information. Consumers, however, do not have direct ac-cess to Sabre.

Until 2002, most airlines (except Southwest) paid an 8% commission to travel agents to market and book airline flights. A friend, Shaun, had a successful travel agency and earned extensive revenue booking flights for business and leisure trav-elers. Shaun came into a meeting with me and said, "The airlines are reducing com-missions on tickets to five percent. That's a forty percent revenue reduction." We talked through his options. He got upset when I asked, "What happens when air-lines reduce commissions to zero?" This happened soon after the first reduction in March 2002.[163] Shaun transformed his business and focused on "business-to-business award travel" and "exotic travel." Many of his competitors ceased to exist. The airlines made the calculation that 8% commissions were too much to give up in an era of reduced demand following the September 11, 2001 attacks, plus increased fuel, labor, and compliance costs.

A similar fate occurred to commissioned stockbrokers. Generally, any business that is an intermediary or broker—including real estate, mortgage and insurance brokers—faces a revenue stream attack.

So, let's look at the likely intentional disruption opportunities to occur in the residential real estate market. This market currently has about 13% cost stack based on the selling price of the house, for a perfectly transparent transaction.

Like a wing experiencing decreasing airspeed and stalling, at some point, a consumer's willingness to pay for this 13% cost stack will diminish. Quickly. It's

---

161 https://www.ibm.com/ibm/history/ibm100/us/en/icons/sabre/
162 https://www.sabretravelnetwork.com/home/solutions/travel_agency/getting_started/
163 https://www.latimes.com/archives/la-xpm-2002-mar-31-tr-digest31.2-story.html

already begun, as we'll see a little later in this chapter. Be certain of this: in the next few years, at least half of the cost stack will be returned to consumers, at the expense of everyone involved in the real estate purchase or rental transaction.

Services will converge, logistics will be perfected, and the current residential real estate ecosystem will face brutal competition to provide converged services efficiently, with great customer experience, and with little friction at greatly reduced prices. Current participants in the real estate ecosystem will lose $100 billion of revenue. That's $100 billion.

It won't happen overnight, but as surely as an aircraft wing will stall with decreasing airspeed, consumers will demand cost reduction, convenience, and better, faster service. So residential real estate participants (realtors, lenders, title insurers, appraisers, inspectors, service providers, builders, employees, and contractors of these businesses) can continue their present business models, which will work until they don't. Or they can become an active participant in creative destruction.

A Thesis on Creative Destruction and Disruption in the Real Estate Business

One needs only to look at Amazon to see an example of using convergence and logistics to rapidly and intentionally disrupt a large swath of previously discrete businesses. If a reader can imagine being transported back to 1995 and ask, "How and when will Blockbuster, Borders bookstores, department stores, specialty, shopping malls, and multi-tier retail distribution models will be damaged and pushed out of existence?" few would name Amazon, Alibaba, or eBay.

The residential housing market has several characteristics that have thus far prevented the type of transformation that Amazon, Apple, and other companies have brought about. These characteristics include:

- Heavy regulation and licensing of virtually all providers in a labor-intensive process
- Heavily decentralized real estate, lending, and related services that favored local face-to-face relationships
- Government conservatorship of Freddie Mac and Fannie Mae, which inhibits product and service innovation, as well as excluding certain borrower classes due to Dodd-Frank Act including the "ability to repay"
- Consumer misunderstanding of down payment and credit requirements to obtain a mortgage loan
- Industry inertia
- Industry lobbyists

Before I describe the events of how the residential real estate markets will be disruptively transformed, let's examine the economic and employment effects[164] on the market participants:

- Residential real estate purchasers will save over $100 billion in transaction fees.
- The residential real estate market will become more liquid.
- Active real estate agents will decrease from 1.2 million to about 200,000.
- Licensed and/or registered commissioned mortgage loan officers will decline from about 100,000 to about 40,000.
- Licensed residential appraisers will be reduced to about 25% of the current active roster.
- Title agent employment will decrease by 75%.
- Real estate brokerage commissions will decrease by 65%.
- GSE and FHA share of the mortgage business will decline by about 40% from 2018 levels.

I've probably annoyed or offended just about every industry reader at this juncture. And that's my point. Discomfort with the coming reduction in transaction fees is healthy. It spurs creative destruction and disruptive impulses. These are the same feelings that owners and employees of the ancient guilds, modern commissioned stockbrokers, travel agents, taxi drivers, retail shop owners, chain bookstores, department stores, and scores of other categories have experienced.

But we can all see it coming. You can argue that my estimates of impact and timing may be wrong. They undoubtedly are not precise, but the order of magnitude is correct. The effect will be material. Ignore it at your own peril.

---

164 Effects can be postulated easy than events, as discussed earlier.

Chapter Eight
A Disciplined Approach to Intentional Disruption

This chapter is relatively short, as we've developed all of the concepts discussed herein previously in the book. I've kept this chapter brief, too, so that readers can revisit and reread it several times. In it, we will go through the summary steps in my approach to intentional disruption, an approach that has just five steps. We have gone through each step in previous chapters in detail. There are longer footnotes in this chapter to cover some details, but I've kept the body of the chapter direct and concise.

Why read this chapter several times? Mary Ann Kipp, a consultant and researcher on innovation, taught me the benefits of "sleeping on an idea."[165] Try reading this chapter during the day, and again at night right before sleeping. Intentionally think about the chapter. Perhaps read it again. There are neurological reasons that multiple reading on different days is effective in generating creative insights.[166] These creative insights are critical to intentional disruption.

I struggled to write this chapter, deleting the work several times. Last evening, I read my notes. I awoke at 6:30 the next morning and the thoughts and words just

---

165 http://kippassoc.com/about-mary-kipp/

166 Joanne Cantor Ph.D., wrote about the "sleep for success" effect. Writing in Psychologytoday.com on May 15, 2010, Sleep for Success: Creativity and the Neuroscience of Sleep, Cantor noted, "During sleep, rat's brains (and yours) practice what they're recently learned. Researchers have discovered that your brain becomes very active when you sleep, and that during certain phases of sleep, your brain becomes even more active if you've just learned something new. In an early study that identified this process rats were hooked up to measure the electrical activity of their brains while they learned a maze. Later, while the rats were sleeping, the researchers observed that their brains were emitting the same pattern of activity they had emitted during maze learning. Apparently, the rats' brains were 're-running' the maze in their sleep and using this time to consolidate their memories of what they had learned. This same phenomenon has been observed in human learning. In other words, if you learn something and then sleep on it, what you've learned becomes clearer just as a function of sleeping. But what's even more interesting is that sleeping on a problem helps people find better solutions. In a study titled 'Sleep Inspires Insight,' participants were given puzzles that involved finding the final number to complete a series of digits. The way they were trained to solve the puzzle was to compare every two-digit pair in the series. What they were not told was that there was a shortcut that allowed people to identify the solution after only two steps. Participants performed three trials of the puzzle and then were given an eight-hour break before returning for ten more trials. Some of them slept during the break and some did not. The people who slept between the two sessions were twice as likely as the others to discover the easier way to solve the problem. According to the researchers, sleeping on a problem apparently allows for a restructuring of the brain connections, setting the stage for the emergence of insight." https://www.psychologytoday.com/us/blog/conquering-cyber-overload/201005/sleep-success-creativity-and-the-neuroscience-sleep

https://doi.org/10.1515/9783110650471-009

flowed. I have no formal training or credentials in psychology or neuroscience, but I do know the technique works. Thank you, Mary Ann Kipp!

The Skyline of a Home Purchase

Many industries subject their customers to a business process that resembles the New York City skyline, silhouetted in Figure 8.1. The skyline is bounded by the East River to the east and the Hudson River to the west. The customer journey figuratively involves visiting many different buildings to achieve the journey, start to finish.

Figure 8.1: A representation of the New York City skyline.

Consider purchasing a new home. The purchase trip might be likened to a trip from Lower Manhattan to Upper Manhattan. The description below is the path most transactions follow. A few steps may be consolidated, but the process generates a real estate transaction file for the real estate broker, mortgage lender, title agent, insurance agent, and all of the services required. That real estate transaction file can easily exceed one thousand pages of documents.

A customer usually starts a residential real estate search with web research, on a real estate site and a mortgage site. These "sites" were easy to access. The next step may be a face-to-face meeting with a realtor. On to a new site—in this case, the site is an office or other physical site.

The next step generally is to qualify or obtain pre-approval for a mortgage. This can be accomplished by visiting an online site or a physical or phone meeting with a mortgage lender. More site visits are likely, perhaps to get income or asset verification.

On to visiting the actual real estate: the home tour. Pre-work may include on-line reviews of the properties, and then the physical tour. More process sites may be visited to review the options in your price range, in addition to visiting the actual homes under consideration.

An offer is made and accepted. A lender is selected. During the lending process, some sites are visited on your behalf. An appraiser and inspector may be engaged to physically enter the proposed home to be purchased. It is generally advised that you accompany the inspector to the home.

Next, on to the title insurance "site" which can be either a website or a building. The homeowner's insurance "building."

When settlement is conducted, the parties travel to physical settlement, paper is shuffled, checks change hands and the home is now owned by the new owners, subject to the mortgage.

Anyone who has purchased a home is familiar with the journey. But does it have to be this way? As Dave Stevens put it in conversations with me for my previous book, *Strategic Transformation*, "You wouldn't build the model the way it works today. Far too many bodies. Far too much cost."

Buying an automobile is generally a "one-stop shop." You view the cars in a showroom, make a selection, visit the dealer's Finance and Insurance department, obtain a loan, complete the legal title work, and drive away.

A Look Back at Stock Trading in the 1960s

Investing in stocks or mutual funds is now an instantaneous transaction. It wasn't always that way. I visited the New York Stock Exchange museum several years ago and observed the way transactions were done in the "old days," as my grandfather used to say. The description of the processes are my observations of the trading done by my grandfather, as well as my understanding of the processes at the New York Stock Exchange based upon my museum visit, as well as several visits to the trading floor over time.

On business days, early in the morning, my grandfather Frank would walk to the newsstand and buy the *Wall Street Journal*. After returning home, he would read the stock quotes with a magnifying glass and sip coffee. He made notes with his fountain pen.

Frank then walked every day to the E.F. Hutton office to consider investments and make trades. It was a treat when I accompanied him on several of those visits. Taking the elevator to the sixth floor of an office building, we walked into the Hutton office. A group of customers sat in chairs reading the paper, making notes and watching a large chalkboard. Prices for widely owned stocks were written on this huge chalkboard, and updated by an employee who carried a long paper tape in one hand, chalk in the other and wrote the prices on the chalkboard. The employee translated what appeared to me to be inscrutable symbols and numbers from the ticker tape.

Every trade my grandfather executed was done on paper trade ticket listing the stock symbol, quantity, and type of order. "At the market" (meaning whatever the market price was when the trade was executed or at its "limit" (meaning a not-to-exceed price) was checked off. The ticker was time-stamped by a very serious looking employee with a cigar drooping from his mouth.

The stockbroker would then take the trade ticket and call in the order to the trade desk at the Hutton office in New York. The individual at the trade desk would then transmit the trade via an internal phone line to a runner at the stock exchange. The runner wrote down the details and ran to the correct Hutton trader at the "specialist" location on the floor of the stock exchange. The trader would use the "open cry out" system and shout the offer to buy an X number of shares "at the market." Another trader or the specialist would offer the shares at the market price and the process then reversed. The trader provided the trade ticket to the runner, who called Hutton New York office, who called the local office. An employee found the stamped trade ticker, wrote the price and quantity on the ticket, and informed the stockbroker that the trade was done. The stockbroker handed a carbon copy of the trade ticket to Frank. Frank wrote it down on his pad.

In the evening, the paper blizzard generated by all this paper was entered in the books and records of the traders, the Hutton New York office and the local offices of Hutton. It was a great adventure to watch this process and see so many people working on so much paper to trade stocks. At times I peered at the stock ticker machine to see if I could watch Frank's trade make its way through the system. I never was able to actually see his exact trade.

Chris McEntee, CEO of InterContinental Exchange Mortgage Services, a subsidiary of the New York Stock Exchange Owner Intercontinental Exchange, described the process used today. The process is much simpler. The order is often entered by the retail customer or the registered representative online, and is executed almost instantaneously. Few, if any, humans ever touch the trade. Accounting for the transaction is instantaneous too, with the transaction entered in buyer and sellers account almost immediately. No paper. No accounts to balance by hand. No mailed trade tickets. And instead of a commission of about 1.25% of the total trade amount to both buyer and seller, transaction costs today are often pennies per share or less. Instead of what used to be a trip around the Lower Manhattan skyline, stock trades today are electronic.

The disruption brought about by electronic equity trading benefitted the customer with more efficient, more transparent, and lower transaction costs. Of course, many jobs and companies were creatively destroyed in the process. The securities trading skyline became an electronic convergence in the ether with an instantaneous logistics system that is a marvel to behold.

Did this disruption happen randomly, or as part of an overall plan?

Intentional Disruption by Company DNA

"Born digital" company executives may consider the first part of this chapter somewhat obvious. While it may seem obvious, competitors of your born digital company are thinking about how to take your business model out as you read this chapter.

"Born traditional" company executives should read this chapter multiple times on different days. (See the footnote on "Creativity and the Neuroscience of Sleep.") I've informally noted in discussions with born digital companies that the intentional focus on developing disruptive ideas involves both collaboration and "sleeping on it."

The process is presented in Figure 8.2.

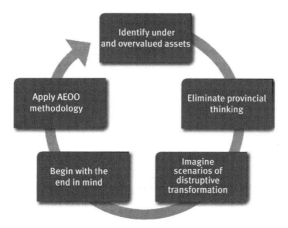

Figure 8.2: A process for intentional disruption.

1. **Identify Undervalued and Overvalued Assets**: A careful inventory and identification of undervalued and overvalued assets is the elixir of intentional disruption. Evaluate undervalued and overvalued assets from a customer's point of view. Identify the critical parts of your service or product that provide true value. Ask yourself, "Would a customer intentionally value and pay for my contribution if it were itemized on a bill?"

In residential real estate, much of the compensation for products and services have the fingers of regulation tipping the value scales by adding complexity, barriers to competition, and layers of cost. A favorite strategy of disrupters is to identify how to eliminate friction. Apply "friction elimination" thinking when identifying undervalued and overvalued assets.

Think about the "cost stack" of a real estate transaction, discussed at length in prior chapters. Would the customer consider the cost stack more expensive than the value provided? How would the consumer value each element of the real estate buying or renting process? Will disruptive competitors find ways to attack the current value proposition?

For example, a neighbor of mine listed his home and sold it the next day. He was very upset because the realtor found a buyer that worked with his wife. His wife was not aware that her fellow employee was looking for a home. In my friend's mind, "paying $20,000 to a realtor to make one call was an outrage." The realtor was an overvalued asset in my friend's mind. The realtor likely believes they completed the transaction as agreed, and delivered a willing and able buyer quickly. My neighbor said, "Next time, I'll market my house myself first."

2. **Reduce "Provincial" Thinking**: Dr. Chris Caplice's provincial thinking model has application here. My interpretation of the provincial thinking model in intentional disruption follows. Begin by intentionally recognizing and minimizing the elements of provincial thinking.

First, reduce recency bias. Like the directors of Motorola dismissing a touchscreen mobile phone, it's easy to dismiss potentially disruptive opportunities because our minds are flooded with recency bias. I was speaking with a Learjet charter pilot who experienced a malfunction of a fuel computer on the first fare-carrying flight after a major overhaul and upgrade of the aircraft. The pilot said, "I couldn't believe there could be a problem after the upgrade and extensive test flights." This is an example of recency bias. The pilot's training kicked in, and they diverted back to the airport and made an uneventful landing.

"Recency bias" is defined by Dave Manuel as "the phenomenon of a person most easily remembering something that has happened recently, compared to remembering something that may have occurred a while back. For instance, if a person is asked to recall the names of thirty people that they have just met, they will usually remember the names of the people that they most recently met first."[167] Stan Middleman has another definition of recency bias: "Some people are bad historians."

Recency Bias at Work

I made a bad decision in acquiring a mortgage banking division in 2004. It was a financial and operational disaster. I became exceedingly skeptical of any acquisition. This was recency bias at work. And the root cause of the bad decision of the 2004 acquisition? A string of successful acquisitions where I was lulled into thinking that

---

167 https://www.davemanuel.com/investor-dictionary/recency-bias/

acquisition is a great business model because of recent successes. Recency bias was also at work.

As another example of minimizing the impact of recency bias, the Oakland A's needed a player to replace their star first baseman Jason Giambi, who was the American League Most Valuable Player in 2000 and who used free agency to sign a $120 million contract with the Yankees at the end of the 2001 season. Giambi was an "All Star" for five straight years during this time, hitting over .300 four straight years and over 30 home runs seven of eight years (except when injured in 2004). In addition, he led the league in base on balls four times.[168] At that point in time, when traded to the Yankees, he was the arguably the best hitter in baseball. He was an "overvalued" (or highly appreciated) asset to the A's, who could not pay the free agency $100 million plus contract offered by the Yankees.[169] The A's needed to replace Giambi's hitting ability.

Enter Scott Hatteberg. Hatteberg had a successful career with the Boston Red Sox, with a batting average of .267 until rupturing nerves in his throwing arm effectively ended his career as a catcher.[170] He was released as a free agent.

The A's intentionally managed their recency bias in using a data-driven approach to identify undervalued player talent. Other teams passed on Hatteberg because he was a career catcher. Catchers with injured arms are not valuable.

Was there a position that Hatteburg could play that didn't need his throwing arm? The A's paid $950,000 to hire Hatteberg with a one-year contract for the 2002 season. The A's then trained him to play first base, where a strong throwing arm was not required. He was a "good" hitter and a naturally good fielder, having been a catcher. Recency bias conquered.

Midway through the 2002 baseball season, the A's began their way to a historic 20-game winning streak never before achieved in the American League. The game that would be their twentieth win was played on September 4, 2002 against the Kansas City Royals. The stadium was electric as the A's jumped out to an 11 to 0 lead. As the game progressed, the Royals began scoring. During the top of the ninth inning, the Royals tied the game 11 to 11. The win streak looked like it might come to an end.

Scott Hatteberg entered the bottom of the ninth inning as a pinch hitter. He hit a walk-off home run to right-center field, securing the twentieth win and the A's historic winning streak. . . a streak that still stands.

Recency bias can be reduced in several ways, the most effective of which is to recognize it as a subtle factor always at work in your mind. Intentionally thinking beyond recent events and into a longer historical context is beneficial for intentionally disruptive thinking.

---

168 https://www.baseball-reference.com/players/g/giambja01.shtml
169 https://www.baseball-reference.com/players/g/giambja01.shtml#all_br-salaries
170 https://www.baseball-reference.com/players/h/hattesc01.shtml

Reducing Availability Heuristic

Second, reduce the "availability heuristic." Behavioral economics defines the term as follows: "Availability is a heuristic whereby people make judgments about the likelihood of an event based on how easily an example, instance, or case comes to mind. For example, investors may judge the quality of an investment based on information that was recently in the news, ignoring other relevant facts... physicians' recent experience in diagnosing a condition increases the likelihood of subsequently diagnosing the condition."[171]

The residential real estate market of the mid-2000s is a great example. Recency bias was evident in the residential real estate market in the mid-2000s. The subprime mortgage market crash occurred in part due to the availability heuristic. Home prices appreciated since the 1940s. The availability heuristic encouraged real estate agents, homeowners, lenders, and the general public to take home price appreciation as a given. Conventional thinking was that real estate prices could ratchet only upward.

Appreciating real estate prices meant that even poorly underwritten loans to unqualified buyer would be bailed out by the rising tide of real estate. If the buyer couldn't make the payments, no worries—the home could be sold at a profit. Home prices continued upward, fueled by loose underwriting standards and the entry of many real estate speculators using "no money down" financing. The market appreciated until it didn't. This triggered the worst real estate and economic bust since the 1930s.

The unprecedented actions that the federal government took to stave off a full-blown depression is described in Appendix 2, along with a listing of other financial crises since the birth of the United States. As you will note, the United States had its fair share of crises.

One useful counterweight to the availability heuristic is data-driven analytics. Seek out data and use a fact-based approach to examine assumptions and current data. One data-driven concept is "mean reversion." Statistically, trends revert to their long-term averages. Investopedia defines mean reversion as "a theory used in finance that suggests that asset prices and historical returns eventually will revert to the long-run mean or average level of the entire dataset. This mean can pertain to another relevant average, such as economic growth or the average return of an industry." The returns in the stock market during the dot-com run-up eventually reverted to the mean with a brutal drop in stock prices.

Review Table 8.1 to compare housing price appreciation by selected markets from 2000 until the housing price peak in 2006 to 2008, and the fall of prices peak to

---

171 https://www.behavioraleconomics.com/resources/mini-encyclopedia-of-be/availability-heuristic/

Table 8.1: Housing price growth rates for various MSAs since 2001.

MSA	HPI CHANGE ()			
	2000 TO PEAK	PEAK TO TROUGH	TROUGH TO CURRENT	ABOVE PEAK
United States	75.9	(25.6)	48.3	10.3
New York-Jersey City-White Plains, NY-NJ	128.0	(22.3)	43.6	11.6
Los Angeles-Long Beach-Glendale, CA	180.6	(38.2)	78.5	10.3
Chicago-Naperville-Arlington Heights, IL	67.1	(38.4)	42.2	(12.4)
Atlanta-Sandy Springs-Roswell, GA	32.6	(35.8)	72.3	10.7
Washington -Arlington -Alexandria, DC -VA-MD-WV	149.3	(28.3)	30.8	(6.2)
Houston-The Woodlands-Sugar Land, TX	29.4	(6.7)	44.0	34.4
Phoenix-Mesa-Scottsdale, AZ	113.4	(51.2)	85.4	(9.5)
Riverside-San Bernardino-Ontario, CA	177.1	(51.8)	81.2	(12.7)
Dallas-Plano-Irving, TX	26.5	(7.2)	62.4	50.6
Minneapolis-St. Paul-Bloomington, MN-WI	69.2	(30.2)	51.1	5.4
Seattle-Bellevue-Everett, WA	90.6	(32.9)	93.3	29.6
Denver-Aurora-Lakewood, CO	34.1	(12.1)	84.1	61.7
Baltimore-Columbia-Towson, MD	123.7	(23.9)	18.1	(10.2)
San Diego-Carlsbad, CA	148.5	(37.5)	69.2	5.7
Anaheim- Santa Ana-Irvine, CA	163.4	(35.3)	59.8	3.4

trough in 2009 to 2010. Subsequent appreciation of home prices now has the average of U.S. home prices 10% above the prior peak. But some markets have not returned to prior peaks, and some markets have heated up far above prior peaks. This dataset offsets some of the availability heuristic bias by using data-driven analytics.

3. **Imagine Scenarios of Disruptive Transformation:** Humans are not very effective at projecting events. We examined how far the prediction of events made by Lester Thurow missed the mark. There is a method, however, for seeing more clearly "around the corner" of the future.

That method is to prepare scenarios of the effects of change rather than the events of change. Focusing on effect can be very useful. Gordon Moore conceived "Moore's Law" by looking at effect. Loosely stated, Moore identified the effect that the speed and capability of microprocessors double every two years. Moore's Law did not identify the events that would occur to cause speed and capability to double every two years. The "how" of events was not as important as the effect.

Moore's Law enabled software and technology designers to use a scenario where computing speed and capability would double every two years, effectively reducing costs. The effect of falling costs allowed designers to develop advanced features that would be cost ineffective today, knowing they would be cost effective in the foreseeable future. Designers did not worry about how events would unfold to increase microchip density, substrate purity, etching method efficiency, or other events necessary to increase computing power. Designers assumed the scenario that falling costs would make their designs commercially viable.

Scenario Magic Wanding

Scenario *"magic wanding"* can be a useful tool. Magic wanding works like this: Assume you have a magic wand capable of three wishes to be granted instantly and without cost. How would you use those wishes?

The magic wand can open your thinking. Your mind can be released from recency bias and availability heuristics. For example, you could use a wish to eliminate half the cost of a real estate transaction. It's not important at this stage to determine how that wish could be granted. What would a residential real estate transaction look like when conducted from a customer experience standpoint?

You can then think about how friction and costs could be reduced. Under what circumstances can you achieve a 50% reduction in speed and cost?

Magic wanding helps develop scenarios where cost, speed, and experience improvements are described from a customer's point of view. It encourages you to think about what a customer would want as if the customer could instantly be gratified. It permits you to think about the effects of a magic wand transformation, not events that drive it.

Magic wanding lets you shift from prediction to preparation for what could occur. We'll use magic wanding in the next chapter to develop scenarios about the residential real estate market.

4. **Begin with the End in Mind**: Steven Covey explained the basis of this approach in his book *Seven Habits of Highly Effective People*.[172] His second habit is "Begin with the End in Mind." According to Covey, this habit is "based on imagination— the ability to envision in your mind what you cannot at present see with your eyes. It is based on the principle that all things are created twice. There is a mental (first) creation, and a physical (second) creation. The physical creation follows the

---

172 Steven R. Covey, *Seven Habits of Highly Effective People*, Chapter 2, Franklin Covey Co., 1990.

mental, just as a building follows a blueprint. If you don't make a conscious effort to visualize who you are and what you want in life, then you empower other people and circumstances to shape you and your life by default."

Defining the backend or destination helps shape the overall process as a conscious choice, not as something that is left to circumstances. To implement, begin with the end in mind.

The end in mind can be described as the future state of the customer experience, speed, and cost of a particular process. For example, one end in mind might be a hypothesis that a buyer of residential real estate could complete a real estate purchase in less than a day with a total transaction cost under 1%. This sounds like a crazy idea—but not quite as crazy as an idea proposed in 1962.

Kennedy's 1962 "Travel to the Moon and Return Safely" Speech

On September 12, 1962, former president John F. Kennedy delivered a speech at Rice University that outlined his plans to fly a man to the moon and back safely by the end of the decade.

> But why, some say, the moon? Why choose this as our goal? And they may well ask, why climb the highest mountain? Why, 35 years ago, fly the Atlantic? Why does Rice play Texas?

> We choose to go to the moon. We choose to go to the moon in this decade and do the other things, not because they are easy, but because they are hard, because that goal will serve to organize and measure the best of our energies and skills, because that challenge is one that we are willing to accept, one we are unwilling to postpone, and one which we intend to win, and the others, too...

> But if I were to say, my fellow citizens, that we shall send to the moon, 240,000 miles away from the control station in Houston, a giant rocket more than 300 feet tall, the length of this football field, made of new metal alloys, some of which have not yet been invented, capable of standing heat and stresses several times more than have ever been experienced, fitted together with a precision better than the finest watch, carrying all the equipment needed for propulsion, guidance, control, communications, food and survival, on an untried mission, to an unknown celestial body, and then return it safely to earth, re-entering the atmosphere at speeds of over 25,000 miles per hour, causing heat about half that of the temperature of the sun—almost as hot as it is here today—and do all this, and do it right, and do it first before this decade is out—then we must be bold.[173]

Kennedy understood the challenges and amount of new technologies required to perform his vision. He addresses them in the body of the speech.

It was a huge undertaking to send a man to the moon and return him back safely, by December 31, 1969. Some thought Kennedy's idea was not possible. Yet

---

173 https://www.jfklibrary.org/asset-viewer/archives/JFKPOF/040/JFKPOF-040-001

the celebration of the fiftieth anniversary of Commander Neil Armstrong and lunar module pilot Buzz Aldrin setting the Apollo Lunar Module Eagle on lunar soil on July 20, 1969 is at hand. Armstrong's first recorded words upon stepping onto the moon's surface were, "One small step for man, one giant leap for mankind." I think the vision, ingenuity, coordination, and courage to accomplish this feat with the technologies of the 1960s is truly impressive, especially as the fulfillment of Kennedy's speech outlining vision and mission was seven years earlier.

Small Steps

Against the backdrop of the lunar landing, how hard should it really be to consummate a real estate transaction in one day? Beginning with the end in mind doesn't mean one takes one gigantic step. The following is a process to evaluate your entire business process, looking for opportunities of convergence and logistic improvement as precursors to perhaps finding a disruptive thought leadership idea(s).

EAOO

The residential real estate transaction activity is labor intensive. The labor intensity is well suited to the methodology to reduce the cost stack. In essence, we'll look at a defined process to consider each activity within the real estate transaction with an eye towards disruptive achievement. I call this process the "EAOO process," pronounced "yooo."[174] In short, evaluate the entire business process from the end (start with the end in mind) to the beginning.

Document the process by breaking the process into milestones. Break each milestone into the tasks that comprise the milestone. Then consider if the process can be improved by taking each milestone and each task within the milestone through the EAOO regimen.

The EAOO regimen is a waterfall, as described below:

- **E**liminate the task by considering how the task could be eliminated or consolidated into another task; if the task cannot be eliminated, consider the next step of automation
- **A**utomate the task internally using robotics process automation, workflow management, or similar automation tool; if the task cannot be automated internally, consider the next step—to outsource

---

174 It may sound like dialogue from the movie *Rocky*, as in, "Yooo, Adrian," but let's keep it just "yooo" for now.

-   **O**utsource the task externally to a specialized outsourcer. Outsource doesn't mean offshore. You can outsource to onshore or offshore vendors; if the task cannot be outsourced, then consider optimization of the task
-   **O**ptimize means finding the most efficient, least cost method to accomplish the task

Once EAOO is completed, repeat the EAOO evaluation on the overall process again. It is likely that the best outcome will require three or more passes of the entire process through EAOO.

EAOO is an intentional process that will fertilize your attempts to achieve disruption impact. But there is no shortcut with the EAOO process. You can't achieve disruptive impact by tolerating bad processes. Jonathan Corr, CEO of EllieMae, notes that toleration of bad process ultimately leads to "human spackle" being used to patch over the automated bad process, with "checkers checking the checkers," and workflow laboring under multiple passes through manual processes.

EAOO is a different approach to intentionally disrupt your own business. EAOO is an intentional walkthrough of an entire business process, starting at the back end of the process and walking forward.

Begin with the End in Mind: An Example

Why start at the back of the process with the end in mind? A former boss, George Groves, was an avid golfer. He often spoke of walking a golf course from the green of the 18th hole forward to the first tee. According to George, walking from the end to the beginning lets you see all of the hazards and opportunities of each hole, with the end in mind of achieving your best golf score. That end, to a golfer, is putting the ball into the hole on the green, with as few strokes as possible.

I tried George's process at arguably the best golf course in the United States, Augusta National. When the spectator gates opened at 8 a.m. on Monday, April 9th on the first day of the 2009 Masters Tournament, I quickly made my way to the green of the 18th hole and walked backwards, planning how I'd play the course.[175]

The green of the 18th hole at Augusta is named "Holly"[176] and features an elevated, relatively small putting surface which golfers call the "green." The green is guarded by two large sand traps, one directly in front of the green, and the other on

---

[175] Augusta is likely the toughest course to get invited to play as a guest. Only a member can extend the invitation, and it is considered incredibly bad taste to ask a member for an invite. However, if a member reads this book, please note that I am available any time, any day to accept your gracious invitation.

[176] Holes at Augusta are named after native vegetation, as explained to me by a member of Augusta.

the right side. There are small grass mounds in front of the sand trap in front of the 18th green. Land a shot short of the green, and there are lots of opportunities to end up in the sand trap, or have your golf ball kicked offline by one of the small grass mounds in front of the sand trap.

I've never played Augusta, but when I do, I have a plan devised on my walk from back to front in 2009. For example, to play the 18th hole within my mediocre ability, I started at the green of the last hole described in the previous paragraph. Beginning with the end in mind, I need to have my approach shot to the green at about 120 yards so I can ensure my ball flies over the sand and grass mound hazards and has a reasonable chance to land on the correct portion of the green near the hole.

Working backwards, this means I need to land my second shot about 120 yards from the hole on the 465-yard par four. That means the first two shots have to travel about 365 yards. Working backwards, the 6 to 7% elevation change[177] on the second shot means that I'll get about 15 to 20 yards less on the second shot than on a flat surface, because the ball travels uphill. So, I need about my normal 190-yard shot that will actually travel about 170 yards up hill. That's a fairway wood for me. Then off the tee, I need about 195 yards up the hill from the very narrow tee box, lined by trees on both sides. That's a driver hit with a moderate swing tempo that produces a consistent 220 yards. Uphill, that's about 200 yards.

That's the end in mind, ending up on the green using three shots, then 2 putts for a one over par 5, and so on for the rest of the remaining 17 holes. If I played exactly to my game plan, I'd end up 18 over. Of course, things happen, and bad shots end up out of position in hazards, vegetation, or dribbling down the course due to poor technique.

But that's my plan, constructed with the end in mind. The golf game is broken down into shot objectives, the golf club to achieve the objective, in what I consider to be a good process. I used the same process at Pine Valley Golf Club in New Jersey, and scored in two digits.

Bad process? Back to the 18th at Augusta. Without starting with the end in mind, I'd be standing on the tee box, looking at the long uphill fairway. That view tells my mind I have to hit my first shot drive as far as possible. For me, swinging to hit the ball as far as possible sacrifices control. Couple that with performance pressure of other golfers watching, and the results are predictable. More likely than not, the shot will go offline and end up in the trees lining both sides of the fairway. I'd

---

177 https://www.pgatour.com/news/2014/04/08/player-perspectives-on-augusta-national-holes.html

be well on my way to an 8 or 9 on the hole and would hear groans from fellow golfers. Bad process leads to bad results.

Figure 8.3: A process for intentional disruption.

Recap of a Disciplined Approach Intentional Disruption

The following recaps this chapter and those that precede Figure 8.2, which shows the disruption process and is repeated here in Figure 8.3 for your convenience.

1. Identify undervalued and overvalued assets, focusing on undervalued assets that could represent opportunities for disruptive effect.
2. Reduce or eliminate provincial thinking. Some may argue this is the first step to intentionally creating a disruptive effect. You can actually start anywhere, because intentionally creating disruptive effect is a process, not an event.
3. Imagine scenarios of disruptive transformation. Think effects driven by scenarios, and not about anticipating events. Dr. Thurow, in my opinion, became too focused on events, which led him down a path that never materialized.
4. Begin with the end in mind. This arguably is the easiest element of my process, because you can visualize future success and what success looks like. President Kennedy did it in his Rice University speech. The millions of steps that culminated in a successful lunar landing seven years later were created with that end in mind.
5. Use EAOO. The discipline it provides can provide the sparks to ignite a disruptive effect.

This process can eliminate about $100 billion of labor and compensation annually in the residential real estate marketplace, improve liquidity, and make real estate more affordable for consumers. The $200 billion in annual fee revenue in the residential real estate marketplace invites competitors both inside and outside of the industry to see opportunity to enhance their profit margin from that pool of revenue.

Chapter Nine
Your Margin Is My Opportunity

"Your margin is my opportunity." This quote is attributed to Jeff Bezos of born-digital Amazon.

My interpretation of this is as follows: In a business segment where there is a large pool of revenue largely consumed by frictional costs like compensation and overhead, a target appears on the backs of businesses in this space. Not all labor is "friction." Direct labor to install air conditioning and heating equipment is not friction. A surgeon performing major surgery is not friction. An airframe and powerplant technician diagnosing and repairing a turbofan engine on an airliner is not friction. However, most intermediation labor is friction. Much overhead in intermediation businesses is also overhead friction. What are we defining as "intermediation labor"? Transactional sales are intermediation labor. More on that in a minute.

Steve Sheetz, CEO of born-traditional Sheetz convenience stores at the time (a mid-Atlantic based chain of convenience stores), had the best explanation of overhead friction I've ever heard. Sheetz was a successful businessman, and a director of a regional bank. At a board meeting of the bank, a long discussion ensued on the value of bank branches. Paraphrasing Mr. Sheetz:

> They're [bank branches] just overhead, as most banks operate them. We call our stores a store because we sell a lot of product in them every day. Most banks perform recurring transactions with existing customers in their branches, as opposed to selling products and getting new customers.

The bankers pushed back, highlighting the desire to build relationships, and that relationships lead to sales. Sheetz noted that you need not have a physical location to build a relationship:

> A convenience store is there to sell products, whether gasoline, prepared food, or convenience needs. Your bank branches rarely sell new products and recruit new customers. Think of how profitable a convenience store would be if half of the visitors came in, used the restroom, and left. Not very profitable. But that's what happens in your bank. The most valuable bank product are deposit accounts. Only banks can sell deposit accounts by regulation. You're protected. But most branches don't open many new, profitable deposit accounts. Customers come in and figuratively use the "restroom" by doing transactions on existing accounts. Your branches are overhead the way you operate them.

Frictional Labor and Overhead in Intermediation Activities

Frictional labor and overhead are essentially the ingredients of many intermediation activities. Definitionally, a "broker" acts as a compensated agent arranging for the sale of products and services on behalf of principals. Retail sales differs from brokerages in

https://doi.org/10.1515/9783110650471-010

that the retailer buys in quantity at a discount and sells at retail to a customer. But retailing is essentially an intermediation activity of buying in bulk to sell at retail.

So where can we apply "my opportunity is your margin" in this scenario? Amazon and Alibaba applied it by disintermediating the retailer "middleman" and going direct to consumers, thereby eliminating retail space, inventory carrying costs, and labor—all expensive, frictional costs. Born-digital Amazon established a convergence and logistical platform that started in books, and spread eventually to almost any consumer product. Born-traditional retailers attempted to catch up. Some have been successful. Walmart and Target have created omni-channels (web-based and traditional retail). From my point of view, the reason Walmart and Target have success in the omni-channel is they already had a nationwide logistics system in place—in other words, the convergence element on the web was much easier with a national logistics channel in place.

Web-based platforms can overcome frictional labor and overhead by providing the convergence of product and logistics needed to sell and deliver them. So, let's look at residential real estate and the related financial services tied to real estate in this light.

Real estate brokerages sell product on behalf of real estate owners. Mortgage brokerages sell product on behalf of mortgage loan investors. Title agents sell title insurance on behalf of title insurers. Insurance agents sell insurance contracts on behalf of casualty insurers. The $160 billion of annual intermediation activities are viewed by born-digital companies as their opportunity. As an order of magnitude comparison, this $160 billion in intermediation revenue is roughly 60% of Amazon's total 2018 revenue selling physical goods. A born-digital company looks at frictional labor and overhead as essentially the ingredients of great opportunity to take out costs and grab market share.

In 2020, about $165 billion in residential real estate transaction revenue is largely from brokerage-type activities—that is, buying and selling goods and services on behalf of the owner of the property. The owner is often referred to as a "principal." Brokerage includes selling the real estate property, brokering mortgages to finance the real estate, and title insurance to protect legal ownership of the real estate. These are all intermediation activities performed on behalf of the principal. The risk is that the principals can decide to "insource" the buying and selling of the property, the financing, and insurance to themselves.

Airlines eliminated travel agent commissions unilaterally. Discount stockbrokers facilitated the end of high securities commissions by disintermediating the long-standing, highly paid stockbrokers. Similarly, Tesla eliminated retail automobile dealers in favor of direct distribution to consumers. Amazon purchased "PillPack"[178]

---

[178] PillPack packages prescription medications into individual packages with time and date instruction, while checking for adverse interactions of medications. This helps patients to take the right medication at the right time and improves compliance to dosage instructions. PillPack has pharmacy prescription distributions licenses in 50 states, so the regulatory logistics were in place.

to disintermediate the distribution of common prescription medications by retail pharmacy chains. Will the brokerage type activities of residential real estate and related financial services be disintermediated, and if so, by whom?

Some larger homebuilders offer one-stop shopping that disintermediates brokerage type activities. The homebuilders use in-house real estate agencies, in-house mortgage lending with low-cost loan officers, and in-house title agencies with noncommissioned title agents.

Deb Still, CEO of Pulte Mortgage, stated:

> Pulte uses an affiliated builder business model. Our lead generation is from the Pulte Homes parent company's business. None of our loan officers go pound the pavement. We have a fulfillment center that we consider origination order entry. We consider the manufacturing of the loan our order fulfillment process. We pay [loan officers] salaries and we pay them incentive for discretionary performance. But we don't pay them like a commission loan officer because they're not sourcing the customer's business. You could argue that all the builder affiliates were the first consumer direct model that ever existed. At Pulte Mortgage, we're a little unique because we're centralized [the whole process]. Some builders still have local loan officers but don't pay them like a typical commissioned loan officer.

Don Salmon, CEO of Toll Brother Mortgage, commented on the benefits of a onestop shopping experience with builders:

> There is significant cost savings to Toll Brothers when consumers use TBI mortgage as opposed to other lenders. Our systems are integrated, and we employ a lot of discipline in our organization to make sure that our loan officers communicate early and often with the Toll Brothers home sales team and the customer. And we pass savings onto our customers.

> So, our mission is twofold. Number one, make sure that the consumer can qualify for the loan for the home they are building. And two, make sure that the consumer experience meets our high level of expectation. It means that we have to be as efficient as possible, and provide an outstanding value to our customers.

The Disruptive Effect of Fintech

Humans are notoriously poor at forecasting events, thanks to provincial thinking affected by the previously discussed recency bias and availability heuristic. Forecasting effects seems to be a more accurate human undertaking. This segment will summarize my hypothesis of how fintech will spark the coming wave of innovation in financial services and residential real estate, and the effects this will have on customers and industry participants. My hypothesis is an informed opinion that forecasts the effects of forces playing out in the industry. For the purposes

---

Amazon's convergence of customers coupled with the logistics of PillPack may spell price competition for traditional pharmacy chains.

of this immediate segment, I'll describe the effects, but not much of the reasoning. In the remainder of the chapter, we will cover the reasoning.

Apples to apples, here's my hypothesis of the effects of fintech over the next three to five years on a pro-forma of 2020 housing and mortgage expectations. It should be noted that pro-forma fee levels below are illustrative and are intended to stimulate robust discussion. The pro-forma amounts are not a forecast or prediction of the future.

Table 9.1 shows the pro-forma revenue generated on $1.6 trillion of home sales after these disruptive events have occurred, assuming the same level of real estate sales activity as in 2018. This assumption is designed to show the possible fee changes based upon a constant volume of real estate sales. The data sources were discussed earlier, and recall that 2018 fees were about $160 billion, resulting in about $100 billion of savings to consumers:

Table 9.1: Proforma fees for real estate transactions post-disruption.

REVENUE TO PROVIDER OF THE FOLLOWING SERVICES	FEE AS A PERCENT	HOME SALES OR MORTGAGE VOLUME	DOLLARS
Total Real Estate Commissions	2.000%	$1,595,250,000,000	$31,905,000,000
Total Loan Origination Fees	1.250%	$1,273,000,000,000	$15,912,500,000
Total Title and Related Fees	0.500%	$1,595,250,000,000	$7,976,250,000
Appraisal and Inspection Fees	0.100%	$1,595,250,000,000	$1,595,250,000
Total Private Provider Fees			$57,389,000,000
Savings versus Prior Estimates			$111,986,312,500

I'm ignoring appraisals and government-imposed taxes and fees for now, as appraisals will likely be replaced with valuation models. As for government fees and taxes. . . well, they are what they are.

As of this moment, I may have no friends left in real estate brokerage, mortgage banking, and title insurance. But I'm just the messenger. Here's how it may happen.

Real estate commissions fall from 6% to about 2%

With the listing side of transactions already under pressure, the listing fee will fall to one-half to one percent, depending on the price of the property. Cookie-cutter homes like those purchased by Invitation Homes will be at the lower end of the scale. Unique properties may be higher, but the linkage between a fixed percentage of the property and the listing fee will fall away in the same way that fixed percentage commissions on stock fell away. There's too much free information available on the internet to have a listing agent provide much value beyond proposing a price, staging concepts, and getting the data on the MLS.

On the selling agent side of the table, the selling commission will fall to 1% or so, or maybe a bit more if the agent can find unique properties. In some cases, it will fall to zero. Why? Unless the customer hires a specific buyer broker, customers buying real estate usually don't understand that the selling agent also represents the seller and not just the buyer. Customers are becoming much more self-service oriented. In some cases, online real estate providers are permitting direct access to listings without the customer using an agent. The customer doesn't really have an agent who represents their interest solely in dual agency. With the emergence of a variety of real estate-oriented websites with free property search and valuation estimates, some customers are comfortable with "do it yourself."

The genie is out of the bottle, so to speak. Multiple Listing Service data of homes for sale, selling prices of homes that recently sold, and estimated values of any homes are all available on many websites for free. Neighborhood characteristics, school quality ratings, crime rates, property tax rates, income tax rates, and unemployment rates—all information to review neighborhoods is available to anyone with a mobile device or a computer. A large part of the neighborhood knowledge base of listing and selling agents is now available for free. The Amazon effect makes shopping online de rigueur.

An acquaintance buying a home with 5% down once said to me while reviewing a settlement statement on the purchase, "Isn't it crazy that the real estate commission is greater than my down payment?" Yes, it is crazy. And it won't last.

Mortgage fees and costs fall from 4% or so to 1%

This is already happening in the jumbo loan market. Money center banks want to attract high-income prospective wealth management clients to the bank. They'll use the jumbo loan to attract this cohort of borrowers to the bank.

One exasperated independent mortgage banker exclaimed, "The damn banks must be losing money on the jumbo loans. I can't touch their rates." The bank is being rational and isn't losing money. It's making a jumbo loan that is a quarter to three eighths of a percent under the conventional mortgage rate because the borrower has high credit quality, the borrower will likely buy other services from the bank and the customer will be targeted by wealth management and insurance salespeople employed by the bank.

The bank also isn't wasting its time collecting all of the documentation required by secondary market agencies and securitizers. The bank isn't paying a commissioned loan officer to take the loan application. Rather, a salaried "private banker" (who is actually a credit analyst) takes the loan application. Finally, the jumbo rate is about 75 basis points above the FannieMae mortgage-backed security of the same duration. So, no, the bank isn't losing money on jumbos.

Fintech will also reduce the cost of loans made to non-high net worth individuals sold into the secondary market. Rocket Mortgage taught customers that they could "press a button, get a mortgage." In reality, it may not be that simple, but getting a preapproval is pretty fast. Customers have free access to their credit scores from credit card companies and other sources. Customers generally know their FICO scores and what is required for a mortgage. Account Check, Day1 Certainty, and other verification technologies will reduce the time and paper required to qualify for a loan. That means quicker loan approval and no hassle. Quicken Loans and a host of other large lenders are already well down this path.

A loan officer friend of mine asked me what I thought the future held for him. I asked him how much he earned in the last three years. He replied that he earned about $1.3 million. I asked him how long he thought he'd continue to earn more than many surgeons, data scientists, physicians, dentists, airline captains, and a host of other professions. He looked at me sheepishly. My reply: "You can earn $1.3 million in the next three years, but you'll have to do a hell of a lot more loans, maybe five to six times as many. After that, who knows?"

Title fees will fall from 1.5% to about 0.5%

About 5 to 10% of the typical title insurance charges on a closing disclosure are actually remitted to the title insurer to insure the title. The rest goes largely to labor and profit for title agencies and attorneys. Title rates are regulated by the state, so perhaps this won't happen so quickly. . . or will it?

Builders have perfected legal bundling and/or discounting of real estate commissions, mortgage and title fees. As a principal owning the real estate, builders usually have salaried listing real estate agents representing their offerings. If a buyer walks into a builder's open houses and showrooms, the buyer can register with the builder and thus eliminate the selling agent real estate commission. Builders often offer an incentive to the buyer of the home to use their mortgage and title companies. Because the builder controls the leads and they own the real estate, they can use salaried mortgage loan officers and title agents. Builders eliminate friction and high sales commissions in the transaction so can pass a significant portion of the fee savings onto their customers. The fee savings can be realized because the builder owns the real estate, the real estate brokerage agency, the mortgage lender, and the title agency. Most important, the builder "owns" the customer and can provide a one-stop shopping experience that eliminates friction and cost to the homebuyer.[179]

Why will this hit the general real estate and financial services market in a similar fashion? Because Zillow can now approximate the same legal structure as a builder, and then some. Through Zillow Offers, Zillow will own the real estate and pay no commissions to independent realtors. Zillow owns a mortgage company and will likely enter the title business in the future.

Zillow is an iBuyer. And iBuyers will change the balance of power in the real estate brokerage, mortgage, and title businesses.

The First Real Estate "iBuyer"

The first time I heard the term "iBuyer" in connection with real estate, it didn't resonate. Could someone actually perform an "instant purchase of real estate"?

Arguably, the first iBuyer was Blackstone's Invitation Homes Inc., a born-traditional company started in 2012 to buy what it believed to be undervalued single-family homes at the tail end of the subprime mortgage crisis. Invitation Homes is now one of the largest owners and operators of single-family homes for lease in the United States. Invitation Homes owns more than 80,000 homes for lease in 17 markets across the country as of December 31, 2018, according to the company's 2018 Form 10-K filed with the Securities and Exchange Commission.[180]

According to the Form 10-K:

> Invitation Homes is meeting changing lifestyle demands by providing residents access to updated homes with features they value, such as close proximity to jobs and access to good schools. Our mission statement, "Together with you, we make a house a home," reflects our commitment to high-touch service that continuously enhances residents' living experiences and provides homes where individuals and families can thrive.

The business model focused on locations with:

> ...strong demand drivers, high barriers to entry, and high rent growth potential, primarily in the Western United States, Florida, and the Southeast United States. Through disciplined market and asset selection, as well as through the Mergers, we designed our portfolio to capture the operating benefits of local density as well as economies of scale that we believe cannot be readily replicated.

---

179 In addition, the builder owns the new home, and the profit margin on the new home is significantly higher than the profit margin of the sale, financing, and insuring. Because the builder "owns" the buyer, the commissions for listing, selling, financing, and title insuring the property are replaced with lower salary and bonus employees as the builder is providing the leads for the listing, sale, financing, and title insuring of the property.

180 Invitation Homes Inc. Form 10-K, December 21, 2018, page 47.

Within our 17 markets, we target attractive neighborhoods in in-fill locations with multiple de-mand drivers, such as proximity to major employment centers, desirable schools, and transporta-tion corridors. Our homes average approximately 1,850 square feet with three bedrooms and two bathrooms, appealing to a resident base that we believe is less transitory than the typical multi-family resident. We invest in the upfront renovation of homes in our portfolio in order to address capital needs, reduce ongoing maintenance costs, and drive resident demand. As a result, our portfolio benefits from high occupancy and low turnover rates, and we are well-positioned to drive strong rent growth, attractive margins, and predictable cash flows.[181]

Invitation Homes used the mortgage crisis, with the sometimes brutal reduction in home prices, to purchase homes that met its selection requirements. Invitation de-scribes its typical target as a three-bedroom, 1,850 square foot home with appeal for younger families with children in neighborhoods with desirable public schools and sited near transportation corridors. Blackstone was an acquirer of single-family real estate as the mortgage crisis began to abate.

Since its founding in 2012, Invitation Homes Inc. was acquiring what it believed to be undervalued assets that could be renovated as necessary, rented for premium prices, and ultimately liquidated at a profit.

The details on Invitation's current inventory of homes as of year-end 2018 is set out in Table 9.2. The occupancy rates are enviable for any landlord and include the downtime required for acquisition, renovation, and rental ramp up. The ramped-up occupancy rate is 95.9%. Said another way, units on average are vacant just 15 days per year.

Table 9.2: Invitation Homes Inc.'s current inventory of homes as of year-end 2018.

MARKET	NUMBER OF HOMES	AVERAGE OCCUPANCY RATE	MONTHLY RENT
Western U.S.	28,685	95.40%	$1,838
Florida	25,172	94.60%	$1,780
Southeast U.S.	17,773	94.40%	$1,483
Texas	4,577	92.60%	$1,625
Midwest	4,600	94.60%	$1,918
Total	80,807	94.60%	$1,735

Invitation's Form 10-K lists the net value of the homes owned as $16.7 billion. That's an average value of $206,000 per unit. The average rental is $1,735. Excluding esti-mated maintenance and taxes of $400, per month, the remaining $1,335 per month

---

181 Ibid.

supports a mortgage payment at 4% of $279,000. The families renting these homes appear to be well-qualified.

Qualification as an Invitation tenant is pretty stringent. According to Invitation's website, tenant eligibility includes:[182]

- **Income** – Applicants must have a minimum combined gross income of 3.0 times the monthly rent.
- **Credit** – A credit report will be obtained on all applicants to verify credit ratings. Income plus verification of credit history will be entered into a credit-scoring model to determine rental eligibility and security deposit levels. This credit-scoring model will include positive and negative payment history for lines of credit, usage of credit, credit history, credit availability, inquiry history, and student loans. Unfavorable accounts which will negatively influence this score include but are not limited to collections, foreclosures, charge-off, repossession, absence of credit, and current delinquency. Debt to previous landlord and open bankruptcies will result in an automatic denial of the application.
- **Criminal History** – A criminal background check will be conducted for each applicant and occupant ages 18 years or more. The application will be denied for any felony conviction up to six (6) years prior to the application date (subject to local laws/requirements), or any felony conviction for sex- and terrorism-related offences, regardless of time.
- **Rental History** – Some credit scoring results will necessitate an evaluation of verifiable rental or mortgage payment history. Applications for residency will automatically be denied for current outstanding debt or eviction.

iBuyer Defined

An iBuyer is usually a corporate entity that uses big data and algorithms to estimate the market value of a home in order to make an instant offer. iBuyers act as principals when buying real estate. Unlike brokers, iBuyers take legal ownership of the real estate. In some ways, iBuyers mimic the role of "specialists" at the New York Stock Exchange, who buy and sell securities on their own account to provide the liquidity and price discovery essential to an orderly market and to profit as a market maker in designated securities.

iBuying is a quantum change to the process of buying and selling homes. iBuyers include the standard 6% commission since sellers like iBuying as a transparent and convenient alternative to a traditional home sale. Two things drive seller acceptance: First, the iBuyer takes over ownership costs such as mortgage payments, taxes, maintenance, and the hassle of staging, showing, and selling a home. Second, the seller can

---

182 https://www.invitationhomes.com/Qualification-Requirements/

now easily buy a replacement home and qualify for a mortgage without the burden of qualifying for and carrying two mortgage payments.

iBuyers for the General Public

Blackstone is one of the world's largest asset managers and had the resources and logistics to purchase and manage a large number of single-family homes for its own account. Could other iBuyers work with the general public?

I started to think of eBay's "Buy It Now" feature. An eBay user can become an instant buyer by agreeing to the seller's "Buy It Now" price. Transparent and easy. No waiting, with a guaranteed purchase. I've used "Buy It Now" on eBay to ensure that I was the successful buyer of certain collectible coins. I didn't want to let the auction continue and possibly be outbid by an auction "sniper" that placed a winning bid just before the bidding closed. But what about a "Buy It Now" for real estate?

Of course! It's a role reversal, where the "Buy It Now" is actually "Sell It Now" to an iBuyer. Instead of coins, stereo gear, and other eBay merchandise, it's real estate. With $1.6 trillion of real estate predicted to change hands in 2020 (assuming a 6% real estate commission), there will be up to $96 billion dollars in fees on the table. That's before another $65 billion of mortgage, title, homeowners' insurance, and related services are available. Enter the iBuyer, looking to scoop up these fees and potentially profit from flipping real estate.

Make no mistake: the iBuyer is a honeypot, aiming to capture real estate sellers before they list. Once a seller is identified and a relationship is formed, the seller can be offered a direct purchase or be referred to cooperating real estate agents, mortgage lenders, and providers of ancillary services. iBuyers are taking clear and disruptive aim at national real estate franchise operators to fundamentally change the real estate selling process.

The iBuying concept of an instant, guaranteed sale of an existing home is not new. Pete Slaugh, owner of a large national real estate brokerage franchise, used a form of iBuying with a branded product called "CertainSale." CertainSale guaranteed the homeowner a sale after a certain period of time. CertainSale advanced the equity in the home, but did not pay off the mortgage. CertainSale solved the problem of ensuring a sale after a certain period, but the homeowner remained liable for ongoing mortgage payments. The homeowner knew the home would sell for CertainSale's price, but the homeowner also had to put up with the staging and showing of the home.

CertainSale and similar programs lacked two ingredients of scalability to be disruptive. Convergence was not possible, as each "guaranteed sale" was conducted locally, or regionally at best, and the logistics lacked enough funding and technology to make the process easy and transparent. Jeff Rutt, CEO of Keystone Customer

Homes operating in Pennsylvania and Maryland, used a form of an instant, guaranteed sale to make it easy for a potential buyer of a Keystone new home to deal with their old homes since 1999.

iBuyers may bring convergence and logistical expertise to the market and obtain scale through venture capital and private equity. Convergence is aggregating seller and buyer leads combined with the logistics to value and purchase homes, the network and methods to repair any home defects, and the capital to hold properties in inventory.

The following is a partial list of iBuyers as of June 2019:

- Digitally born Opendoor describes itself as "the revolutionary way to buy and sell your home. In 2014, we set out to reinvent life's most important transaction with a new, radically simple way to buy and sell your home. Our mission is to empower everyone with the freedom to move, and we've served more than 40,000 customers who have come to Opendoor to make that move easier . . . . Opendoor currently operates in 20 cities, including Atlanta, Austin, Charlotte, Dallas-Fort Worth, Denver, Houston, Jacksonville, Las Vegas, Los Angeles, Minneapolis-St. Paul, Nashville, Orlando, Phoenix, Portland, Raleigh-Durham, Riverside, Sacramento, San Antonio, Tampa, and Tucson."[183] Opendoor uses salaried on-demand tour agents [to] accompany customers with home tours for any property listed on the MLS and to handle other real estate on-site or local activities. Opendoor has capital from SoftBank,[184] General Atlantic, Access Technology Ventures, Andreessen Horowitz, NEA, Norwest Venture Partners and homebuilder Lennar, among others.[185]

- Founded in 2015, digitally born Offerpad describes itself as a company to "reinvent the home sale process and provide sellers with the convenience, control, and certainty they'd been lacking under the outdated system. Pairing groundbreaking real estate technology with fundamental industry experience, they created a platform where sellers could receive a strong purchase offer for their home, quickly contract and close, and avoid the hassles associated with traditional real estate selling. Since 2015, Offerpad has provided the best way to buy and sell a home, helping thousands of homeowners move freely."[186] Offerpad currently buys homes in Tucson, Phoenix, Atlanta, Tampa, Las Vegas, Salt Lake City, Charlotte, Raleigh, Dallas-Fort Worth, Tucson, Orlando, and Los

---

183 https://www.opendoor.com/w/about

184 https://techcrunch.com/2018/09/27/opendoor-just-raised-400-million-in-funding-from-softbanks-vision-fund/

185 https://www.pymnts.com/news/investment-tracker/2018/opendoor-funding-round-real-estate-investments-venture-capital/

186 https://www.offerpad.com/about/

Angeles. Offerpad is more secretive about funding; public documents describe LL Funding leading a debt and equity round in May 2018.[187]

– Digitally born Zillow Offers describes itself as "a home-selling option for homeowners who want a certain and predictable sale on their timeline. Homeowners in participating markets can request an offer from Zillow by providing their address and answering some questions about their home. If the home is eligible, Zillow will review the home details and local market conditions, then respond with a cash offer within a few days. If the homeowner accepts the offer, a dedicated Zillow Offers Advisor will schedule a home evaluation and be a resource throughout the closing process. If the homeowner decides to list their home for sale instead, Zillow can connect them with a trusted local agent. Not a seller? We have answers for real estate agents too."[188] Zillow is publicly traded.

– Digitally born Knock describes itself as being "on a mission to make it as easy to trade-in your home as it is to trade-in your car. We bring certainty, convenience and cost-efficiency to home buying and selling. Homeownership is the symbol of the American dream, but ironically it is often what holds people back. Our home is our largest purchase and most valuable asset, but it is also the most difficult to buy and sell. Traditional U.S. residential real estate is complex and outdated, making it stressful, expensive and time-consuming for the average consumer to buy and sell homes. Knock envisions a world where mobility is easier and simpler for the 71% of home sellers who are also buying their next home at the same time. And we're making it possible with the Knock Home Trade-In, currently offered in and between Atlanta, GA, Charlotte, NC, Raleigh-Durham, NC, Dallas-Fort Worth, TX and Phoenix, AZ. We buy your new home on your behalf so you can move in before we represent you in the sale of your old home on the open market."[189] Knock is funded by Foundry Group, RRE Ventures, Corazon Capital, WTI, FJ Labs, and Company Ventures, among others.[190]

– Digitally traditional Abodewell (formerly Amne Real Estate) describes itself as follows. "Abodewell buys your home when you're ready to sell. We make you a competitive offer based on national trends, a deep understanding of the local real estate market, and your home's special features—all within 48 hours. You get to skip the burden of finding the right buyer, the inconvenience of arranging showings and open houses, and the stress of an uncertain timeline. When you sell to Abodewell, you can close in as few as 10 days." Abodewell operates

187 https://www.forbes.com/sites/omribarzilay/2018/05/16/offerpad-secures-150-million-in-new-financing/#6ae4234a4b15

188 https://www.zillow.com/offers/

189 https://www.knock.com/about-us

190 https://www.vcnewsdaily.com/Knock/venture-capital-funding/gcjcglxqnk

in Austin, Texas.[191] Abodewell completed a $4 million seed round with undisclosed investors.[192]

- Digitally born Perch describes itself as "transforming the way people buy and sell their homes. Simplifying it all, to the way it probably should have always been; fair and true to market, straightforward, easy. We're helping customers find and purchase their dream home." Perch operate in Dallas, San Antonio, and Austin, Texas.[193] Perch is funded by FirstMark Capital, Accomplice and Juxtapose, among others.[194]
- Traditionally born Keller Williams is a real estate brokerage entering the iBuyer space, as has Coldwell Banker and many other traditionally born real estate brokerages. There are so many announcements that I won't cover them individually. The question is whether "adding on" an iBuying process can truly transform the existing brokerage model.

iBuying as Disruptors

iBuyers are disruptive because iBuyers offer a simple one-step process for selling a home. It's a compelling story:

1. Receive a cash offer with no contingencies, or;
2. Go through the time, frustration, and inconvenience of meeting with listing real estate agents, evaluating their "competitive market analyses," staging the home to make it attractive to buyers, going through the hassle of potential buyers walking through your home, waiting for offers, countering a buyer's offer, clearing buyer's contingencies, negotiating who pays for alleged defects discovered during the inspection and appraisal process, waiting for a buyer's mortgage to be approved, scheduling settlement, dealing with the walkthrough of the home immediately prior to closing, going through the hassles of the settlement process, and finally emerging with a check for your equity after closing. Or, if anything goes wrong in the process, having the transaction fall through and start over.

A cash offer has its disadvantages—mainly the possibility that the cash offer may be less than the net amount of selling a home traditionally, as previously described. If a seller wants to buy a new home, the iBuying offer may offset the possibility of a lower net cash price, because the replacement home buying process becomes much

---

191 https://www.abodewell.com/how-it-works
192 https://www.crunchbase.com/organization/abodewell#section-funding-rounds
193 https://perch.com/about/
194 https://perch.com/press/perch-raises-220-million-to-transform-the-consumer-home-buying-experience/

easier. Qualifying for a mortgage with a home to sell is much more difficult for most buyers. The buyer must be able to qualify for a new mortgage while carrying both payments, or have a contract in hand from a buyer of the old home, as well as arrange for a near simultaneous sale of the old home and purchase of the new home. This can be a logistical nightmare in many cases.

One firsthand experience I had with selling a home involved the sale of a beach property in Bethany Beach, Delaware. Three listing agents made presentations and pricing suggestions. I listed the home. Several offers were made and rejected. The agent, so confident in her listing presentation of value, was now talking about why the price was too high. Eventually a well-qualified buyer presented a reasonable offer, which I accepted. We went back and forth with inspections, actual and perceived "defects." A closing date was scheduled for late December. I was anxious to close the sale.

My wife Judy and I were visiting family in California. The phone rang while I was driving to Palm Desert to meet our son and his wife. The listing agent told me that during the walkthrough, the buyer noted that the heat pump was not working correctly and needed an immediate repair before closing. The prior inspection had not detected any problems. The agent estimated the corrective repairs at $2,000.

After a lot of back and forth, I simply told the agent I wasn't paying for the repairs. The agent then said the buyer must close by year-end as the buyer was doing a tax-free exchange transaction. Finally, the agent offered me something of value, by tipping the buyer's hand.

I told the agent that she could pay for the repairs out of her commission, the buyer could pay for them, or the buyer could walk away. If the buyer walked away, I'd let the listing expire and I'd find a new agent. I politely hung up, put the phone on silent, and enjoyed the visit with our family. Later, I received an email that the transaction had closed. The settlement sheet showed the agent made a small commission concession to the buyer for the alleged heat pump issue.

My wife told me I was being difficult to the agent. My response was that the realtor was receiving a $30,000 commission, and she needed to do something to earn it. My experience in the business was helpful, and I was pretty confident the agent would find a way to get the deal to close. The whole process was frustrating and time-consuming. It mirrored previous home sales we had concluded. It's a messy, elongated, stressful, and time-consuming process.

Would I have taken an iBuyer's offer for the beach property? Most likely.

iBuying is in the early stages of adoption. The amount of venture funding flowing into the real estate space chasing the $150 billion plus in fees seems to point to greater adoption. The iBuyer is seeking a potential home seller or buyer early in the process, before a realtor or lender has gotten to the seller or buyer.

iBuying is the most disruptive threat to real estate brokerages, lenders, title providers, and appraisers. Over the past 50 years, the residential real estate market has been based on one-on-one relationships and referrals to a variety of service providers like mortgage lenders and title providers. More importantly, the national real estate franchises first and foremost used brick and mortar as well as national advertising to generate potential homebuyers. The traditional first stop was a realtor, who then referred the buyer to a lender and title agent.

The History of Traditional Real Estate Brokerages

A local real estate brokerage pays fees to a national franchisor to generate leads for buyers and sellers of real estate. The real estate agents take these leads and does the leg work for the local brokerage owner as independent contractors to obtain listing contracts and potential homebuyers. Lender's loan officers build relationships with realtors to get referrals for mortgages. Title agents do the same. In some cases, the real estate brokerage owner owns an interest in a title agency and/or mortgage lender to capture profits from these activities.

We discussed Sears as an early mover to centralize the real estate buying and selling process through its Coldwell Banker, Sears Mortgage, and Allstate Insurance ownership, as discussed previously. Cendant purchased multiple real estate franchise operators, including Coldwell Banker, Century 21, and ERA real estate. Cendant Mortgage served the real estate franchisees. The subprime mortgage crisis ended Cendant's attempt to create a one-stop shopping experience.

The real estate franchises were spun off into publicly traded Realogy Holdings Corp. Realogy describes itself as "the leading and most integrated provider of residential real estate services in the U.S. that is focused on empowering independent sales agents to best serve today's consumers. Realogy delivers its services through its well-known industry brands including Better Homes and Gardens® Real Estate, CENTURY 21®, Climb Real Estate®, Coldwell Banker®, Coldwell Banker Commercial®, Corcoran Group®, ERA®, Sotheby's International Realty® as well as NRT, Cartus®, Title Resource Group, and ZapLabs®, an in-house innovation and technology development lab. Realogy's fully integrated business model includes brokerage, franchising, relocation, mortgage, and title and settlement services. Realogy provides independent sales agents access to leading technology, best-in-class marketing and learning programs, and support services to help them become more productive and build stronger businesses. Realogy's affiliated brokerages operate around the world with approximately 193,600 independent sales agents in the United States and approximately 106,400 independent sales agents in 112 other countries and territories."

Sounds great, except Realogy's stock price has declined from a high in May 2013 of about $53.50 to price of just over $6 as of the end of June 2019.[195]

---

195 https://www.google.com/search?q=realogy+stock+price&rlz=1C1GGRV_enUS751US751&oq=
realogy+stock+price&aqs=chrome..69i57.3301j0j4&sourceid=chrome&ie=UTF-8

Why? In my opinion, the traditional real estate franchise is losing leads to online real estate websites, and more recently to iBuyers. Andrea Riquier writing in *MarketWatch* on June 30, 2019, and quoting John Campbell, a stock analyst for Stephens Inc., explains it:

> "...Most importantly, we believe that iBuying opens to the doors to so much more for Zillow, particularly the sell-side lead opportunity," Campbell wrote. Zillow won't just show you a home—it will sell it to you. Specifically, Zillow could dominate the add-on services that anyone in the market to buy or sell a home needs: mortgage lending, title insurance, and so on, he said. But Zillow is so powerful it's disrupting the entire industry as it goes, Campbell argued. "Partly due to Zillow, we believe that the power pendulum has clearly swung towards agents and away from brokerages."[196]

The pendulum that Campbell is speaking about is the power of real estate franchisee operators to set the percentage of compensation to agents, and the power to capture mortgage and title leads. Brokerages are losing control of the initial consumer contact with consumers to iBuyers. This has become a trend, as well as a quirky regulation covering real estate transactions.

Real estate agents are independent contractors, not employees of most real estate franchisee operators. The Real Estate Settlement Procedures Act prohibits consumer referrals from a real estate agent to any other service provider for any "thing of value," such as cash, entertainment, and related inducements. There is a carve out for referrals from a licensed real estate agent to another licensed real estate agent for listings or buyer referral. The iBuyers jump into these carve outs, and can offer sellers the instant buy, or offer the seller a suggested real estate agent. The agent referral generates income for the iBuyer. Either by instant buy or referral, the iBuyer gets paid. Who is getting disintermediated? The traditional real estate franchisee: the Coldwell Banker, Century 21, Keller Williams, and other national franchisees. Downstream, disintermediated participants include mortgage lenders and title agents who rely on realtors for an ongoing stream of referrals.

Reversing the Flow of Customer Leads

Traditional lenders attempt to reverse the lead flow from realtors in a number of ways. Phil DeFronzo, CEO of Norcom Mortgage, also founded RealtyQuest Inc.[197] in Southwest Florida to generate home purchase leads. These leads are prequalified or preapproved for mortgage loans, and are then provided to selected realtors that meet RealtyQuest Inc. requirements for customer service.

---

196 https://www.marketwatch.com/story/real-estate-sector-at-the-tipping-point-prompts-stock-analyst-to-flip-his-ratings-2019-06-11?mod=mw_latestnews
197 https://www.realtyquestinc.com/about

Home Captain was founded by CEO Grant Moon. Grant described Home Captain:

In 2011, I decided to purchase my first home. The loan officer and the realtor were not working together, resulting in a frustrating home buying process that was complex, disjointed, and time-consuming.

Home Captain is a technology-enabled real estate platform that helps guide prospective home-buyers through the home buying process. The model is lender centric. The lender works with the borrower on financing. Our Home Captain concierge rep acts as the liaison connecting the loan officer, real estate agent and homebuyer, making sure that all parties communicate well and are informed throughout the purchase process.

The Home Captain platform is designed specifically to help homebuyers have a better purchasing experience. Real estate agents are matched with higher quality homebuyers. Lenders are able to increase conversions on home purchase loans.

Brutal Competition for the Residential Home Buying Customer

Real estate agents are not employees, so the owner of a brokerage cannot compel the agent to use his mortgage company or title agency. The agent can refer their buyers and sellers to any provider based on the agent's relationship, but not legally for any "thing of value." This puts every independent real estate brokerage, independent realtor, lender, title agent, aggregation site, as well as literally any lead source in brutal competition.

This is the most acute emerging problem for real estate brokerage franchisors. iBuyers, services like Home Captain, and Mortgage Rate aggregation sites are getting to potential consumers early in the process and then delivering the leads directly to realtors. This reduces the value of the real estate brokerage franchisors, as the independent agents demand higher commission rates to offset the cost of the leads the independent realtor purchases.

iBuyers can sell leads to real estate agents, mortgage lenders, and other parties legally for fair value. Or an iBuyer can become an owner in a real estate brokerage, mortgage lender, or title agency and refer buyers and sellers in compliance with RESPA as the services are under common ownership.

The iBuyer generates the initial contact with the consumer, and can sell or direct that lead to a real estate agent though the iBuyer's real estate brokerage, mortgage lender, or title agency. This explains Zillow's purchase of Mortgage Lenders of America. In my opinion, iBuyers will seek to enter mortgage and title insurance, as well as other services, upsetting the long-held structure of many parties linked together in one transaction. This will put tremendous competition on the $160 billion of fees to be generated from real estate transactions in 2020, and for years to come.

Hybrid Real Estate Brokerage Models

Real estate brokerages have been attempting to optimize commission splits and generate additional income by selling mortgages and title insurance for years. My former bank established joint venture partnerships with a number of large real estate brokerages and builders in the early 2000s. These were joint ventures among born-traditional companies, and they worked well enough. New "hybrid" real estate companies are attempting to use a digital platform to reduce the frictional costs of labor and overhead. Some of the frictional costs saved are being passed back to consumers as an inducement to use the hybrid service. Specifically, listing fees are being discounted, and selling agent fees are being effectively discounted in the form of closing cost rebates to customers.

Redfin is a born-digital company that initially worked on map-based search technology. Redfin's patents include U.S. Patent number 9,760,237 for user interfaces for displaying geographic information. The patent has its genesis in 2005, overlaying data as images on a map in different layers.

Though Redfin was born digital, the company undertook the transformation of the traditional real estate agent-based model in what I'd call a "hybrid," linking a digital platform to traditional agents. Being a real estate brokerage had some advantages, including access to Multiple Listing Source data. Holding agents accountable by encouraging consumer reviews helped with quality. Redfin paid bonuses based on consumer reviews.[198] One bold move was adding for-sale-by-owner listings to its website, becoming the first site to combine complete listings from the Multiple Listing Service with homes listed by owners.[199] Redfin is publicly held.

Redfin began testing 1% listing fees in various markets, directly challenging traditional real estate franchisees. "Discount" real estate agencies existed in the past, but never gained much traction due to their small scale, small marketing budgets, and minimalist technology.

Redfin began offering mortgage through Redfin Mortgage in 2017. Redfin's initial public offering raised $138 million on July 28, 2017. Redfin's approach is two-pronged: It attacks the traditional listing fee by discounting it to 1% from its usual 3%. The hybrid brokerage has the data provided by technology tools to estimate a selling price, and to market a home, possibly supplanting much of the value-add of a listing real estate agent. This capability may make the listing fee the logical first target.

The traditional fee for the selling agent—the agent who shows buyers the houses available for sale—is not directly challenged, though homeowners are offered a rebate toward closing costs as a legal way to discount the selling agent's fee. Why

---

198 http://press.redfin.com/company-timeline
199 http://press.redfin.com/company-timeline

would a selling agent consent to a lower commission? Because the leads are provided by Redfin.

Redfin's strategies of reducing the listing fee and rebating part of the selling agent's fee are existential threats to traditional real estate brokers. The better real estate agents demand the highest commission splits because these agents source business. Less prolific agents that cannot source sufficient business are more likely to work with Redfin due to Redfin's lead sourcing.

Redfin's discount listing strategy is more customer-focused—after all, what seller would rather pay 3% for listing a home on the MLS as opposed to 1%? The rich data on a variety of internet sites makes the traditional listing agent's value proposition difficult to sustain.

Redfin announced a partnership with RE/MAX, a born-traditional, full-service brokerage. According to a press release dated March 18, 2019, RE/MAX and Redfin announced an Exclusive Referral Relationship in the United States and Canada. "In areas where Redfin does not have capacity to serve customers, Redfin refers customers to approved partner agents at other brokerages, including participating RE/MAX agents. When the customer closes on a home purchase or sale, Redfin receives a referral fee. participating RE/MAX agents will have the exclusive opportunity to meet customers from almost 5,000 U.S. postal codes where Redfin.com currently does not promote any agents. In addition, Redfin will only partner with RE/MAX in Canada."

Interestingly, the press release deals with channel conflict among Redfin, RE/MAX agents and competing agents: "Where both companies have agents, the current spirit of competition will continue, and the agreement does not prevent either brokerage from serving clients anywhere. Where Redfin already works with partner agents from different brokerages, those partner agents can continue to participate in the Redfin Partner Program. Agents from different brokerages can continue to apply to become Redfin partner agents in areas not covered by the exclusivity agreement."

The culture clash between born-digital and born-traditional companies is apparent, as the current spirit of competition lasted but two months. According to an account of RE/MAX's termination of its agreement with Redfin published by RISMedia on May 13, 2019:[200]

> Given Redfin's recent announcement regarding a program that would encourage buyers not to use agents on listings where the seller is represented by Redfin, we cannot continue with an official, corporate-level relationship at this time. We have begun the process of dissolving our exclusive referral agreement with them beginning today.

> According to a statement from Redfin, an issue between the two companies is Redfin Direct, a new service Redfin is piloting in Boston for Redfin's listing customers to get offers from unrepresented buyers. "Redfin understands this concern, as we employ thousands of licensed

---

200 https://rismedia.com/2019/05/13/re-max-redfin-exclusive-partnership-terminated/

professionals and believe the vast majority of homebuyers need professional advice, and will happily pay for it. But we also have a duty to get as many offers for our customers' listings as we possibly can, and to give those listing customers the best value. We believe in consumer choices; our mission is to redefine real estate in consumers' favor."

Disintermediation of labor and overhead is in a born-digital company's DNA. RE/MAX apparently objected to Redfin's test to work with buyers who bypass a real estate agent, thus disintermediating the most defensible element of the traditional real estate brokerage's fee structure: the logistics of shuffling buyers around to look at real estate. That just had to be too much for real estate agents to take, and the pressure on RE/MAX appeared to be such that the Redfin deal had to be terminated. It's ironic that the test market was Boston, the birthplace of another economic revolution 250 years ago.

Continuing with born-digital real estate brokerages, Clever is a discount listing service, currently offering $3,000 flat fee listings, or 1% if the home has a listing price greater than $350,000. The selling agent side offers a rebate on closing costs.[201] There is a variety of local and regional companies with a value proposition similar to Clever, so I won't elaborate here. Clever is privately held.

eXp Realty appears to be a hybrid by birth. It uses virtual offices instead of physical offices for real estate agents. This eliminates much of the overhead friction of traditional realtors. eXp purchased VirBella, a born-digital online campus and collaboration technology, and integrated its real estate operation onto VirBella's platform.[202] eXp focuses on an agent web-based technology to support a virtual office and to foster collaboration among agents. Agent loyalty appears to be built by this platform as well as eXp World Holdings' Sustainable Equity Plan continues to share equity with eXp Realty agents and brokers to promote longevity. eXp is publicly traded.[203]

Compass, a born-traditional real estate brokerage, is not quite a hybrid in the sense of reducing commissions to consumers. Rather, it focuses on exclusivity and building excitement of its forthcoming "exclusive" listings. Compass claims to provide the Compass web-based portal so agents have more time for advising their clients, and changing how agents and clients navigate the process of finding or selling a home.[204]

Redfin, Clever, eXp, Compass, other hybrids, and the iBuyers are all aiming at the traditional 6% real estate commission model. These models always have a real estate agent to build their own brand and source leads from internet traffic, as opposed to the traditional signs in the year and referral basis of traditional real estate franchisees.

---

201 https://clever.com/

202 https://www.virbela.com/use-cases#exp

203 https://expworldholdings.com/2019/05/09/exp-world-holdings-reports-first-quarter-2019-financial-results/

204 https://www.compass.com/about/

The stock prices of Zillow and Realogy tell it all. Since 2013, Zillow is up 292%, while Realogy is down 82%.

But will there be a role for traditional realtors and loan officers? John Hedlund of Amerihome has a view on this:

> As long as the majority of real estate transactions continue going through a traditional realtor, the brick and mortar loan officer will continue to be relevant because you need boots on the ground to build those relationships. However, as digital real estate brokers gain traction, the local realtor will start losing their grip on the borrower and no longer be able to direct them to their favorite loan officer. Once that's happens in force, the ability for increased purchase business in "consumer direct" lending will be a reality.

A View from Integrated One-Stop Providers

Born-traditional Trident Mortgage Company is a full-service mortgage banker and is one of the largest realtor-affiliated mortgage companies in the United States. Trident is affiliated with born-traditional Berkshire Hathaway HomeServices Fox & Roach, which has 4,000 independent realtors.[205] In discussion with Marie Gayo, President of Trident Mortgage Company, she and I went through some of the intricacies inherent in unifying real estate, mortgage, title and homeowner's insurance under one roof. She had some interesting observations about the competitive aspects inherent in this model:

> I will say that because of this integrated model, our margins are thinner than most independent mortgage bankers and banks that are out there. And the reason the margins are thinner is because we have to compete. A big competitive point obviously is price and the only way you can come back having your competitors come through your doorways—sometimes it barrels down to price. If service and technology are the same, then price becomes the key competitive advantage.

> We have to compete on every level. We have to be the best in service. We have to be the best in turn times. We have to be the best in price. We have to have the depth of products. It absolutely eats into your margins.

> We've had to create a lot more efficiencies here. You've got to take advantage and leverage technology in the best way possible. We operate with a very low-cost structure. But we've been introducing layers of technology to improve that efficiency even more.

> When we talk about other competitors that are newer to the landscape, such as Zillow, I believe that real estate agents have their choice. Consumers have their choice and in the end, and you still have to deliver on all facets of the business, whether it is competing on price, whether it's competing on products, whether it's competing on service.

---

205 https://www.foxroach.com/about-fox-roach

> I go to conferences and talk to a lot of my peers. They sometimes look at our model and think I've got it easy. We have it harder because when your real estate sales associates, your customers, they're both our clients. We see them every day. Our loan officers have to deal with their clients day to day in a very intensive way. It's not just catering to our consumers, but it's also catering to the agency. Our [one-stop-shop] model is harder.

Roy George of born traditional Taylor Morrison Home Loans, an affiliate of born-traditional TaylorMorrison Homes, sees the one-stop shopping market requiring significant technology investment:

> Competition is going to increase. We are going to see more fintechs. Traditional companies that exist today will have to become like the fintechs. The playing field is going to even itself out a little bit. You can see well-known CIOs and CTOs moving over to mortgage companies that are looking to digitize everything.

> We're not just going to slap some new customer-facing technology out there. Leaders are truly trying to innovate the space. I think you're seeing some true consolidation over the next five years. My former employer is a mortgage fintech company and is very, very focused on not just the customer's digital experience, but also the digital experience for both the internal and external customer. It's going to be robotics, it's going to be AI, it is going to be a lot of things like that and only those companies that embrace technology in full are going to capture market share.

Banks May Become More Formidable Competitors

Recent changes by Congress expanded the Qualified Mortgage[206] (QM) imprimatur to any mortgage loan funded by a bank with less than $10 billion of assets. This may change the calculus for portfolio lending by mid-sized banks. The loan must meet Ability to Repay but is otherwise a QM loan. These changes were brought about by Congress to expand the availability of mortgage credit from banks.

How many banks have less than $10 billion of assets? 4,160 banks in the US, not including credit unions and mutual banks not insured by the FDIC. These expanded QM opportunities are available only to federally regulated banks and are not available to independent mortgage bankers.

---

206 According to the Consumer Finance Protection Bureau, a "Qualified Mortgage" is a category of loans that have certain more stable features that help make it more likely that you'll be able to afford your loan.

A lender must make a good-faith effort to determine that you have the "ability to repay" your mortgage before you take it out. This is known as the "ability-to-repay" rule. If a lender loans you a Qualified Mortgage, it means the lender met certain requirements and it's assumed that the lender followed the ability-to-repay rule. https://www.consumerfinance.gov/ask-cfpb/what-is-a-qualified-mortgage-en-1789/

According to Dave Stevens, former CEO of the Mortgage Bankers Association, that may take some time. "Bankers are still shell-shocked from the regulatory on-slaught from the crisis. The risk appetite just may not be there for a lot of banks."

Part of the shell shock is that regulators have a knee-jerk reaction when a banker mentions "mortgage banking." But less so when a banker states that the bank is con-sidering expanding first and second lien portfolio lending to residential homebuyers. It's all in how one says it. And there is plenty of balance sheet capacity in the bank-ing system to make one–four family residential loans.

In short, the transition of mortgage lending to primarily purchase-driven trans-actions—together with builders and iBuyers representing a growing market share of purchase financing business—means that mortgage lending will be transformed, with friction costs of labor and overhead being reduced from about 4% to 1% of the mortgage amount.

Opportunities in Mortgage Servicing and Origination Recapture

Mortgage servicing—the collection of monthly payments, escrow administration, and so on—provides an opportunity to interact with the customer each month. Yet mortgage servicing appears to be an underutilized gateway into getting to the cus-tomer first. The customer's current payment history, loan balance, loan origina-tion data, and even current credit report are available for use anytime.

Yet this treasure trove of data and relationship-building opportunity appears to be an undervalued asset. J.D. Power 2019 U.S. Primary Mortgage Servicer Satisfaction Study rated overall industry satisfaction with mortgage servicers is 777 (on a 1,000-point scale). Life insurance is about the same at 779, and health insurance plans are at the bottom of the industries rated by J.D. Power.[207]

Some servicers scored well, as Quicken Loans ranked highest among servicers for the sixth consecutive year, with a score of 878. Regions Mortgage followed with a score of 848, and Guild Mortgage ranked third at 828.[208]

MBA NewsLink quoted John Cabell, Director of Wealth and Lending Intelligence with J.D. Power:

> Mortgage servicers are really missing an opportunity to build the kind of goodwill with their customers that has proven to translate directly to increased advocacy and repeat business. The industry's laser focus on lowering costs, managing regulatory compliance and minimizing

207 https://www.mba.org/servicing-newslink/2019/august/servicing-newslink-tuesday-8-6-19/ news-and-trends/jd-power-primary-loan-services-have-trust-issues-with-customers?_zs=VCbwB1&_ zl=fxXE5

208 https://www.mba.org/servicing-newslink/2019/august/servicing-newslink-tuesday-8-6-19/ news-and-trends/jd-power-primary-loan-services-have-trust-issues-with-customers?_zs=VCbwB1&_ zl=fxXE5

delinquencies has come at the expense of customer experience. It is negatively affecting customer trust in their brands.[209]

MBA NewsLink noted that mortgage servicers "occupy a unique slice of the consumer finance marketplace" in which many of their customers do not select them but are acquired when the servicers purchase loans in the secondary market. The involuntary nature of this relationship, combined with an industry-wide focus on efficiency and cost controls, resulted in low customer satisfaction.

Transferred customers seek the same basic customer experience criteria as those who actively choose a mortgage servicer, yet their satisfaction scores are lower. They also have a significantly higher incidence of problems with payment and escrow accounts. The study said that 54% of first-time homebuyers say they are confused, angry, or irritated when transferred. This phenomenon spotlights the unique communications and customer experience challenges mortgage servicers still need to address with transferred customers.[210]

Many large loan servicers have relayed to me that their "recapture rate"—providing new financing when an existing borrower pays of their loan—is significantly less than 40%. This means that the time and expense acquiring the loan servicing is lost more than 60% of the time. This strikes me as very low, especially since a servicer has borrower historical financial data, demographic data and current credit data. Servicing recapture is a great opportunity to get to the customer first. A goal of recapturing 80% or more of customers seems like a reasonable target to pursue. Achieving this recapture rate would likely be a very profitable endeavor.

And it's not just servicing recapture. The lender who originated the loan has a large amount of data about the borrower. This data includes income, job history, family statistics, asset and real estate holdings, education, creditors, marital status, children's ages, interest rate, and balance of the mortgage. That snapshot of data could power an ongoing campaign to provide relationship-based information to a customer.

I don't mean birthday cards or anniversary cards for the home purchase. You could use the static data to project when children may be entering junior high, high school, or college. Whether a debt consolidation loan may make sense. How much the borrower's home has appreciated and whether there is available equity. When the borrower might be ready to trade up to a new home.

---

209 https://www.mba.org/servicing-newslink/2019/august/servicing-newslink-tuesday-8-6-19/news-and-trends/jd-power-primary-loan-services-have-trust-issues-with-customers?_zs=VCbwB1&_zl=fxXE5

210 https://www.mba.org/servicing-newslink/2019/august/servicing-newslink-tuesday-8-6-19/news-and-trends/jd-power-primary-loan-services-have-trust-issues-with-customers?_zs=VCbwB1&_zl=fxXE5

You could also supplement the static data with purchased data to obtain a more contemporaneous view of the customer. But few are doing even the most rudimentary attempt at origination recapture. Mortgage Cadence, a loan origination system provider, uses anonymized data of its users to develop a benchmarking study on various performance metrics, including borrower recapture.[211] According to Mortgage Cadence, borrower share is the percentage of existing borrowers recaptured in a given year for a new loan.

The Mortgage Cadence Benchmarking Study found:

> Borrower share has historically been a challenge for lenders. When we performed our initial analysis in 2012, lenders were capturing 1.31% of their existing borrowers each year for a new mortgage. By 2017, that share had fallen to just 0.86%. Fast-forward to this year, and not much has changed, with the 2018 average borrower share measure at 0.85%.

> This metric shines light on an incredible opportunity for lenders, as customers who already enjoyed a positive experience with the institution are much easier to market to than acquiring an entirely new customer. Our top performer knows this, and capitalized on it, by working with 3.29% of its previous customers in 2018.[212]

Let's do the math on Borrower Share. There are 126 million households in the United States, according to Statista.[213] About 65% of the households are homeowners, as shown previously. Multiplying households by the home ownership rate, there are about 82 million homes owned by households in the United States. About 6 million homes are sold per year as discussed in this book. Dividing 6 million home sales by 82 million homeowners, about 7.3% of homeowners buy a new home each year.

According to Mortgage Cadence, in 2018 lender recapture of existing borrowers was just 0.85%. That means repeat business of an existing lender is just 11.5%. Meaning 88.5% of borrowers that used a lender to get a loan use a different lender on their next transaction. Lenders spend $8,000 plus to obtain a borrower, and then let that investment walk to another lender 88% of the time. This is just crazy. But recapture or lending and servicing clients represents a very large opportunity to cut customer acquisition cost and increase customer loyalty. If you take nothing else from this book, resolve *right now* to increase your retention to increase your return on equity!

Regulation of the Residential Real Estate and Related Financial Services Market

As Dave Stevens noted, residential real estate and related real estate financial services are perhaps one of the most regulated industries in the United States. These

---

211 Mortgage Cadence Annual Lending Performance Benchmarking Study Results: 2019
212 Ibid.
213 https://www.statista.com/statistics/183635/number-of-households-in-the-us/

regulations, coupled with aggressive enforcement, monetary penalties, and "shaming" of purported violators increase costs to consumers and stifle competition. The following is a partial list of regulations covering the industry.

- The Fair Housing Act protects people from discrimination when they are renting or buying a home, getting a mortgage, seeking housing assistance, or engaging in other housing-related activities. Additional protections apply to federally-assisted housing.
- The Dodd-Frank Wall Street Reform and Consumer Protection Act (also known as Dodd-Frank) is a variety of consumer protection legislation that established the Consumer Financial Protection Bureau.
- The Real Estate Settlement Procedures Act prevents referral fees in a federally regulated mortgage transaction and sets requirements for disclosure in lending and servicing transfers, among other things.
- The Truth in Lending Act requires disclosures regarding the cost of credit.
- The Gramm–Leach–Bliley Act focuses on consumer privacy protections in financial services.
- The Fair and Accurate Credit Transactions Act addresses credit reporting accuracy and consumer access to their credit histories.
- The National Affordable Housing Act requires that borrowers must be notified whenever the servicing of their loans is transferred to another institution. Borrowers must be notified of the transfer at least 15 days before it becomes effective.
- The Equal Credit Opportunity Act prohibits discrimination in the granting or arranging (for example a mortgage broker) of credit.
- The Community Reinvestment Act requires banks to address the financial needs of the communities where they are located and makes "redlining," or lending exclusion areas illegal.

A material part of the cost stack in real estate is, in my opinion, the result of the unintended consequences of the plethora of regulatory restrictions imposed on real estate sales and financing. Some costs arise from excessive and duplicative regulation. Consumer disclosure is important, but one hundred pages of disclosure for a mortgage transaction can be confusing to consumers. The stringent mega-regulation and the risk of strict punitive enforcement likely costs lenders about $2,000 in compliance costs per loan.

The Real Estate Settlement Procedures Act (RESPA) prevents referral fees in federally regulated transactions. Referral fees are permissible among real estate agents, but are not permissible if made by or paid to mortgage lenders or title agents. Referral fees are permissible in most other industries.

Given the complexity of regulations, they often have perverse effects. For instance:

- A mortgage loan originator cannot reduce his or her commission income to lower fees or rates for a mortgage, even though the beneficiary is clearly the borrower.
- "Qualified Mortgage" regulations are designed to ensure borrowers can repay obligations. The unintended effect is that underwriting and documentation standards are strict in that certain borrowers are not eligible for loans because they can't document certain forms of income. Lenders, particularly banks, are so risk averse due to very aggressive enforcement that there has been little product innovation in the past ten years.
- FreddieMac and FannieMae remain wards of the federal government, while enjoying material exceptions to the "Qualified Mortgage" regulations that reduce private competition and product innovation.
- Federal bank regulators stifle bank innovation in the residential lending space with excessive regulations on the investment in mortgage servicing rights, slow movement on fintech bank charters, discouragement of monoline banks focusing on residential lending, and continuing aggressive enforcement of minor exceptions to disclosure regulations.

First off, most customers do not understand that a no-fee or no-points mortgage has a higher interest rate than one paid with origination fees and other costs directly. Borrowers have been trained to use a "no points, no fee" loan. A no points, no fee loan makes sense if the borrower only plans on being in the home about five years or less. Otherwise, there's no point in increasing the rate on a 30-year fixed rate loan to cover points and fees.

In my opinion, mostly due to RESPA, mortgage finance has remained outside of a point of sale environment. The evidence is automobile finance. It seems that few consumers go to a bank or car loan broker to get a loan. They walk to the finance and insurance department of an automobile dealer, get approved in a few minutes, and, within the hour, complete the paperwork so that they can drive off the lot. Why? The dealers are paid referral fees by the lender, the dealer shops lenders for a competitive rate to make sure the sale closes and customers are delighted because of the absence of hassles and mountains of paperwork.

I once had a conversation with a senior mortgage finance regulator who shall remain nameless. I used the example of car finance point of sale with minimum disclosures, and the customer being the judge of what is a fair price for the car and the loan. I suggested a similar approach for mortgages. The regulator was aghast. The regulator's thoughts were, in so many words, that lenders would take advantage of the customer without consumer protections, like all of the disclosures. I pushed back, and said most customers don't read the disclosures—they only look at the loan terms and cash to close. I got more looks of disbelief. I finally asked her how many consumers could actually understand all of the disclosures. A red face, and then reality... "Not too many," was the answer. And that's after the "simplification" brought about by TILA-RESPA Integrated Disclosures, or TRID.

Sensible regulation fairly applied in a constructive manner will also go a long way in reducing consumer costs incurred in residential real estate transactions.

Chapter Ten
The Disruptive Path Forward

This final chapter describes possible scenarios of the effects of disruption that may occur in the next ten years. The scenarios won't unfold exactly as described. They never do.

I am firm in my conclusions, however, that two effects of disruption will occur:

- First, the winners in the race to get to the customer first will establish considerable competitive advantage. If you can establish a one-stop-shopping convenience and control over the whole real estate transaction process with a customer, you can control a large part of the revenue to be earned in the transaction. This is doubly important due to the second effect described.
- Second, the cost stack in residential real estate transactions will be substantially reduced at virtually every process, milestone, and task that comprises the $200 billion revenue residential real estate industry. You will have to control a greater portion of a greater number of transactions to earn the same dollar revenue you currently earn.

The reasons are straightforward:

Consumers want instant gratification, and the "tipping point" of adoption of fintech that removes friction is rapidly approaching. Malcolm Gladwell, author of *The Tipping Point: How Little Things Can Make a Big Difference*, described a tipping point as the moment when an idea, practice, or trend hits a threshold and then spreads like a wildfire. Examples include touchscreens on mobile devices, patient zero in an epidemic, streaming video, and streaming music.

We may be witnessing the approach of a tipping point in residential real estate brokerage and lending industries. With that in mind, the following are several sub-scenarios that play toward the transformation of the residential real estate and lending business.

Just as transportation speed was increased and costs were reduced in the early 1900s by the tipping point transition from horse-drawn carriages to automobiles and trucks, so too will the real estate industry. What will likely unfold is a unique combination of technology and touch that maintains the human factor where necessary, while ameliorating friction via fintech. As Tom Faughnan of Associated Bank put it, "I don't think you're ever going to take people out of the equation . . . we've got to have a combination of both . . . and if you haven't invested in one or the other, you're going to be left behind."

The scenarios I've presented don't have specific time frames associated with them. It's the "what," "how," and "why" we are going to delve into here, not the "when." While the "when" is up in the air, however, this impending disruption is inevitable, rest assured.

https://doi.org/10.1515/9783110650471-011

Why Fintech Will Create a Wave of Innovation

Consumers have become seduced by immediate gratification. Streaming video and music. Instant purchase and one-day delivery from internet retailers. Information and research on demand. Walk into a car showroom, pick out a car, finance it, and drive it away. Research and book an airline ticket, rental car, and hotel instantly and travel tomorrow. All available now.

So instant gratification is coming to residential real estate buying, selling, and financing. We see some of it already. Zillow, Opendoor, and Offerpad deliver instant offers to buy a home from its owner. Rocket Mortgage and others offer "press a button, get mortgage approval" for consumers, riffing off of the Amazon concept of "one-touch" purchasing.

Like all disruptive competitors, the instant gratification promise has some significant contingencies. The largest contingencies arise from archaic regulation. The most restrictive barrier to innovation in the real estate buying and financing marketplace is RESPA. RESPA was enacted in 1974, the same period as the first OPEC Oil Embargo; as such, its application in the real-world scenarios of today is antediluvian. More to the point, it is a huge barrier that segregates the natural market ecosphere.

There are other equally archaic artifacts. Fannie and Freddie were created in two periods of crises involving financial and real estate liquidity: the 1930s and the late 1970s, respectively. RESPA, Freddie, and Fannie were created before Apple Computer existed. In fact, Freddie and Fannie predates personal computers, the internet, cell phones and electronic engine controls in automobiles. The Douglas DC-3 two-engine propeller driven 25 seat airliner was developed just after Fannie was created. The Boeing 707 and McDonnell Douglas DC-9 were modern jet aircraft at Freddie's birth.

The regulatory infrastructure in most Western democracies is designed against creative destruction. Its bureaucrats are guardians of the past. Nothing happens fast. But creative members of a democracy find legal ways to innovate around guardians of the past.

For example, I mentioned the home I jointly owned with my siblings in Bethany Beach, Delaware. The subprime mortgage market ignited huge growth in vacation homes. Prices and building skyrocketed. Real estate transfer taxes were used by the Town of Bethany to finance operational matters. The vacation real estate market went bust, and so did transfer tax revenue. The town's solution? Raise the transfer tax.

Predictably, the higher transfer taxes further depressed real estate sales. Buyers found a way to work around confiscatory transfer taxes by buying the real estate within a single purpose limited liability corporation (LLC). You could now transfer the real estate without those pesky transfer taxes, and at any time. No need to wait for the courthouse to open to record the sale of the LLC membership interest. Fannie and Freddie now facilitate mortgages on real estate in closely held, single-purpose LLCs.

Stewart Title is a leader in electronic mortgage closings. Mortgage Electronics Real Estate Services facilitates transfers of mortgage servicing, eliminating the need to manually record transfers in the local courthouse. This consolidation of services will take the friction and cost out of real estate transactions, a prime example of convergence and logistics at work.

I live near Lancaster, Pennsylvania, where many Amish settled two hundred years ago to avoid religious persecution. Today, many sects follow Amish traditions of not using electricity or powered vehicles for personal comfort. The horse and buggy are still frequent users of Lancaster rural county roads. I've seen a horse and buggy at a drive-up window of a bank, which was a bit of a culture shock. I've seen gas-powered threshing equipment pulled by horse-drawn teams. But even strict Amish have adapted to modern business, maintaining computers and cell phones for business use only in outbuildings. Why mention this? Because fintech is so powerful that observers of even the strictest faith codes have found a faithful way to adapt to the benefits of fintech. If the Amish can adjust, surely the residential real estate ecosphere will transform in the face of fintech.

Real Estate and Lending Industry Commissioned Jobs: Value Versus Compensation

No one disputes the positive impact that a good realtor, loan officer, title agent, appraiser, or inspector can have on a real estate transaction. This book has a presupposition that this good work will continue. Instead, I posit that it is the scope of the work and the value proposition that will be disruptively transformed by fintech. Much will be automated, and some positions could be consolidated into a broader scope. Again, as Tom Faughnan asserted, the future will be a combination of both human touch and fintech.

Looking to history, commissioned travel agents, commissioned stockbrokers, commissioned Tupperware salespersons, and other door-to-door salespeople are largely historical footnotes. Why? The disproportionate cost of finding and selling to customers became uneconomic. In every case, buyers found substitutes and sellers found a new manner to interact and transact with customers.

Expedia and similar websites killed off the commissions travel agents earned on airline reservations. In response, some travel agents moved into other niches of experience travel, award travel, and the like. The 8% needed to book an airline fare gave way to the lesser friction and lower cost of a website.

Commissioned stockbrokers were largely replaced by internet-enabled discount brokers. Stockbrokers are now largely "wealth management" advisors, and are compensated on an annual fee basis calculated on assets under management. The portfolio value goes up, as does the advisor compensation, and vice versa. Low-cost mutual funds and 401(k) accounts also democratized equity investments, and the broadened customer base expanded the industry. High commissions essentially killed the commissioned stockbroker model.

Tupperware salespeople operated door-to-door on a high commissioned based multi-level marketing system. Changing lifestyles, department stores, and demographics killed off door-to-door Tupperware and a host of similar multi-level marketing models.

There are other examples and plenty of them. The point is that transaction-based commission models are ripe for disruption. Many high-compensation positions in residential real estate home sales, mortgage finance, and insurance are heavily commission-based.

The result of this highly commission-based ecosphere is that disruptors are looking to make the salesperson's margin (i.e., commission) their opportunity. Congress passed laws against referral fees and steering consumers to a particular product or salesperson in federally regulated real estate and mortgage transactions. A laudable goal.

Initially, authorities promulgated RESPA, Dodd-Frank, and similar regulations in order to curb abuses created by commissioned product sales: title agents paying referral fees to realtors and mortgage loan officers, mortgage lenders paying referral fees to realtors, loan officers steering of consumers to high commission products like subprime mortgages, realtors steering consumers to lenders and title agents who pay referral fees, and so on.

But the results of these good intentions were that RESPA and Dodd-Frank created regulatory cost friction and reduced innovation, competition, and availability of credit. Once again, laudable goals spoiled with unintended consequences.

Car dealers can build an integrated distribution system because they own the asset being sold. The ancillary services are easy for a consumer to purchase as a one-stop shop. Do the consumers always get the best car price, best trade-in price, and best lease or loan rate and terms in a one-stop shopping experience? I don't know. Yet it is the predominant model of how cars are sold, thanks to its inherent convenience. Customer expectation of this convenience can only continue to grow in the residential real estate sector.

Some of these changes will be industry-initiated, some will be consumer-initiated, and some will arise from regulation and litigation. Let's take a look at the litigation impact.

Real Estate Brokerage Litigation

Often times, an industry under stress from competitive forces attracts a variety of competitors. Six percent on $1.6 trillion of home sales per year is a lot of revenue with a lot of fingers seeking to catch a part of the fees. For example, Redfin, iBuyers, and many others are attacking traditional real estate brokerages. Fintechs have their eye on the prize and are putting pressure on the industry in ways we haven't seen until now.

Other pressures might take the form of legal attacks. Legal attacks can advance theories of alleged harm that may not be obvious to market participants, and totally transform a marketplace. The subprime mortgage crisis created these opportunities, and the bankruptcy and securities litigation created a tipping point that defined alleged "toxic mortgages." Once "toxic mortgages" and "liar loans" became popular descriptions, the mortgage industry was forever transformed.

The same phenomenon could be emerging in real estate brokerage. Litigation regarding alleged anticompetitive practices has a way of attracting plaintiff attorneys, who have a way of attracting legislators and regulators.

Take Realogy as an example. Realogy is the defendant in a class action suit seeking compensation for investor losses. You might recall the stock price decline of Realogy stock price. According to a press release from the Rosen Law Firm:

> ...a global investor rights law firm announces it has filed a class action lawsuit on behalf of purchasers of the securities of Realogy Holdings Corp. (NYSE: RLGY) from February 24, 2017 through May 22, 2019, inclusive (the "Class Period"). The lawsuit seeks to recover damages for Realogy investors under the federal securities laws.

> According to the lawsuit, defendants throughout the Class Period made false and/or misleading statements and/or failed to disclose that: (1) Realogy was engaged in anticompetitive behavior by requiring property sellers to pay the commissions of a buyer's broker at an inflated rate; (2) Realogy's anticompetitive actions would prompt the U.S. Department of Justice to open an antitrust investigation into the real estate industry's practices regarding brokers' commissions; and (3) as a result, defendants' statements about the Realogy's business, operations and prospects were materially false and misleading and/or lacked a reasonable basis at all relevant times. When the true details entered the market, the lawsuit claims that investors suffered damages.[214]

The core of the Rosen litigation has its roots in litigation regarding the seller payment of buyer's brokerage fees. Attorneys initiated the class action litigation based on alleged anticompetitive practices at the National Association of Realtors. In a May 18, 2019 press release, the National Association of Realtors (NAR) moved to dismiss this litigation:

> ...moved to dismiss the Moehrl v. NAR lawsuit on the basis that the complaint misrepresents NAR rules for the operation of Multiple Listing Services (MLSs), which have long been recognized by the courts across the country as protecting consumers and creating competitive, efficient markets that benefit home buyers and sellers. The filing was made in federal court in Chicago.

---

214 https://www.rosenlegal.com/cases-1600.html

NAR's brief points out that, as the centerpiece of their case, the seven class action law firms who represent one plaintiff have resorted to fundamentally mischaracterizing NAR's rules. That mischaracterization, according to the NAR's filing, led the class action attorneys to "dream up" purportedly anticompetitive rules that simply do not exist in NAR's Handbook or Code of Ethics. In reality, NAR rules specifically direct listing brokers to determine—in consultation with their clients—the amount of compensation to offer buyers' brokers in connection with their MLS listings. Furthermore, under NAR rules, a buyer's broker is free to negotiate a commission from the listing broker that is different from what appears in the MLS listing. Neither NAR nor any MLS has any say in setting broker commissions.[215]

The core of the modern real estate brokerage business model is under attack by consumers demanding lower fees, fintech alternative real estate sales models, and plaintiff class action attorneys.

Consumers are the ultimate arbiters in fees. Fintech options, whether iBuyers or the plethora of mixed channel models of Redfin and others, will ultimately converge the market, and better logistics will empower faster service and lower fees.

My partner, Alex Henderson, is an attorney and often says litigation is always unpredictable, expensive, and has unintended and unforeseen consequences. I'll leave the real estate brokerage litigation there, but I do sense the impact will be far-reaching.

Convenience Versus Price

Do customers care about convenience and accept the higher price? Why do consumers pay for Starbucks and bottled water? Convenience and perceived quality. Regulators have not yet fully realized that consumers not only have more choices but also now have access to more information—in other words, most consumers are an order of magnitude more educated and served by more buying options than when RESPA was written. And yet, we are still stuck with RESPA, and likely will be for the foreseeable future.

If we are stuck with RESPA and similar regulations, then fintech will redesign the fact pattern so that some elements of the current regulatory regime are effectively minimized. In real estate, you can observe the adaption of builders to how builders sell homes. The builder owns the asset and offers a discount to use the builder's mortgage and title affiliates. Other facets of the real estate ecosphere have undervalued owning the asset (the home) because they are brokers, not principals. In my opinion, the iBuyers understand the power of owning the assets as a key to providing a one-stop shop for homebuyers.

---

215 https://www.nar.realtor/newsroom/national-association-of-realtors-moves-to-dismiss-moehrl-suit-shows-lawsuit-is-based-on-rule

Disruptive Scenarios

Earlier in the book, the difficulty of forecasting future *events* was covered in detail. The outcome of that discussion was that the use of scenarios to forecast the future *effects* could provide useful insights into the future. As my friend George Brubaker used to say, "How can we profit from this?" My hope is that these scenarios help readers anticipate how they can position themselves and their companies to profit from the impact of the coming wave of fintech innovation.

iBuyers and Technology Increase Liquidity and Reduce Transaction Costs

Treating a house as a fungible asset to be held as inventory changes everything. Builders have mastered this concept, as they are a manufacturer of housing and the house is the final product. Investment buyers form an additional group similar to builders in taking possession of residential real estate, either to own as an investment or to "flip" it short-term for profit. Therefore, iBuyers might be considered both instant buyers as well as institutional investors.

iBuyers have grasped how providing liquidity, speed, flexibility, and convenience can appeal to potential home sellers. iBuyers can use valuation technology to find undervalued assets to purchase, upgrade, and re-sell.

Institutional investors in residential single-family real estate have the same advantage. Invitation Homes, for instance, could move its business model into acquiring, renting, managing, and selling single-family homes as a one-stop shop.

According to Shawn Tully writing in *Fortune* magazine on June 21, 2019, "over the past seven years, [institutional] investors have amassed a substantial portfolio— some 300,000 houses in all. The biggest players include Invitation Homes, a REIT that's the product of a merger of rental divisions of several investment firms, including Blackstone [Invitation Homes], Starwood Capital, and Colony Capital; American Homes 4 Rent; and Amherst. All these landlords use automated house-hunting to fuel their growth."[216]

Artificial intelligence (AI) will augment iBuyers' ability to identify, price, rehabilitate, and either flip or hold residential real estate for short- or long-term investment. For example, Amherst describes its residential real estate investment activities as follows:

> Amherst Residential manages multiple pools of capital that invest in single family rental homes. Since the platform was created in 2012, it has raised more than $4 billion of debt and equity capital in support of its acquisition, stabilization and portfolio sale activities."[217]

---

216 https://fortune.com/longform/single-family-home-ai-algorithms/
217 https://www.amherst.com/our-business/single-family-equity/

To manage its portfolio of single-family homes and support its development and sale activities, Amherst founded Main Street Renewal, an internally managed, vertically integrated property acquisition, repair and management business. The U.S. housing market is undergoing a shift away from ownership toward single-family home leasing. The underlying fundamentals show that this trend will continue, creating a significant opportunity for investors. The single-family leasing market has historically been fragmented with little scale or institutional management. Based on an extensive history of analytical research, Amherst actively participates in the Single-Family Equity sector.[218]

Amherst uses AI to provide a "deep understanding and proprietary analytics on single-family home and mortgage markets, a scalable, high-volume acquisition capability that leverages multiple purchase channels and a unique combination of national scale with local market knowledge and execution."[219]

AI's adoption rate in residential real estate is increasing. According to James Julius, Founder and Managing Partner AI of an analytics company Visimo:

Real estate disintermediation will be powered by immense amount of public data available. This data can be used to develop an online learning model. AI, when fully utilized, is more than a 'Netflix suggestion engine' type of way to improve the intelligence in your experience. It can learn from itself and provide better feedback based upon the outcomes that are being collected.

One can look at another industry—healthcare—to see the possibilities of AI exploitation. Healthcare is an industry that is flushed with data and is beginning to exploit its full potential. A huge opportunity arises from leveraging existing data from wearables—things like Apple Watch, FitBit, and others—and including personal consumer data alongside of provider data to be able to deliver an improved overall patient experience. The advancement of adjacent technologies has opened the door for AI to be leveraged in a better way. Technical, pharmaceutical, and overall medical advancements—alongside AI's advancements—have allowed this industry to really benefit from using AI.

Residential real estate is ripe for AI exploitation. The cost trend of accessing AI is nonlinear and disproportionally negative over the past couple of years. Previously, access to AI was limited to large organizations or academic institutions. Future trends suggest the data collection costs are relatively inexpensive and both quantity and quality of software packages are improving.

Steve Butler, General Manager of AI Foundry, a business unit of Kodak Alaris stated:

AI Foundry creates software solutions that makes data "'actionable," by automating and streamlining enterprise business operations. The technology applies visual cognitive document automation, AI and deep learning in the residential lending space. It is important to automate manual, labor-intensive mortgage processes through AI to replace multi-week manual processes to speed up mortgage approval.

---

218 https://www.amherst.com/our-business/single-family-equity/
219 https://www.amherst.com/our-business/single-family-equity/

There are many ways an AI platform can increase efficiency in mortgage lending. AI can intake document images, identify and classify those images, and then extract data from electronic images and documents with superior accuracy and minimal manual intervention. This can streamline or eliminate manual processes.

AI can deploy Intelligent robots to automate manual processes. Machine learning can automate more complex processes. All of this permits employees to spend more time helping build the relationship with customers.

As opposed to static automation technology of the past, AI enables machines to learn. With mortgage lending, the technology is capable of learning, and is able to create validation rules and identify data anomalies. It is even possible that the process is capable of making decisions.

iBuyers will deploy AI throughout the market analysis, collateral analysis, and demographic data to quickly and efficiently speed execution of real estate transactions. These factors will reduce transaction costs, provide liquidity, and increase visibility to everyone in the residential real estate market. This includes individual homebuyers and sellers, intermediaries, lenders, and service providers.

This time of transition puts me in mind of the Manhattan skyline. Sometime in the 2000s, large glass structures started going up in Chelsea. Eventually, they spread, even popping up in Brooklyn. Old school New York took umbrage. What were these glass structures (primarily residential units) and who would want to live there? Why did they need to stand out so defiantly against the traditional New York skyline of brick and stone? Disruption never feels natural at first, but eventually it convinces even the most stalwart traditionalist. Let's take a moment to see how disruption is already playing out on the other side of the country in the Southwest.

The fintech impact is playing out quickly in Phoenix. According to Redfin, in a report written by Dana Olson,

> Institutional or instant buyers, known as iBuyers, are taking up a growing share of Phoenix home sales. iBuyers are companies—like RedfinNow, Zillow and Opendoor—that make instant cash offers to home sellers and close within days without any listings or showings, with the intent to re-sell for a profit.
>
> In Phoenix, iBuyers purchased an estimated 6.9 percent of homes that sold in December 2018, according to a Redfin analysis of public records. That's up from 4.2 percent in December 2017 and it makes Phoenix home to the largest iBuyer market share of any metro area in the U.S.
>
> Overall, iBuyers had an estimated 4.8 percent market share in Phoenix last year, versus 2.7 percent in Dallas and 2.2 percent in Atlanta, two other markets that have been popular with iBuyers.[220]

Figure 10.1[221] illustrates the growth in the iBuyer market share in Phoenix.

---

220 https://www.redfin.com/blog/ibuyer-impact-phoenix-housing-market/
221 https://www.redfin.com/blog/ibuyer-impact-phoenix-housing-market/

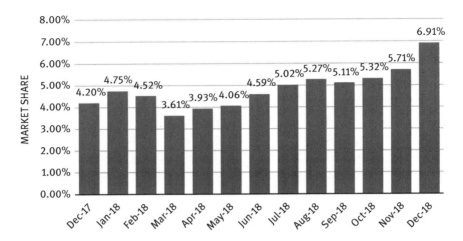

Figure 10.1: Growth of the iBuyer market share in Phoenix.

The factors driving iBuying in Phoenix include rapid growth in real estate sales, the availability of a large, mid-tier price range segment built in the last 15 years, comparatively low real estate taxes, and a reasonable price per square foot value proposition. Think of the home characteristics that attract an Invitation Homes investment. I call this segment the "shelter" segment, meaning that the home is primarily for a family to live in a safe, convenient neighborhood. "Shelter" describes the Phoenix iBuying subject properties.

This price segment is very affordable from a down payment standpoint, and the availability of new housing developments makes pricing relatively transparent. The relatively recent construction provides for cosmetic repairs for the iBuyer, as opposed to major repairs of much older homes. The value proposition may be attributable to the collapse of Phoenix home prices during the sub-prime mortgage crisis.

iBuyers typically do not seek properties in very high-priced or tight real estate markets such as the Bay Area, nor do iBuyers typically seek vacation homes or multi-unit properties. iBuyers seek shelter real estate that has a broad appeal to families.

The iBuyer phenomenon is laying the groundwork for a car-like buying experience. The iBuyer as a property owner can better couple one-stop shop products such as mortgage, title, and insurance.

In short, the effect of iBuyers as principals will be to increase adoption of technology, put downward pressure on transaction costs, and drive all market participants more quickly to the one-stop shopping experience. The iBuyers experience is best in larger markets where housing is homogenized, and automated valuation models can yield fairly precise market value estimates. My experience bears this out, as my home in Pennsylvania is in a homogenized market and the automated valuation models appear to be accurate. My home on the water in Florida is more unique, and the automated valuation models appear to be much less accurate.

The value appears to be impacted by homes not on the water, and thus my home appears to be undervalued.

My belief is that many of the individual elements in the residential real estate market will transform into a true one-stop shopping experience, similar to car buying. Homes will become inventory held for resale by iBuyers and investors. Hedge funds provide the financing for the iBuyers. Transaction speed and certainty increases. A one-stop shop is achieved, with much activity happening how and when the consumer chooses, from self-serve to fully relationship-oriented, and everything in between. The many discrete steps and parties involved within real estate brokerage, mortgage, appraisal, inspections, title insurance, and hazard insurance will merge into a more seamless transaction. Some elements, such as appraisals, will be replaced with technology. The human elements of advice, empathy, and relationships will not.

The opportunity for profit is to identify where in the value chain one fits and aggressively drive transaction costs down, while simultaneously finding ways to increase relationship and engagement with homebuyers.

The Cost of Shelter Will Shape Public Policy

The effects of this scenario are borne out by the colloquial saying that, "Real estate values depend on location, location, and location" is becoming more pronounced. This is borne out by the wide disparity in shelter (mortgage or rent payment) costs in different areas of the country. The disparity in the cost of shelter, in my opinion, is at the heart of the discussion on income inequality. Disparity in shelter costs has the potential to re-shape the population demographics of major metro centers as well as low-cost states. Shelter costs include mortgage payments to own a home as well as rental payments for rental housing.

You may recall Figure 10.2, which was previously discussed in Chapter 6. It's worth revisiting in the context of the cost of shelter as it relates to population and demographics. Figure 10.1 illustrates that the percentage of median family income expended on owning a home in various locales. In Detroit, about 15% of median family income is spent on mortgage payments, when the family puts 3.5% as a down payment. In San Francisco, it's 78%.

It's even more dramatic when you consider that Detroit's estimated median family income in 2018 was $55,500 versus San Francisco's $116,400.[222] Said another way, a family with median income in Detroit family would spend about $8,500 - per year on mortgage payments. In San Francisco, a family with median income would spend about ten times that—almost $80,000 per year on mortgage payments due to the much higher cost of housing in San Francisco. That explains the high

---

222 https://www.ffiec.gov/Medianincome.htm

percentage of renters in San Francisco, and the out-migration of population from the San Francisco environs.[223]

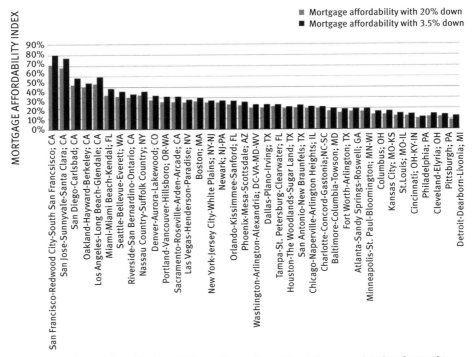

Source: National Association of Realtors, US Census Bureau, Current Population survey, American Community Survey, Moody's Analytics, Freddie Mac Primary Mortgage Market Survey, and the Urban Institute.
Note mortgage affordability is the share of media family income devoted to the monthly principal, interest, taxes, and insurance payment required to buy the median home at the Freddie Mac prevailing rate 2018 for a 30-year-fixed-rate mortgage and property tax and insurance 1.75 percent of the housing value.
Data for the bottom chart as of Q3 2018.

Figure 10.2: Mortgage affordability by metropolitan statistical area.

Figure 10.2 shows mortgage affordability in the form of the percentage of median family income that is required for the mortgage payment on a home at the median price for the respective locale. The higher the percentage, the less affordable the locale.

State and local income tax disparities and "millionaire taxes" can affect the migration of high earners. The federal income tax limitations on state and local tax deductions may be one of the matches that lights significant migration away from high-cost locales. As of this writing, there are 6 locations that have adopted millionaire taxes: California, Connecticut, Maine, New Jersey, New York, and Washington, D.C.

223 https://www.sfgate.com/expensive-san-francisco/article/bay-area-exodus-fleeing-moving-cost-census-13778557.php

"The millionaire tax is designed to 'catch' the higher earners that the legislatures feel are not paying their fair share," said Tim Gagnon, a certified public accountant who teaches at Boston's Northeastern University. "Most millionaires receive much of their income from investments, which do not always get assessed the additional rates and surcharges."[224] Many high earners are mobile and can simply move their legal residence to lower tax locales.

Want a 4% increase in take home pay? Move your residence or place of employment out of the Philadelphia area. According the Philadelphia Inquirer, Philadelphia has the highest city wage tax in the country at 3.89% of gross wages.[225] That may explain the growth of the Philadelphia suburbs.

Across the Delaware River, New Jersey lost a significant portion of taxable income in December 2015 when hedge fund billionaire David Tepper left New Jersey for warmer climes. According to Robert Frank writing in the *New York Times*, "Mr. Tepper declared himself a resident of Florida after living for over 20 years in New Jersey. He later moved the official headquarters of his hedge fund, Appaloosa Management, to Miami. New Jersey won't say exactly how much Mr. Tepper paid in taxes. But according to Institutional Investor's Alpha, he earned more than $6 billion from 2012 to 2015. Tax experts say his move to Florida could cost New Jersey—which has a top tax rate of 8.97 percent—hundreds of millions of dollars in lost payments."[226]

Expect the issues of affordable housing and income inequality to come to the forefront in the residential real estate marketplace. Be aware of both opportunities to help resolve the issues as well as incidences of exposure to reputational and financial risks in an industry that at times has been a favorite target of regulators and legislators.

The Need for Exceptional Human Talent

Billy Beane of the Oakland A's pioneered a methodology to identify and develop undervalued assets. The ability to sign a baseball player that may not "look like a baseball player" but appears to be an undervalued asset has propelled the A's to exceptional performance in the "cost per win" metric.

How will the residential real estate industry find talent to transform the industry profitably? Since many customer-facing real estate industry employees, brokers, and agents are licensed by a state, one scenario revolves around the need to retool the skills of a large number of licensed participants already in the residential real estate market.

---

224 https://turbotax.intuit.com/tax-tips/state-taxes/state-tax-tips-for-millionaires/L15HLnPCB
225 https://www.inquirer.com/news/wage-tax-rate-philadelphia-business-jobs-reduction-reform-20190515.html
226 https://www.nytimes.com/2016/05/01/business/one-top-taxpayer-moved-and-new-jersey-shuddered.html

There is an acute need for exceptional talent in the residential real estate space. The size and scope of the $1.6 trillion market for homes to be sold annually, as well as the $160 billion in fees related to the home sale activity will draw competitors, whether fintech or iBuyers or other innovators.

The traditional roles of realtors, loan officers, title agents, loan processors, and mortgage underwriters will be significantly transformed. It may occur more slowly due to state licensure requirements that form a barrier to entry.

Inertia of the federally imposed 90% market share of federal mortgage guarantors will be transformed by new private-capital market players and a reduced role of the federal mortgage finance behemoths. Such change will be powered by fintech entrepreneurs, engineers, and data scientists.

Many current industry participants will have to engage in ongoing education and skills development. Randall Stephenson, Chairman & CEO AT&T is quoted in the *New York Times*: "'There is a need to retool yourself, and you should not expect to stop,' he said in a recent interview at AT&T's Dallas headquarters. People who do not spend five to 10 hours a week in online learning, he added, 'will obsolete themselves with the technology.'"[227] Simply put, it will be difficult for many well-paid employees who perform intermediation activities such as brokerage services, or manual data analysis activities such as appraisers, loan processors, or loan underwriters. This effect is evident in other industries where technology has replaced human talent, including supply chain and logistics managers in warehouse locations.

Joseph Schumpeter's creative destruction will be at work. Resistance, as they say, will be futile. The internal combustion engine displaced the farriers, blacksmiths, and teamster horse drivers of the 19th-century equestrian transportation system. Many blacksmiths transitioned to ironworkers, building skyscrapers and subway infrastructure. Teamsters moved from driving horses to driving trucks. But the residential real estate industries have many highly paid personnel for whom the transition into a fintech-driven economy will be more difficult. It's not easy to transition from a realtor or commissioned loan officer into a data scientist. Expect the fight to be bloody. Litigation by incumbent companies attempting to protect their favorable boundaries may be common. Businesses trying to make an old model work risk irrelevance and failure.

The biggest fight will be for talent. According to PwC, the demand for data scientists and analytics personnel will outstrip available talent in 2021 by a factor of 2 to 1.[228] Hiring from competitors will be an expensive proposition. Establishing a pipeline

---

227 https://www.nytimes.com/2016/02/14/technology/gearing-up-for-the-cloud-att-tells-its-workers -adapt-or-else.html

228 Gallup and BHEF, Data Science and Analytics Higher Education Survey (December 2016) in Investing in America's Data Science and Analytics Talent, 2017, BHEF and PwC.

direct from education is another strategy. Retraining and upskilling existing employees will play a large role.

Also playing a large role is tapping into a broader pool of talent through diversity and inclusion initiatives. This is necessary because it's good business. The Mortgage Bankers Association has long played a role in developing talent over the past 20 years through its "Emerging Leaders" program.

More recently, the Mortgage Bankers Association launched a new networking platform for women in the real estate-finance industry, mPower, which stands for "MBA Promoting Opportunities for Women to Extend their Reach." According to Marcia Davies, Chief Operating Officer at the Mortgage Bankers Association:

> mPower was initially informal in nature. It became clear that there was tremendous interest in expanding the talent pool for women. We struck a nerve in the lending community to help identify and nurture female talent. mPower is designed to recognize and promote the rise of women in the real estate finance industry, as well as the overall workforce.

> You really need to take care of people that are working hard to help you advance company objectives. It's your job to make sure that you treat them well and you listen to them and you help meet their needs. As I rose into leadership, sadly my father died very young so he wasn't there for me to get his advice. But I'll never forget that adage to treat people the way you want to be treated. A lot of times you show up with empathy seeking to understand somebody else's point of view. Even when I'm frustrated because you never know what may have happened that morning. And you never know what's going on with someone else.

> Relationships and empathy are a priority and a key strategic plank. People show respect to one another. Diversity would be considered as something that's required in order to get to the best result. And we would really listen and factor in the contributions of the whole team by developing trust and relationship.

> Respect in the workplace translates to growth and development of people. And I mean both women and men. The industry has to develop skilled leaders and to empower these leaders to help change our industry for the better.

One of the treats I had while writing this book was to interview a multigenerational management team and to discuss how younger talent is developed in the industry. That team was Chris George, CEO of CMG Financial, and his son A.J. George, Chief Administrative Officer of CMG Financial. A.J.'s insights into his own development were instructive:

> When I was younger, I thought it'd be really cool to go to work with my dad every day because he seems to really dig whatever it is that he does. [Once I entered the business], I found a need to always a need to respect everybody's position, and we're not always going to agree on everything. My father inspires us to be good businesspeople. But he really inspires us on how to really, truly make a difference. Here's how to do the right thing, but do it creatively. Here's a way to proceed so you're proud to tell your brothers how you'd do something. Should I have kids one day, to be proud of how to say here's how I handled something.

Kristy Fercho, Executive Vice President and President of Mortgage at Flagstar Bank is an influential woman in the mortgage industry. Kristy is the only female African American president of a major mortgage company in the United States and has an important perspective for expanding and sustaining home ownership. In a discussion at the 2019 MBA Chairman's Conference, and a follow-up conversation, Kristy shared her views:

> By 2025, there will be 17 million new first-time homebuyers. 14 million of those buyers will be people of color, who may be lacking trust in the traditional mortgage or real estate professional. Having people that look like and understand the values of people of color builds trust.

It's important that the industry prepares for the 14 million new people of color as potential homebuyers. It is a huge opportunity that requires employing, training, and licensing new employees to serve that market.

Building trust through diversity and inclusion is important. Kristy relayed a story about an uncomfortable moment, a moment that will become rarer through diversity and inclusion efforts:

> I was being interviewed with several other CEOs at an event. I was the only African American in the group. On the stage I commented that I was the only African American female to lead a mortgage company. The interviewer stumbled, unsure as to whether it was okay for him to call me Black or African American. It's okay to call me what I am. The cameraman helped out and said, "Hey, she knows she's Black." That broke an awkward moment, and provided some levity. More importantly, diversity and inclusion require that you to see people for who they are, not as a label.

Trust can also be broken easily, Kristy noted:

> In the late 1990s, an executive of an acquired company told a terribly offensive "joke" during a company meeting of 200 employees [of various ethnicities] of the acquired and existing companies. Trust among the employees of the two companies was under stress as a result of the "joke."

> Shortly after the meeting, the executive that told the "joke" was fired. The CEO of the overall company sent a personnel letter of apology to each of the attendees. The quick action spoke volumes. Trust and respect weren't words on a piece of paper, they were core values that were required.

Building an effective and diverse team requires work and intentional effort:

> You need grace, and to be open to authentic dialogue. You can discuss differences in perspective and experience. It's okay to say, "This is how an action or comment made me feel." Ninety-nine percent of the time, people did not mean to offend. Grace in your dialog goes a long way in building a relationship.

Kristy's effectiveness as an executive and role model will be more publicly displayed. The Mortgage Bankers Association nominated Kristy as MBA's Vice Chairman for the

2020 membership year.[229] If past is prologue, Kristy will serve as MBA's Chairman in 2021.

So, whether it's mPower, CMG, or your own business, mentoring and developing talent will be a required competency as the wave of fintech washes over our industry. The talent need will be acute, and strategies to attract, upscale, and retain talent will be "table stakes" within the industry.

Convergence, Logistics, and the New Skyline

There are hundreds of fintech-powered services employing convergence and logistics tools to put pressure on the traditional real estate brokerage, mortgage lending, appraisal, title insurance, and related services. Not all will be successful, but all are populating the skyline with more and different ways for consumers to approach real estate ownership.

The power of successful convergence and logistics cannot be underestimated. Does anyone recall the Netscape Netbusiness Marketplace? According to a Time Warner AOL March 28, 2001 Press Release, the Marketplace was to be a one-stop, global e-commerce community of hundreds of thousands of businesses. Many competitors envisioned this goal, but only Amazon got there. A summary of the press release is in a footnote.[230]

As you think about fintech innovation, consider that fintechs are usually either a convergence or logistics play. In some scenarios, they are both. With so many fintechs innovating in different ways, it is certain that the traditional value proposition of 12% to 13% fees to consummate a real estate transaction will fall. The industry will consolidate any individual steps currently used in a residential real estate

---

229 https://www.mba.org/2019-press-releases/july/kristy-fercho-of-flagstar-bank-nominated-to-be-2020-mba-vice-chairman

230 America Online, Inc. and PurchasePro (Nasdaq: PPRO), a leading enabler of business-to-business, e-commerce solutions for companies of all sizes, today announced ten new strategic agreements, including deals with Hewlett-Packard Company, Homestore.com and Spherion Corporation, to accelerate their B2B and e-commerce efforts, and jointly-develop the Netscape Netbusiness Marketplace. The Netbusiness Marketplace is a one-stop, global e-commerce network of hundreds of communities and marketplaces that allow small, medium and large businesses to buy, sell and interact online. AOL and PurchasePro also announced a joint sales, marketing and product development operation in support of the Marketplace. The joint sales team will include both the PurchasePro sales force and the AOL Interactive Marketing Group. Leveraging PurchasePro's industry-leading e-commerce technology, and AOL's expertise in developing user-friendly services, tools and technology to support commerce online, the Netbusiness Marketplace provides business users with advanced features in a familiar and convenient environment. Moreover, the initiative builds on PurchasePro's extensive network of private-label marketplaces that encompass more than 140,000 businesses—all of which will be connected to the Netbusiness Marketplace.

transaction. Whether the transaction becomes an instant one-stop shop remains to be seen, but the trip will be substantially shorter.

The rapid evolution of Amazon illustrates what is possible, where convergence and logistics effect rapid change to the landscape of products and services. Moving back to the Manhattan skyline, it's been remarkable to see how the city has evolved its attitude and perceptions. In the years since the first glass Chelsea tower went up, old school New York has adjusted. While once jarring, the glass buildings now seem to be setting the tone for a new New York, one of transparency and clarity. The glass skyline on the West Side now seems to be an augur of the future, a bright one—disruption can ultimately be viewed as a clarifier. My hope is that this is a lesson many industries will embody in the coming years through fintech, transforming our economy once again and offering consumers a more transparent experience.

Appendix 1 The Mavericks

AJ George

Mr. George is the Chief Administrative Officer for CMG Financial, a privately-held mortgage banking firm. Mr. George began his career in 2005 with CMG Financial, where he gained a comprehensive lending background with abundant experience in correspondent, wholesale, and retail lending. He was instrumental in the creation, development, and growth of CMG's correspondent lending channel and led it to becoming the largest channel within the company and the sixth largest correspondent lender nationwide in 2018, per Scotsman Guide. Mr. George has shaped many fundamental principles of the organization that CMG Financial is today, building his career on the idea that "hard work works."

Barrett Burns

Mr. Burns serves as the President and Chief Executive Officer of VantageScore Solutions, LLC. Over the years of serving in the industry, he developed extensive experience in banking and finance that allowed him to hold executive positions in a variety of companies. He serves as a board member for numerous industry associations, including the Mortgage Bankers Association, the Structured Finance Industry Group Executive Committee, America's Homeowner Alliance, the Corporate Board of Governors for the National Association of Hispanic Real Estate Professionals, and the Asian Real Estate Association of America's National Advisory Council.

Bill Emerson

Mr. Emerson serves as the Vice Chairman of Rock Holdings Inc., the parent company of Quicken Loans, the nation's second-largest mortgage lender. Bill joined Quicken Loans in 1993 and served with passion and commitment to helping customers. The strong leadership skills led Quicken Loans to become the largest retail mortgage lender and closed nearly $300 billion in home loan volume across all 50 states since 2013. Bill is a member of the Board of Directors of Xenith, Inc., the Detroit Economic Club, the Parade Company, and the Skillman Foundation.

Brent Chandler

Mr. Chandler is founder and CEO of FormFree. He is a widely recognized innovator in mortgage and financial services technologies and has 25 years' experience on the leading edge of trading, personal finance, wealth management, and consumer financial services. Chandler created AccountChek® by FormFree® in 2007 after his own frustrating home-buying experience fueled an obsession with making loans simpler and safer for everyone. Prior to that, he was part of the team that created the world's first online trade while at CheckFree (acquired by Fiserv). He's also held senior-level

https://doi.org/10.1515/9783110650471-012

positions on Wall Street at Merrill Lynch and Fidelity. Chandler serves on the advisory board of Jawdrop, is a member of FourAthens Tech Incubator, and is an active mentor for Georgia's Terry College of Business Entrepreneurship Program.

Chris George

Mr. George is the Founder, President, and CEO of CMG Financial, a privately held mortgage banking firm. Mr. George has over 35 years of experience in the mortgage industry. He has spent three and a half decades cultivating an organization capable of sustaining and thriving through cyclical market fluctuations. The company operates in all 50 states and the District of Columbia and holds federal agency lending approvals with HUD, VA, RHS, GNMA, Fannie Mae, and Freddie Mac. Mr. George has held many advocacy positions within the industry, including the Chairman of the Mortgage Bankers Association (MBA), a member of the MBA's Board of Directors, past Chairman for California Mortgage Bankers Association (CMBA), a member of the CMBA's Board of Directors, and other advisory boards and task forces within the industry. In 2011, Mr. George created the CMG Foundation to support nonprofit organizations through ongoing fundraising efforts. To date, the CMG Foundation has raised over $3 million for its beneficiaries including the Gary Sinise Foundation, the Cancer Support Community, and the MBA Opens Doors Foundation.

Chrissi Rhea

Ms. Rhea is the President and CEO of Mortgage Investors Group. She has over 35 years of experience in the mortgage banking industry. Ms. Rhea is a member of the Mortgage Bankers Association IMB and sits on the board of directors for the Tennessee Housing Development Agency. She started her career in the mortgage industry as a loan officer in the early 1980s. Nine years later, Ms. Rhea and co-founder Chuck Tonkin started Mortgage Investors Group and turned a company with five colleagues to a company with 400 employees in 26 branch locations. MIG is known as a leading provider of single-family residential mortgages in the Southeast.

Dave Stevens

Mr. Stevens is a former Chief Executive of the Mortgage Bankers Association (MBA) and is currently a mortgage policy consultant. Mr. Stevens served as the Chief Executive Officer and President of the MBA from June 2011 through August 2018. He has a well-rounded background from working with Long & Foster Real Estate, Inc. in the role of Senior Vice President, then as the President and Chief Operating Officer. In addition, he served as the Senior Vice President of Mortgage Sourcing and Single-Family Lending at Freddie Mac. He sits on the Board of Directors for the National Association of Mortgage Brokers (NAMB) and on the lender's advisory council for the Mortgage Bankers Association. He was the founding executive sponsor of the

Woman's Mortgage Industry Network and coordinated the first Latino initiative joint venture with Freddie Mac and Latino mortgage industry leaders.

David Motley

Mr. Motley, a Certified Mortgage Banker, has been working with Colonial Savings for more than 15 years. He has been the Executive Vice President and moved his way up to serve as the President of Banking and Mortgage Operations at Colonial Savings, F.A. in May 2006. Mr. Motley has more than 25 years of mortgage production management experience. David serves on the board of the Texas Mortgage Bankers Association as the Secretary/Treasurer.

Deb Still

Ms. Still is the Chief Executive Officer and President of Pulte Mortgage LLC. She has been serving the mortgage industry for more than four decades. Her background has allowed her to take many roles in Pulte Mortgage LLC. She was an Executive Vice President of Loan Production; Corporate Secretary, and Chief Operating Officer and is a member of the Board of Directors. Ms. Still served as Chairman of the Residential Board of Governors at Mortgage Bankers Association and was the Chairman of the Mortgage Bankers Association in 2013. She is currently is a member of the MBA's Board of Directors and the Chairman of MBA's Opens Doors Foundation.

Don Salmon

Mr. Salmon is the retired President and CEO of TBI Mortgage Company. TBIM is a wholly owned subsidiary of Toll Brothers, Inc., a publicly traded homebuilder based in Horsham, PA. Don began his mortgage banking career in 1977 as a loan officer and has served in various management and executive positions since 1981. Mr. Salmon was founder and CEO of Phoenix Mortgage Co., in Fort Washington, PA.

Eddy Perez

Mr. Perez has over ten years' experience in the mortgage banking industry as a top-producing loan officer, sales/branch manager, and executive. Prior to his career at Equity Prime Mortgage, LLC, he operated the top producing branch at Global Mortgage, Inc. Eddy holds a B.B.A. degree in Finance with a concentration in Mortgage Lending from Georgia State University.

Grant Moon

Grant Moon is the Founder and CEO of Home Captain, a real estate technology company that provides tools, services, and data that lenders need in a competitive and ever-changing digital world. Within its suite of products and services, Home

Captain boasts a one-stop-shop with web and mobile MLS integrated home search app, an AI-powered chatbot for re-engaging mortgage leads, world-class real estate concierge services, lender centers, and Realtor® match technology. These services result in Home Captain borrowers purchasing homes two weeks quicker than the national average, partners increasing purchase conversions by up to 10x and lender portfolio recapture rates of 43.5% of clients who sell and simultaneously purchase a home. Grant is also a Major in the US Army Reserves who had dedicated himself to assisting home buyers in navigating the realty transaction by providing education centers, multiple books, lender rate tables, and concierge services that streamline the process.

Jay Plum

Mr. Plum is Executive Vice President of home lending and card products for Huntington Bank, a Columbus, Ohio-based regional bank. Mr. Plum is a 30-year veteran of the lending industry. Under Jay's leadership, Huntington has become the top mortgage lender in Ohio and the third largest in its eight-state region across the Midwest. The bank is currently ranked eighth nationally for home equity and has been honored by J.D. Power for customer satisfaction. Before Huntington, Jay was president of Home Lending Solutions at RBS Citizens. Focusing on credit and customer service, his team originated more than $10 billion in total loans in 2009 during his final year at the bank.

Jerry Schiano

Mr. Schiano is the Chief Executive Officer with over 25 years of entrepreneurial experience in the mortgage industry, including founding and leading multiple lending organizations. Mr. Schiano founded (1999) and served as CEO of Wilmington Finance Inc., which grew into a top-15 originator of non-agency residential loans. Mr. Schiano sold Wilmington Finance to American General Finance, in 2002 and continued to manage the company through 2006. Mr. Schiano went on to found New Penn Financial in 2008. New Penn was sold to Shellpoint partners and in the second quarter of this year Shellpoint and New Penn announced that they would be sold to NRZ. Currently, Mr. Schiano is founder of a new venture focused on direct-to-consumer home equity originations, Spring EQ.

John Hedlund

Mr. Hedlund is the Chief Operating Officer and Managing Director for AmeriHome Mortgage and one of the original founders (2013). He has led the Correspondent Lending business from inception, now the third largest nationally. He oversees and has responsibility for all areas of the business including sales, business development and marketing, loan quality, operations, compliance and underwriting. Mr. Hedlund is an experienced C-level business executive, specializing in the strategic design, execution, and leadership of large, diverse financial services organizations. He has successfully led numerous businesses through major transformational change over the past 30 years, displaying a unique ability to drive sustainable revenue growth and productivity improvements through innovation and continuous improvement while fostering a loyal and cohesive leadership team. Prior to Amerihome, Mr. Hedlund held executive positions with Bank of America, Countrywide, New Century and RBC Mortgage.

Jonathan Corr

Mr. Corr serves as the Chief Executive Officer and President of Ellie Mae. Before he became CEO and President, Jonathan served as the Chief Strategy Officer and Executive Vice President of Business Development and Product Strategy for Ellie Mae. He is recognized for his mortgage industry expertise and technology knowledge and has served in management positions for PeopleSoft, Inc., Netscape Communications Corporation, and Kana/Broadbase Software/Ruberic.

Kristy Fercho

Kristy Fercho serves as Executive Vice President, President of Mortgage at Flagstar Bank. She joined Flagstar Bank in 2017 after 15 years with Fannie Mae, where she served as Senior Vice President, Customer Delivery Executive, responsible for the strategy and business performance of all single-family customers in the western United States. Prior to Fannie Mae, she worked for PepsiCo and Baxter Healthcare.

Fercho has a bachelor's degree in finance from the University of Southern California, and a Master of Business Administration from the Erivan K. Haub School of Business at Saint Joseph's University in Philadelphia.

Lori Brewer

Ms. Brewer is the Founder and President of LBA Ware, she is an accomplished entrepreneur and technology leader. Ms. Brewer has over 20 years of experience in the mortgage industry. She entered after serving as a captain and information systems manager in the US Air Force, and manifested her forward-thinking vision through the development of more than 25 lending applications. Today, LBA Ware is a Certified Women's Business Enterprise. She has served as the technology chair on the Stratford Academy board of trustees and as a board advisor to the Middle Georgia State College School of Information Technology.

Marcia Davies

Ms. Davies is the Chief Operating Officer of the Mortgage Bankers Association. She ensures cross-organizational alignment and facilitating the implementation of strategic initiatives, as well as maintaining oversight of organizational priorities for the MBA. She is the lead strategist for MBA's external activities, providing leadership, guidance and overall management to the public affairs and marketing divisions. In addition, Marcia provides strategic direction and management of MBA's Conferences, Membership, Education, Information Technology and Office Services divisions. She is also a Board member of MBA's Opens Doors Foundation. Marcia is the founder of mPower—MBA Promoting Opportunities for Women to Extend their Reach—MBA's networking platform for women in the real estate finance industry. Under her leadership, mPower has grown into an engaged community of more than 4,000, providing best-in-class conference and webinar programming, networking events, and online opportunities to stay engaged.

Marie Gayo

Ms. Gayo is the President of Trident Mortgage Company. She manages both sales and operation. She has over 20 years of experience in the mortgage and investment banking industry. Marie joined the company in 2009 and was formerly responsible for managing operations for Trident Mortgage Company. Marie possesses an extensive leadership background in operations, risk management, and administration, and has demonstrated success in the areas of strategy execution and business process improvement. She is a certified Six Sigma Black Belt and past member of the American Society for Quality and Project Management Institute.

Mary Ann McGarry

Ms. McGarry is the President and Chief Executive Officer of Guild Mortgage. Under her leadership, Guild has grown from its base in the West to become one of the top lenders in the nation by putting customers first, offering loan options to meet the needs of any homebuyer and working to strengthen communities through the Guild Giving program. Ms. McGarry began her career with Guild in 1984 as a supervisor in internal audit. She held positions as chief financial officer, chief production operations officer and chief operating officer, before being promoted to president in 2005 and CEO in 2007. Ms. McGarry has been the driving force in the development and execution of Guild's strategic growth plans and objectives. As a result, the company is now one of the largest independent mortgage lenders in the U.S., with close to 4,000 employees and 205 retail branches in 33 states. She currently serves on the investment committee and the servicing committee of the Mortgage Bankers Association, as well as on the Fannie Mae advisory council.

Matt Hansen

Mr. Hansen is the founder and CEO of SimpleNexus. Matt's introduction to mortgage came by fulfilling a family favor. Matt's brother-in-law asked him to develop an app to reduce phone calls from borrowers. Within weeks, more originators wanted the product and Matt began to add more features. Since founding SimpleNexus in 2011, Matt has grown the company from a handful of associates into a thriving business, employing more than 100 people. Matt is continually moving the company forward, not innovating for innovation's sake, but creating solutions that are changing the way the mortgage industry does business—for the better.

Maylin Casanueva

Ms. Casanueva is Teraverde's Chief Operating Officer and is responsible for client service delivery, growth, profitability, and overall business operations. Ms. Casanueva has 25 years of Capital Markets, Mortgage Securitization, and Mortgage Banking experience. She also leads the Coheus Enterprise Solutions, which leverages data for powerful insights into profitability and areas of opportunities for organizations. Ms. Casanueva has been recognized as Housing Wire's 2019 Women of Influence and Progress in Lending Association's The Most Powerful Women in FinTech.

Nima Ghamsari

Mr. Ghamsari serves as Chief Executive and Co-founder of Blend, a Silicon Valley Technology company empowering lender to originate efficiently and keeping user-friendly surface. Prior to his position at Blend, Nima was a business development engineer and worked as an advisor for the CEO at Palantir Technologies.

Patrick Sinks

Mr. Sinks has been President, Chief Executive Officer, and Director of MGIC Investment Corporation and its principal subsidiary MGIC since 2015. Prior to that, he held a variety of positions in accounting, finance, sales, and operations.

Phil DeFronzo

Mr. DeFronzo is the founder and CEO of Norcom Mortgage. Through natural leadership Phil was able to grow the company to a well-known regional lender. His achievements include increasing revenue, building brand awareness, and growing the business. In 2011 Norcom was recognized as one of the "Fastest Growing Lenders in New England."

Richard Bechtel

Mr. Bechtel has nearly 30 years of experience in the Mortgage Banking industry. He currently serves as Executive Vice President, Head of U.S. Mortgage Banking for TD Bank. Prior to TD Bank, he served as Head of Mortgage Banking at CIBC and the PrivateBank, as well as leadership at Wells Fargo and Chase. He serves on several industry boards and committees and he recently led the PrivateBank to win the inaugural Mortgage Bankers Association Diversity & Inclusion Award. Mr. Bechtel earned his MBA from the Kellogg School of Business at Northwestern University and has expertise in sales, operations, capital markets, compliance, marketing, technology, and product development.

Rick Arvielo

Mr. Arvielo has over 18 years of experience in the mortgage banking industry. He is diverse in marketing and technology, starting his first company Paradon, Industries. Shortly after, Mr. Arvielo joined the mortgage banking industry and launched New American Funding with Patty Arvielo. Rick is a member of the Mortgage Bankers Association (MBA) and is a part of the Board of Directors. In addition, Mr. Arvielo serves in the Mortgage Action Alliance Committee, RESBOG and is the 2017–2018 Chairman of MORPAC, the MBA's Political Action Committee.

Ross Diedrich

Mr. Diedrich is the Chief Executive Officer and co-founder of Covered. Under his leadership, Covered has been recognized on housing Wire's "Tech100" list of most innovative companies in housing, BuiltInColorado's "Top 50" startups to watch in 2018, and has been featured in *Wired* Magazine. Previously, Mr. Diedrich was the VP of Structured Products and CD Trading at Nathan Hale Capital where he grew revenue 5.6x and achieved the highest ROI in the company. He regularly ranked in the top three traders in the country. During his tenure at Nathan Hale Capital, he achieved the prestigious Chartered Financial Analyst designation.

Roy George

Mr. George is the head of compliance for all financial, mortgage two joint ventures and title services for Taylor Morrison Home Funding. He has over 22 years of mortgage industry experience. He's worked both as an origination and servicing leader to implement various technology initiatives through the use of vendor partners. Mr. George has worked both as an origination and servicing leader to implement various technology initiatives through the use of vendor partners. Prior to joining Taylor Morrison Home Funding, Roy held numerous leadership roles including SVP, Mortgage Operations, and, most recently, Chief Compliance Officer. Roy has led operations with 2,000 plus employees and has been involved with a smaller digital mortgage startup.

Scott Gillen

Mr. Gillian is the Sr. Vice President of Industry Relations & Marketplace Strategy Strategic Initiatives for Stewart Lender Services. Mr. Gillen is responsible for oversight of Stewart's product development and strategy related to product implementation. Prior to joining Stewart, Mr. Gillen served as Director of Sales and Marketing for Mortgage Resource Network (MRN). There, his responsibilities included the ongoing management and oversight of MRN's sales and marketing efforts. Prior to that, Mr. Gillen served in senior management positions with Harbor Financial Mortgage Corporation. He is an active member in industry trade associations, serving as Vice Chairman of the Education Committee for the Mortgage Bankers Association and as a member of the Legislative Committee. He has also served on the Boards of the Houston Mortgage Bankers Association and Texas Mortgage Bankers Association.

Stanley Middleman

Stanley C. Middleman is the founder and Chief Executive Officer of Freedom Mortgage Corporation, a national, full-service mortgage company headquartered in Mount Laurel, New Jersey. The company is one of the largest mortgage originators and mortgage servicers in the United States. Mr. Middleman has over 30 years' experience in the financial services industry. Stan is a member of the Housing Policy Executive Council and serves on the NAHREP Corporate Board of Governors. He has served on numerous advisory boards, including Freddie Mac and Ellie Mae Inc. In November 2018, Freedom Mortgage was presented with the Chairman's Award in honor of their service to our community and their support of Liberty USO. Mr. Middleman is a graduate of Temple University with a BS in Accounting.

Steve Butler

Mr. Butler is Founder and president of AI Foundry, provider of a SaaS-based cognitive business automation platform that can digitally transform and fully automate document-intensive business processes in any industry to boost revenues while lowering costs and building low-term customer retention. He has served in CEO positions for prominent data analysis, enterprise software, system management and CAE companies in the Boston area and Silicon Valley. Steve has built a track record of developing high-growth companies with significant M&A and international expansion. He served on the board of directors for five different companies, including six years as a public company director.

Susan Stewart

Ms. Stewart is the CEO of SWBC Mortgage Corporation. Susan has impacted her company tremendously; she is well known for her commitment amongst her customers and co-workers. She serves as Vice Chair of the Residential Board of Governors of the MBA and is an MBA Board Member and Opens Door Foundation Board Member. Ms. Stewart is a past president of the Texas Mortgage Bankers Association and the San Antonio Mortgage Bankers.

Tim Nguyen

Mr. Nguyen is the CEO & Co-Founder of BeSmartee, the leader in digital mortgage innovation. Using a combination of big data and AI, borrowers can go from application, to approval to disclosures, and enter fulfillment in about 15 minutes. Previously, he was CEO & Co-Founder of InHouse, Inc., a technology-enabled-service company providing appraisal management solutions to the mortgage lending industry. He has served as an advisor to companies ranging from $5 to $500 million in annual revenue. He lives in Southern California with his wife and two boys.

Tom Faughnan

Mr. Faughnan the executive vice president and director of residential lending, consumer & business banking. He has over 30 years of experience in mortgage industry. He is responsible for all aspects of the residential lending business, including first mortgage and home equity programs. Before that, he served as the CEO of an independent mortgage banker and as general manager of a large real estate brokerage affiliate. He is a founding member and Vice President of New York MBA, he has served on numerous non-profit boards and currently serves on the board of directors for Habitat for Humanity Green Bay Chapter and is a member of the Community Banks and Credit Unions Committee of the Mortgage Bankers Association.

MAVERICK	TITLE	COMPANY
AJ George	*CAO*	CMG Financial
Barrett Burns	*CEO & President*	VantageScore Solutions, LLC
Bill Emerson	*Vice-Chair*	Rock Holding Inc.
Brent Chandler	*CEO & Founder*	FormFree Holding Corporation
Chris George	*President and CEO*	CMG Financial
Chrissi Rhea	*President and CEO*	Mortgage Investors Group
Dave Stevens	*CEO & President (retired)*	Mortgage Bankers Association
David Motley	*President Savings, F.A and its divisions*	Colonial National Mortgage
Deb Still	*CEO & President*	Pulte Mortgage, LLC
Don Salmon	*CEO*	TBI Mortgage
Eddy Perez	*President*	Equity Prime Mortgage, LLC
Grant Moon	*CEO & Founder*	Captain Home Realty
Jay Plum	*EVP of Home Lending and Card*	Huntington Bank
Jerry Schiano	*CEO*	Spring EQ
John Hedlund	*Managing Director and COO*	AmeriHome Mortgage Company
Jonathan Corr	*CEO & President*	Ellie Mae, Inc.
Kristy Fercho	*Executive Vice President, President of Mortgage*	Flagstar Bank
Lori Brewer	*CEO & Founder*	LBA Ware
Marcia Davies	*COO*	Mortgage Bankers Association
Marie Gayo	*President*	Trident Mortgage Co. LP
Mary Ann McGarry	*President & CEO*	Guild Mortgage Company
Matt Hansen	*CEO & President*	SimpleNexus
Maylin Casanueva	*COO*	Teraverde
Nilma Ghamsari	*CEO & Co-Founder*	Blend
Patrick Sinks	*Vice Chairman*	Mortgage Guaranty Investment Corporation
Phil DeFronza	*CEO & Founder*	Norcom Mortgage
Richard Bechtel	*EVP, Head of US Mortgage Banking*	TD Bank

(continued)

MAVERICK	TITLE	COMPANY
Rich Arvielo	*CEO*	New American Funding
Ross Diedrich	*CEO & Founder*	Covered Insurance
Roy George	*VP Compliance*	Taylor Morrison Funding
Scott Gillen	*SVP Industry Relations & Marketplace Strategy*	Stewart Lender Services
Stanley Middleman	*CEO*	Freedom Mortgage Corporation
Steve Butler	*Founder and President*	AI Foundry
Susan Stewart	*CEO & Founder*	SWBC Mortgage Corporation
Tim Nguyen	*CEO & Co-Founder*	BeSmartee
Tom Faughnan	*SVP Mortgage*	Associated Bank

Appendix 2   Financial Crises 1775 to 2010

It was Stan Middleman of Freedom Mortgage who rekindled my interest in financial history a few years ago. In a conversation we had for a previous book of mine, Stan warned, "Don't be a bad historian." This idea inspired me to take up my early interest in the origins of financial theory and financial innovation once more and synthesize this historical knowledge with some of the ideas explored in this book.

That early education in financial history I found myself returning to occurred when studying post-masters under Dr. Eli Schwartz. Dr. Schwartz was a fantastic finance professor, and encouraged me to begin doctoral studies in finance. He had a keen sense of history, guiding me toward research on the origins of financial theory. After a semester working as a graduate assistant, I discovered that doctoral studies were not my preferred future, however. I got a job in finance instead, eventually working for Bill Miller (yes, *the* Bill Miller, from Legg Mason and the only human in history to beat the S&P average 16 years running.) In honor of Dr. Schwartz, the following is an annotated history of financial crises in the United States. Financial crises are more the norm than the exception, so enjoy this short history.

Revolution in Crisis

Surprisingly, the first financial crisis on American soil occurred during the Revolutionary War. Perhaps this is not so surprising when you consider that Colonial America had a war with England to finance.

The Continental Congress printed the first paper money, known as Continental. This currency was not backed by precious metal, but was rather backed by the "anticipation of collection of tax revenue."[231] (Sound familiar?) "In specie" payment means that the currency is backed by exchange into hard assets, such as gold or silver bullion. Lacking bullion to offer the exchange in bullion, Congress reneged on its promise and issued notes in such quantity that they led to inflation, which, though mild at first, rapidly accelerated as the war progressed.

The Bank of the United States was conceived in 1790 to deal with inflation, war debt, and to put the government on more sound financial footing. Alexander Hamilton was the architect of the Bank of the United States. Though the intent of the Bank was to facilitate government finances, at the time of the revolution, there were barely any banks in the colonies; Britain had used its authority to protect its own banks and prevent the development of financial rivals. Hamilton's vision was to create a central source of capital that could be lent to new businesses and thereby develop the nation's economy.

---

231 https://www.frbsf.org/education/teacher-resources/american-currency-exhibit/independence/

https://doi.org/10.1515/9783110650471-013

Some argued that the Bank was unconstitutional. The Constitution granted power to tax and print money to Congress, not a private corporation, critics argued. So, in 1811, when faced with the decision to renew the Bank's charter, Congress refused, by one vote, to renew it, and the bank ceased operations.[232]

With the War of 1812, federal debt began to mount again. At the same time, most state-chartered banks, which were issuing their own currency, suspended specie payments. Congress chartered the Second National Bank primarily to ensure a uniform currency. This entity would function as the first regulator of banking in the United States. It held large quantities of other banks' notes in reserve and could discipline commercial, privately owned banks for over-issuing notes with the threat of redeeming those notes.

The First Banking Crisis in the U.S.

The Second Bank was headquartered in Philadelphia; during the time it operated, it had offices in 29 major cities around the country. Unlike the First Bank, however, the Second Bank was poorly managed at its outset and was on the verge of insolvency within a year and a half after it opened. The Second Bank navigated various financial and political crises until its charter expired in 1836.

With the closing of the Second Bank, states passed "free bank laws," which allowed banks to operate under a much less onerous charter. While banks were regulated, they were relatively free to enter the business by simply depositing government bonds with state auditors.

These bonds were the collateral backing the notes free banks issued. Hundreds of new banks were formed. Their bank notes circulated around the country, often at a discount. The discount on a given bank note varied in part with the distance from the issuing bank and in part with the perceived soundness of the bank.

The outbreak of the Civil War and the need to finance the war led to the national banking system. The national banking system was durable, and it survives to this day. With a national charter, banks had to issue government-printed bills for their own notes, and the notes had to be backed by federal bonds, which helped fund the war effort. In 1865, state bank notes were taxed out of existence. This, in spite of all previous attempts, was the first time a uniform national currency was established in the United States.

The system of privately owned national and state banks worked well and promoted a uniform currency throughout the United States. Private ownership, however, meant that banks could fail. A bank panic would often begin when depositors

---

232 https://www.minneapolisfed.org/about/more-about-the-fed/history-of-the-fed/history-of-central-banking#top

would learn that their bank was unable to meet withdrawal requests. The result typically was a "*run*" on the bank, in which a large number of depositors would attempt to pull out their money, causing an otherwise solvent bank to fail. Seeing this, depositors at other banks would withdraw their funds, too, causing a system-wide panic.

In 1893, a bank panic coincided with the worst depression the United States had ever seen. The economy stabilized only after the intervention of financial mogul J. P. Morgan. After another particularly bad panic and ensuing recession in 1907, bankers and the Congress decided it was time to reconsider a centralized national bank.

On December 23, 1913, President Woodrow Wilson signed the Federal Reserve Act into law.

The new Federal Reserve Bank would be a largely public institution. Profits in excess of cost were handed over to the U.S. Treasury. Financial transfers and check processing that were handled by private clearinghouses would now be conducted by the Fed, with the fees for such services going toward the operational costs of the Bank.

The Federal Reserve was decentralized into district banks which operated independently, but with an oversight board located in Washington, D.C. Each district bank issued its own money, backed by the promise to redeem this money in gold. After Congress passed and President Wilson signed the Federal Reserve Act in 1913, Congress established 12 district banks to reflect the distribution of population and banking in the country.

New York Fed President Benjamin Strong began conducting open market operations in the 1920s. While Monetarists delighted in Strong's use of open market operations to stabilize price levels and control the amount of money in the U.S., many historians eventually would blame the Fed's botched monetary policy for the length and severity of the Great Depression.

1929: The Great Crash

Nobody knew, as the stock market imploded in October 1929, that years of depression lay ahead and that the market would stay seized up for years. In its regular summation of the president's week after Black Tuesday (Oct. 29), *TIME* put the market crash in the No. 2 position, after devastating storms in the Great Lakes region. *TIME* described the stock-swoon this way: "For so many months, so many people had saved money and borrowed money and borrowed on their borrowings to possess themselves of the little pieces of paper by virtue of which they became partners of U.S. Industry. Now they were trying to get rid of them even more frantically than they had tried to get them. Stocks bought without reference to their earnings were being sold without reference to their dividends." The crisis that began that autumn and snowballed into the Great Depression would not fully resolve for a decade.[233]

1973: The OPEC Embargo

Need proof that the every-seven-years formulation hasn't always held true? Look at the OPEC oil embargo. This crisis is widely viewed as the first major, discrete event after the Crash of '29 to have deep, wide-ranging economic effects that would last for years. OPEC, responding to the United States' involvement in the Yom Kippur War, froze oil production and hiked prices several times beginning on October 16, 1973. The Saudi Minister of Oil, Ahmed Zaki Yamani, famously indicated that any attempt to invade the oil fields of his country would result in the complete destruction of the oil fields by the Saudis themselves. The Saudis knew they could survive on limited production, but that the West could not. Oil prices eventually quadrupled, meaning that gas prices soared. The embargo, *TIME* warned in the days after it started, "could easily lead to cold homes, hospitals and schools, shuttered factories, slower travel, brownouts, consumer rationing, aggravated inflation and even worsened air pollution in the U.S., Europe and Japan."

1981: The Early-'80s Recession

The recession of the early 1980s lasted from July 1981 to November of the following year, and was marked by high interest rates, high unemployment, and rising prices. Unlike market-crash-caused crises, it's impossible to pin this one to a particular date. *TIME*'s cover story of Feb. 8, 1982 titled simply, "Unemployment on the Rise," examined the dire landscape and groped for solutions that would only come with an upturn in the business cycle at the end of the year. "For the first time in years, polls show that more Americans are worried about unemployment than inflation," *TIME* reported. A White House source told *TIME*: "If unemployment breaks 10%, we're in big trouble." Unemployment peaked the following November at 10.8%.

1987: Black Monday

If the meaning of the Crash of '29 was underappreciated at the time it happened, the meaning of Black Monday 1987 was probably overblown—though understandably,

---

233 Dan Mitchell, "These Were the 6 Major American Economic Crises of the Last Century," *Time Magazine*, July 16, 2015.

given what happened. The 508-point drop in the Dow Jones Industrial Average on October 19 was and still remains the biggest one-day percentage loss in the Dow's history. But the reverberations weren't all that severe by historical standards. "Almost an entire nation become paralyzed with curiosity and concern," *TIME* reported. "Crowds gathered to watch the electronic tickers in brokers' offices or stare at television monitors through plate-glass windows. In downtown Boston, police ordered a Fidelity Investments branch to turn off its ticker because a throng of nervous investors had spilled out onto Congress Street and was blocking traffic."

2001: The Dot-Com Crash

The dot-com bubble deflated relatively slowly and haltingly over more than two years, but it was nevertheless a discrete, identifiable crash that paved the way for the early-2000s recession. Fueled by speculation in tech and internet stocks, many of dubious real value, the Nasdaq peaked on March 10, 2000, at 5132. Stocks were volatile for years before and after the peak, and didn't reach their lows until November of 2002. In an article in the Jan. 8, 2001, issue, *TIME* reported that market problems had spread throughout the economy. The "distress is no longer confined to young dot-commer's who got rich fast and lorded it over the rest of us. And it's no longer confined to the stock market. The economic uprising that rocked eToys, Priceline.com, Pets.com and all the other www's has now spread to blue-chip tech companies and Old Economy stalwarts."

2008: The Great Recession

The extreme stress in the financial markets in the late summer and early fall of 2008 was quantified by the Kansas City Financial Stress Index (KCFSI), a monthly measure of stress in the U.S. financial system based on 11 financial market variables issued by the Kansas City Federal Reserve Bank. A positive value indicates that financial stress is above the long-run average, while a negative value signifies that financial stress is below the long-run average. The KCFSI decreased from 1.47 in April 2008 to 0.94 in May 31, 2008... followed by an almost six-fold increase to an all-time high of 5.55 as of October 2008. This unexpected and unprecedented increase in financial stress as quantified by the KCFSI was the proximate cause of rapid declines in asset prices.

What inspired this rapid uptick? The failure of several subprime mortgage lenders in 2007 reduced the availability of credit to subprime borrowers. New Century Financial Corporation, a real estate investment trust founded in 1995 and headquartered in Irvine, California, declared bankruptcy on April 2, 2007. On July 11, 2007, credit rating agencies S&P and Moody's announced the downgrade of $12 billion and $5 billion of subprime RMBS, respectively. Bear Stearns placed two structured and asset-backed securities hedge funds in bankruptcy on July 31, 2007. American Home Mortgage Investment Corp., a large subprime lender, filed for bankruptcy on August 6, 2007. In 2007, losses on subprime mortgage-related financial assets began to cause strains in the global financial markets. By December 2007, the U.S. economy had entered a recession.

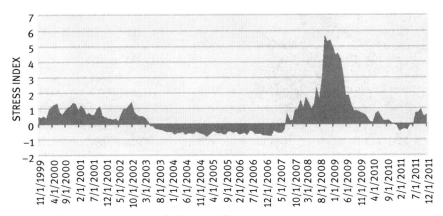

Sources: The Federal Reserve Bank of Kansas City

Figure B.1: Kansas City Federal Reserve Bank Financial Stress Index from 1999 to 2011.

Despite the failures cited above, however, the markets in early 2008 did not act as if the economy was in severe trouble. On January 11, 2008, for example, Bank of America announced an agreement to purchase Countrywide Financial Corp for $4 billion in stock. Bear Stearns was acquired by JPMorgan Chase on March 16, 2008. The Federal Reserve agreed to guarantee $30 billion of Bear Stearns' assets in connection with the government-sponsored sale of the investment bank to JPMorgan Chase.

As of late May 2008, the financial markets continued to show signs of stress, but the stress was largely confined to the subprime market, and significant actions by the Federal Reserve and other central banks appeared to be addressing subprime mortgage matters. For example, the Federal Reserve responded to an apparent lack of liquidity in worldwide financial markets with sharp reductions in the federal funds rate, reducing the rate from 5.25% in May 2007 to 2.00% as of April 30, 2008. The Federal Reserve press release stated, "The substantial easing of monetary policy to date, combined with ongoing measures to foster market liquidity, should help to promote moderate growth over time and to mitigate risks to economic activity." On May 8, 2008, the Federal Reserve provided an increase in the amounts auctioned to eligible depository institutions under its biweekly Term Auction Facility

("TAF") to bring the amounts outstanding under the TAF to $150 billion, again to increase liquidity.

For example, prior to the failure of Fannie Mae, the company issued the following unexpected and extraordinary description of events that occurred after the close of its second quarter 2008. The following note was included in Fannie Mae's June 30, 2008, Form 10-Q, released August 9, 2008:

Market Events of July 2008:

In mid-July, following the close of the second quarter, liquidity and trading levels in the capital markets became extremely volatile, and the functioning of the markets was disrupted. The market value of our common stock dropped rapidly, to its lowest level since October 1990, and we experienced reduced demand for our unsecured debt and MBS products. This market disruption caused a significant increase in our cost of funding and a substantial increase in mark-to-market losses on our trading securities arising from a significant widening of credit spreads. In addition, during July, credit performance continued to deteriorate, and we recorded charge-offs and foreclosed property expenses that were higher than we had experienced in any month during the second quarter and higher than we expected, driven by higher defaults and higher loan loss severities in markets most affected by the steep home price declines. Greater credit losses in July not only reduce our July net income through our actual realized losses, but also affect us as we expect that we will need to make further increases to our combined loss reserves in the second half of 2008 to incorporate our experience in July.

Less than 30 days after this 10-Q release, in early September 2008, Fannie Mae was in unexpected conservatorship. In addition, four other major publicly traded companies were unexpectedly placed in conservatorship, bankruptcy, or acquired under duress. The companies and their impact on the financial services marketplace in September 2008 were extraordinary:

- Freddie Mac and Fannie Mae owned or guaranteed $4 trillion in mortgage loans at the time of their failure, or 40% of all residential mortgage loans outstanding in the U.S.
- AIG had assets of over $1 trillion at the time of its takeover.
- Washington Mutual and Wachovia assets totaled over $1 trillion at the time of their takeover.

The failure of these five financial firms, with a collective total of $6 trillion of assets heavily involved in the U.S. housing market, in one month (September 6 to October 7, 2008), had an overwhelming adverse impact on liquidity and price discovery in financial markets.

The unexpected nature of the stress in the financial markets is illustrated in the sharp climb in bank failures. Total assets of failed banks from the beginning of 2007 through June 1, 2008 were just under $5 billion. By October 1, 2008 the total assets of failed banks had grown to $350 billion, an increase of 70 times. A total of 7 banks failed from January 1, 2005 to June 4, 2008. Another 27 failed from June 1,

2008 to January 31, 2009. Ultimately, 468 banks with total assets of $690 billion failed from January 1, 2005 through December 31, 2012.

Compiling a list now of the events that followed flows with the slow-moving but increasingly sinister terror of a Hitchcock film. On July 11, 2008, IndyMac Bank, F.S.B., Pasadena, CA, was closed by the Office of Thrift Supervision. The Federal Deposit Insurance Corporation was named conservator. Just a little over three months earlier, IndyMac Bank had total assets of $32.01 billion and total deposits of $19.06 billion. The most recent prior FDIC-insured failure in California was the Southern Pacific Bank, Torrance in 2003.

On July 13, 2008, the Board of Governors of the Federal Reserve System announced that it had granted the Federal Reserve Bank of New York the authority to lend to Fannie Mae and Freddie Mac, should such lending prove necessary, and that any lending would be at the primary credit rate and collateralized by U.S. government and federal agency securities. This authorization was intended to supplement the Treasury's existing lending authority and to help ensure the ability of Fannie Mae and Freddie Mac to promote the availability of home mortgage credit during a period of stress in financial markets. At the same time, the U.S. Treasury Department announced a temporary increase in the credit lines of Fannie Mae and Freddie Mac (Government Sponsored Enterprise, or GSE) and a temporary authorization for the Treasury to purchase equity in either GSE, if needed.

On July 15, 2008, the Securities and Exchange Commission issued an emergency order to enhance investor protections against "naked" short-selling in the securities of Fannie Mae, Freddie Mac, and primary dealers at commercial and investment banks.

On July 30, 2008, President Bush signed the Housing and Economic Recovery Act of 2008 (Public Law 110-289), which, among other provisions, authorized the Treasury to purchase GSE obligations and reforms the regulatory supervision of the GSEs under a new Federal Housing Finance Agency.

On July 30, 2008, the Federal Reserve announced several steps to enhance the effectiveness of its existing liquidity facilities, including the introduction of longer terms to maturity in its Term Auction Facility Extension of the Primary Dealer Credit Facility (PDCF) and the Term Securities Lending Facility (TSLF).

The Federal Housing Finance Agency (FHFA) initiated the conservatorships of the Federal National Mortgage Association (Fannie Mae) and the Federal Home Loan Mortgage Corporation (Freddie Mac) on September 6, 2008. The U.S. Treasury Department announced three additional measures to complement the FHFA's decision: 1) Preferred stock purchase agreements between the Treasury/FHFA and Fannie Mae and Freddie Mac to ensure the GSEs positive net worth; 2) a new secured lending facility available to Fannie Mae, Freddie Mac, and the Federal Home Loan Banks; and 3) a temporary program to purchase GSE Mortgage Backed Securities (MBS).

On September 14, 2008, the Federal Reserve Board announced a significant broadening in the collateral accepted under its existing liquidity program for primary dealers and financial markets to provide additional support to financial markets.

On September 15, 2008, Bank of America announced its intent to purchase Merrill Lynch & Co. for $50 billion.

Also on September 15, 2008, Lehman Brothers filed for federal bankruptcy protection.

Credit rating agencies downgraded AIG's long-term credit rating on the afternoon of September 15, 2008. AIG's stock price plunged. AIG could not access short-term liquid funds in the credit markets.

On September 16, 2008, the Federal Reserve Board, with the full support of the Treasury Department, authorized the Federal Reserve Bank of New York to lend up to $85 billion to AIG under section 13(3) of the Federal Reserve Act.

The net asset value of shares in the Reserve Primary Money Fund fell below $1, primarily due to losses on Lehman Brothers commercial paper and medium-term notes, further disrupting liquidity in the money markets.

On September 17, 2008, the Securities and Exchange Commission took several coordinated actions to strengthen investor protections against "naked" short selling. The Commission's actions applied to the securities of all public companies, including all companies in the financial sector. The actions were effective at 12:01 a.m. ET on Thursday, September 18, 2008.

On September 18, 2008, the Bank of Canada, the Bank of England, the European Central Bank (ECB), the Federal Reserve, the Bank of Japan, and the Swiss National Bank announced coordinated measures designed to address the continued elevated pressures in U.S. dollar short-term funding markets and to improve the liquidity conditions in global financial markets.

On September 19, 2008, the Federal Reserve Board announced two enhancements to its programs to provide liquidity to markets. One initiative extended non-recourse[234] loans at the primary credit rate to U.S. depository institutions and bank holding companies to finance their purchases of high-quality asset-backed commercial paper (ABCP) from money market mutual funds. To further support market functioning, the Federal Reserve agreed to purchase from primary dealers quantities of federal agency discount notes, which are short-term debt obligations issued by Fannie Mae, Freddie Mac, and the Federal Home Loan Banks.

On September 19, 2008, the U.S. Treasury Department established a temporary guarantee program for the U.S. money market mutual fund industry. Concerns about the net asset value of money market funds falling below $1 exacerbated

---

234 Non-recourse loans are backed only by any collateral underlying the loans. The loans are not guaranteed by the issuer itself.

global financial market turmoil and caused severe liquidity strains in world markets. In turn, these pressures caused a spike in some short-term interest and funding rates, and significantly heightened volatility in exchange markets. Maintenance of the standard $1 net asset value for money market mutual funds was important to investors. If the net asset value for a fund fell below $1, it undermined investor confidence. The program would provide support to investors in funds that participated in the program so that those funds would not "break the buck." The goal was to enhance market confidence and alleviate investor concerns about whether money market mutual funds could absorb a loss or not.

On September 20, 2008, the Treasury Department submitted legislation to Congress asking for the authority to purchase troubled assets from financial institutions to promote market stability and help protect American families and the U.S. economy.

On September 25, 2008, JPMorgan Chase acquired the banking operations of Washington Mutual Bank in a transaction facilitated by the Federal Deposit Insurance Corporation. JPMorgan Chase acquired the assets, assumed the qualified financial contracts and made a payment of $1.9 billion. Claims by equity, subordinated, and senior debt holders were not acquired, meaning investors in these instruments suffered material or complete losses. Washington Mutual Bank also had a subsidiary, Washington Mutual FSB, Park City, Utah. They had combined assets of $307 billion and total deposits of $188 billion. The combined assets and deposits of these entities represented the largest bank failure in the history of the United States.

On September 29, 2008, central banks announced further coordinated actions to expand significantly the capacity to provide U.S. dollar liquidity. The Federal Reserve announced several initiatives to support financial stability and to maintain a stable flow of credit to the economy during this period of significant strain in global markets. Actions by the Federal Reserve included: (1) an increase in the size of the 84-day maturity TAF auctions to $75 billion per auction from $25 billion beginning with the October 6 auction, (2) two forward TAF auctions totaling $150 billion to be conducted in November to provide term funding over year-end, and (3) an increase in swap authorization limits with the Bank of Canada, Bank of England, Bank of Japan, Danmarks Nationalbank (National Bank of Denmark), European Central Bank (ECB), Norges Bank (Bank of Norway), Reserve Bank of Australia, Sveriges Riksbank (Bank of Sweden), and Swiss National Bank to a total of $620 billion, from $290 billion previously.

On September 29, 2008, Citigroup Inc. announced its intent to acquire the banking operations of Wachovia Corporation; Charlotte, North Carolina, in a transaction facilitated by the Federal Deposit Insurance Corporation and concurred with by the Board of Governors of the Federal Reserve and the Secretary of the Treasury in consultation with the President. (Wells Fargo & Company offered a competing bid on October 3, 2008, which ultimately was accepted.)

The Troubled Asset Relief Program ("TARP") was signed into law by U.S. President George W. Bush on October 3, 2008. TARP provided up to $700 billion to inject equity into the U.S. banks and to purchase "troubled assets."

On October 3, 2008, President George W. Bush signed the Emergency Economic Stabilization Act of 2008, which temporarily raised the basic limit on federal deposit insurance coverage from $100,000 to $250,000 per depositor. The temporary increase in deposit insurance coverage became effective upon the President's signature. The legislation provided that the basic deposit insurance limit would return to $100,000 after December 31, 2009. (In fact, the "temporary" limit has remained at $250,000.)

On October 7, 2008, the Federal Reserve Board announced the creation of the Commercial Paper Funding Facility ("CPFF"), a facility that would complement the Federal Reserve's existing credit facilities to help provide liquidity to term funding markets.

On October 14, 2008, the Treasury announced a voluntary Capital Purchase Program to encourage U.S. financial institutions to build capital to increase the flow of financing to U.S. businesses and consumers and to support the U.S. economy. Under the program, Treasury purchased up to $250 billion of senior preferred shares on standardized terms as described in the program's term sheet. The senior preferred shares would qualify as Tier 1 capital. (Tier 1 capital is considered the most permanent form of bank capital, and included common stock and certain preferred stock.)

On October 24, 2008, PNC Financial Services Group Inc. purchased National City Corporation, creating the fifth largest U.S. bank.

On November 10, 2008, the Federal Reserve Board and the U.S. Treasury Department announced a restructuring of the government's financial support of AIG. The Treasury was to purchase $40 billion of AIG preferred shares under the TARP program, a portion of which was to be used to reduce the Federal Reserve's loan to AIG from $85 billion to $60 billion. The Federal Reserve Board also authorized the Federal Reserve Bank of New York to establish two new lending facilities for AIG. The Residential Mortgage-Backed Securities Facility was to lend up to $22.5 billion to a newly formed limited liability company to purchase residential MBS from AIG; the Collateralized Debt Obligations Facility was to lend up to $30 billion to a newly formed LLC to purchase CDOs from AIG (Maiden Lane III LLC).

On November 18, 2008, Executives of Ford, General Motors, and Chrysler testified before Congress, requesting access to the TARP for federal loans.

On November 20, 2008, Fannie Mae and Freddie Mac announced that they would suspend mortgage foreclosures until January 2009.

On November 21, 2008, the U.S. Treasury Department announced that it would help liquidate the Reserve Fund's U.S. Government Fund. The Treasury served as a buyer of last resort for the fund's securities to ensure the orderly liquidation of the fund.

On November 21, 2008, the U.S. Treasury Department, Federal Reserve Board, and FDIC jointly announced an agreement with Citigroup that provided a package of guarantees, liquidity access, and capital. Citigroup issued preferred shares to the Treasury and FDIC in exchange for protection against losses on a $306 billion pool of commercial and residential securities held by Citigroup. The Federal Reserve was to backstop residual risk in the asset pool through a non-recourse loan. In addition, the Treasury committed up to an additional $20 billion in Citigroup from the TARP.

On November 25, 2008, the Federal Reserve Board announced the creation of the Term Asset-Backed Securities Lending Facility ("TALF"), under which the Federal Reserve Bank of New York would lend up to $200 billion on a non-recourse basis to holders of AAA-rated asset-backed securities and recently originated consumer and small business loans. The U.S. Treasury would provide $20 billion of TARP money for credit protection.

On November 25, 2008, the Federal Reserve Board announced a new program to purchase direct obligations of housing related government-sponsored enterprises—Fannie Mae, Freddie Mac and Federal Home Loan Banks—and MBS backed by the GSEs. Purchases of up to $100 billion in GSE direct obligations were to be conducted as auctions among Federal Reserve primary dealers. Purchases of up to $500 billion in MBS were to be conducted by asset managers.

On December 3, 2008, the SEC approved measures to increase transparency and accountability at credit rating agencies to ensure that firms provide more meaningful ratings and greater disclosure to investors.

On December 19, 2008, the U.S. Treasury Department authorized loans of up to $13.4 billion for General Motors and $4.0 billion for Chrysler from the TARP.

On December 29, 2008, the U.S. Treasury Department announced that it would purchase $5 billion in equity from GMAC as part of its program to assist the domestic automotive industry. The Treasury also agreed to lend up to $1 billion to General Motors "so that GM can participate in a rights offering at GMAC in support of GMAC's reorganization as a bank holding company." This commitment was in addition to the support announced on December 19, 2008.

By any view, it was a hell of a six-month period.

What's Next?

Most people tend to think of financial crises as negative events or something to be avoided. Financial crises are much like summer thunderstorms. Thunderstorms can't occur in stable air. There needs to be instability and moisture in the atmosphere, as well as a lifting mechanism.

In the economy, that instability can occur due to an OPEC oil embargo, real estate price bubbles, armed conflict as well as government policy and intervention.

We've all seen puffy white clouds during the summer. These are cumulus clouds, formed by air heated from the sun near the ground rising into the cooler atmosphere above. As the air gently rises, the water vapor in the atmosphere condenses into the very small water droplets, which form the white cumulus cloud.

The air temperature cools about 2 degrees Fahrenheit for each one thousand feet of altitude in the lower atmosphere. The temperature gradient increases at a higher altitude. It's not unusual for the air temperature to be minus 20 or colder at 36,000 feet.

A thunderstorm occurs when the updraft from heated air on hot days rises quickly to 20,000 feet or more. The instability in the atmosphere is created when humid air is lifted by updrafts, and begins to cool. Small droplets of water form and begin to fall towards earth, but the updraft overpowers gravity and lifts the droplets higher. This cycle continues, and soon the upper parts of the cloud have strong updrafts carrying droplets and the competing warm updrafts and the cooler waterdrops create turbulence. That turbulence results in the bumps that you sometimes feel when flying in the summertime. Updrafts and downdrafts are not neatly separated; various parts of the cloud have updrafts; other parts have downdrafts. The competing forces roil the cloud and create the constantly changing look of the cloud.

Eventually the water droplets become larger and heavy enough to fall to the ground as rain. The cooler water droplets and surrounding air overpower the warm rising air. Rain and cool air form a downdraft that can be quite powerful. That downdraft descends to the earth and spreads out, producing the strong winds that are characteristic of thunderstorms. The friction between the updrafts and downdrafts within the cloud produces static electricity, or lightning.

The stronger the warm updraft, the more violent the storm. That's why very hot days can produce the strongest thunderstorms. Once the downdrafts from the upper reaches of the thunderstorm reach the ground, the air is cooled, the updrafts cease and the thunderstorm ends.[235]

Thunderstorms provide an analog for economic crises. The upward spiral of housing prices eventually reached levels where home buying cooled, and the price of houses fell precipitously. The federal reserve reduced interest rates that heated up the economy, until the asset inflation balloon is popped, as in the dot-com crisis.

You get the idea. Steady and stable economic growth, or asset price growth can be sustainable. Like a thunderstorm, too much of an updraft eventually produces a powerful storm. Once the storm calms, the cycle repeats. Joseph Schumpeter calls

---

235 My description of thunderstorms is intended as a metaphor, not a scientific explanation. Information from the North Carolina Climate Office was a source, as well as knowledge acquired as a light aircraft pilot. See the following URL for a technical description of convective thunderstorm activity: https://climate.ncsu.edu/edu/Thunderstorm

this cycle creative destruction. Excesses are wrung out of the economy, and new growth begins.

So what's next? Disruption is much like a thunderstorm. It may appear as a small cloud on the horizon, but eventually the instability of the economy results in creative destruction. The taxi medallion crisis destroyed many a taxi owner, but the beneficiaries are riders who found the ride hailing services filled an unmet need.

The thunderstorms on the horizon of the residential real estate and lending industries are the result of years of inertia, consumer acceptance of excessive costs, and over-regulation. The creative destruction is coming due to a wave of innovation by fintechs. Once the consumer tastes the benefits, the old models will fall.

What's next in the general economies of the western world? Extended periods of low interest rates and government deficits have produced updrafts in economic activity. Those updrafts have produced disparities in income and wealth among individuals, states, and countries.

Government intervention of this nature will create economic thunderstorms. The economic atmosphere is inherently unstable. You can hear the thunder in the distance. And when the economic thunderstorms present themselves, remember the sage advice from my good friend George Brubaker. "How can we profit from this?"

Index

https://doi.org/10.1515/9783110650471-014